KEN

Highlights

Philip Briggs

Edition 1

Bradt Travel Guides Ltd, UK
The Globe Pequot Press Inc, USA

Bradt

About this book

There are many heavyweight guidebooks to Kenya bloated with long lists of budget hotels and complicated overviews of public transport targeted at backpackers and independent travellers. This 'highlights' guidebook is more selective in the information it offers, and is written for the traveller on (or planning to go on) an escorted tour. The book has two main aims: first, to help those considering a safari to decide what they'd like to see and do, and therefore to construct their itinerary or liaise with tour operators in an informed way; and, second, to provide an entertaining, colourful and informative guide to carry on the trip itself. With that in mind, the book provides overviews of every town, reserve and city that ranks as a possible highlight, a quick summary of practicalities and a short list of recommended accommodation. The selections are made by Philip Briggs, who is one of the world's most-renowned guidebook writers on Africa. In addition, we have called upon the expertise of some of the leading tour operators – those who know best the accommodation Kenya has to offer – to recommend their favourite lodges and tented camps. Those tour operators were carefully chosen by Bradt and invited to contribute on the basis of their reputations for excellence; they also made a payment towards the production costs of the book.

These pages are unique in bringing together the selections of a top writer and top operators, ensuring this is the most useful guidebook available to those planning a safari tour to Kenya.

 ## Lodge/camp accommodation

Accommodation in this guide has been carefully selected and reviewed by the following tour operators: Aardvark Safaris Ltd, Africa Sky, Lowis & Leakey, Rainbow Tours, Safari Consultants and The Zambezi Safari and Travel Company. See pages 64–5 for more information on these operators including details on how to book.

Note: opening hours are daily unless otherwise stated.

Feedback request

If you have any comments about this guide (good or bad), we would welcome your feedback. Please email us on ✉ info@bradtguides.com.

Author

Philip Briggs has been exploring the highways, byways and backwaters of Africa since 1986, when he spent several months backpacking on a shoestring from Nairobi to Cape Town. In 1991, he wrote the Bradt guide to South Africa, the first such guidebook to be published internationally after the release of Nelson Mandela. Over the rest of the 1990s, Philip wrote a series of pioneering Bradt guides to destinations that were then – and in some cases still are – otherwise practically uncharted by the travel publishing industry. These included the first dedicated guidebooks to Tanzania, Uganda, Ethiopia, Malawi, Mozambique, Ghana and Rwanda (co-authored with Janice Booth), all now in their fourth–sixth editions. Philip has visited more than two dozen African countries in total and written about most of them for specialist travel and wildlife magazines including *Africa Birds & Birding*, *Africa Geographic*, *BBC Wildlife*, *Travel Africa* and *Wanderlust*. He still spends at least four months on the road every year, usually accompanied by his wife, the travel photographer Ariadne Van Zandbergen, and spends the rest of his time battering away at a keyboard in the sleepy village of Bergville, in the uKhahlamba-Drakensberg region of South Africa.

Author's story

My own relationship with Kenya dates back to 1986, when I arrived there as a first-time backpacker escaping the climatic vagaries of the English winter. It wasn't quite love at first sight - a cockroach-infested budget hotel on the noisiest street in Nairobi's dodgy River Road area did less than match up to advance images of East Africa - but within a couple of days, I was smitten. Highlights of that first trip remain with me to this day: sitting on a jetty watching the grunting hippos of Naivasha, exploring the forested slopes of Mount Kenya, a herd of elephants treading delicately around my tent in Tsavo East, snorkelling in the coral gardens of Watamu, and above all perhaps the many gracious Kenyans who made me feel so welcome in their delightful country. Since that formative first visit, I have returned to Kenya on the slightest pretext, and have spent more than a year there in all, exploring every accessible corner of a country that remains something of a first love and still enthrals me to this day.

Contents

(NC/D)

Kenya Highlights 101

List of maps

(EWL)

Introduction

Kenya is the home of the safari. Hemmed in by the swooning Indian Ocean beaches of the Swahili coast, overlooked by the sensational snow-capped peaks of Mount Kenya and Mount Kilimanjaro, and scarred by the mile-deep continental schism that is the Great Rift Valley, this is a land of exceptional scenic variety and beauty. Its geographic diversity embraces vast inland seas and intimate palm-lined rivers, dense tropical forests and parched rocky deserts, rolling mountain meadows and tortured volcanic plugs... but, above all, those hypnotic tracts of acacia-studded African savanna, protected within some of the world's most celebrated wildlife reserves.

And what reserves they are. There is dust-blown Amboseli, where peaceable herds of tuskers march majestically below the iconic outline of Kilimanjaro. There is beautiful Lake Nakuru, shores grazed by prehistoric-looking rhinos, shallows tinged pink by more than one million flamingos. And of course there is the Masai Mara, arguably the finest safari destination in Africa, home to incredible concentrations of lions and other predators, and host to the world's greatest wildlife spectacle, which unfolds annually as millions of wildebeest hurtle across the Mara River from the neighbouring Serengeti plains.

Further north, we have the scorched rocky plains of Samburu-Buffalo Springs, where typical African plains mammals are replaced by dry-country specials such as Grevy's zebra, reticulated giraffe, and the impala-meet-giraffe anomaly that is the gerenuk. We also have the haunted volcanic landscapes of Tsavo West, the incomprehensible vastness of Tsavo East, the untrammelled expanses of Meru, along with more intimate and low-key gems such as Shimba Hills, Kakamega Forest and Hell's Gate... The list goes on, but for those swayed by statistics rather than superlatives, there is perhaps no better index of Kenya's biodiversity than a national bird checklist comprising 1,136 species – this is the second-highest for any African country, a figure made all the more remarkable when you realise that Kenya doesn't even make the top 20 in terms of surface area.

The ideal complement to the wildlife reserves of the interior is Kenya's sultry coastline, which consists of more than 500km of idyllic beach frontage lapped by the warm waters of the Indian Ocean. Studded with mysterious medieval ruins and dense tropical jungles, the coast is hemmed in by offshore reefs whose kaleidoscopic array of colourful fish is as delightful to snorkellers and divers as the country's more familiar terrestrial wildlife.

(SMC)

It would be something of a stretch to tag the Kenyan coast as some sort of 'best-kept secret'. Nevertheless, even the relatively developed beaches around Mombasa seem refreshingly uncrowded by comparison with their Mediterranean counterparts. And there are many exclusive beach resorts sufficiently isolated and low-key to sustain fantasies of being stranded on an uninhabited tropical island – albeit an island equipped with sumptuous accommodation, a bank of amply stocked refrigerators, a world-class chef, and an entire legion of Men Friday to provide service with a smile.

Socially and economically, Kenya can come across as a mass of contradictions. By African standards, it is a notably developed country, boasting an unusually high level of education, a genuinely substantial middle class, world-class tourist facilities, and the semblance of an industrial belt sprawling out from its bustling capital. Yet for all the modernity of the cities and towns, Kenya is also perhaps the most visibly traditional of African nations. Indeed, there remain vast tracts of the north where one can drive all day without seeing another vehicle, without passing a single person dressed in contemporary clothing, and – perhaps the benchmark of obscurity – without seeing a solitary Coca-Cola sign.

Elsewhere, and to the average tourist more accessibly, Kenya's unforced blend of the traditional and modern is epitomised by the red-robed Maasai pastoralists who roam the age-old southern savannas armed with traditional spears and a mobile phone. Or by the cosmopolitan and adaptive legacy of the coastal Swahili, which reaches its apotheosis in the small island town of Lamu, a richly atmospheric and remarkably laidback settlement that's barely changed its shape in centuries. It is this fascinating cultural dimension that completes the appeal of a country that is already justifiably renowned for its beaches, wildlife and scenery.

Introducing KENYA

1 History and People

Kenya, together with neighbouring Ethiopia and Tanzania, has one of the longest records of human habitation of any country on earth, encompassing several million years. Ironically, however, the documented history of the interior barely stretches back into the 19th century, while what little is known about coastal history prior to the arrival of the Portuguese in 1499 is based as much on archaeological evidence as on the handful of relevant Arabic documents that survive. Today, the country's long history is reflected in its rich cultural diversity, which includes about 40 different tribes belonging to three different linguistic groupings, the result of at least half-a-dozen different waves of immigration to present-day Kenya from neighbouring territories.

Kenya at a glance

Location Equatorial East Africa, bordered by Somalia to the northeast, Ethiopia and Sudan to the north, Uganda to the west and Tanzania to the south. The southeast is on the Indian Ocean.

Size 582,645km^2 (22nd largest in Africa)

Status Republic

Population 40 million (2010 estimate)

Life expectancy 58 years

Capital Nairobi (population 3-4 million)

Largest towns Nairobi, Mombasa, Nakuru, Kisumu, Eldoret, Machakos, Meru, Nyeri, Kitale, Kericho

Economy Mainly agriculture, including tea, coffee, horticultural products, but some service and manufacturing industry, tourism

GDP US$29.5 billion; per capita US$838 (2008 estimate)

Languages English and KiSwahili are the official languages; others include Kikuyu, Luo, Akamba and Maa

Religion 45% Protestant, 35% Catholic, 10% Islamic, 2% Hindu, and the remainder follow various traditional beliefs

Currency Kenya shilling (Ksh)

Rate of exchange US$1 = Ksh81; £1 = Ksh125; €1 = Ksh103 (Sep 2010)

Head of state President Mwai Kibaki

Prime minister Raila Odinga

National airline/airport Kenya Airways/Jomo Kenyatta International (Nairobi)

International dialing code 254

Time GMT+3

Electrical voltage 220-240V 60Hz. Round or square three-pin British-style plugs

Weights and measures Metric

Flag Black, red and green vertical stripes, separated by two narrow white bands, with a shield in the centre

Public holidays 1 January, 1 May, 1 June, 10 October, 20 October, 16 November, 12 December, 25 December, 26 December; also Good Friday, Easter Monday and Eid al-Fitr

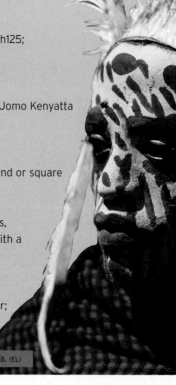

A Kikuyu wearing face paint and feathered regalia. (EL)

History

It would be misleading, and problematic, to treat Kenya as a distinct historical entity prior to the late 19th century, when the political map of Africa more or less took its present shape. To give but one example, the ports of Mombasa and Malindi share a great deal of common history with their counterparts in Mozambique, Tanzania and Somalia, but their links to most parts of the interior were practically non-existent until the colonial era. For this reason, the earlier sections in the historical account frequently range beyond the modern borders of Kenya to place events in a broader perspective.

Prehistory of the interior

A near-incontrovertible body of fossil evidence, much of it unearthed in Kenya, supports the accepted theory that the entire drama of human evolution was enacted in East Africa. The most ancient Kenyan hominid fossils include many *Australopithecus* bones from the Turkana region, some more than four million years old, and the more recently discovered remains of an arboreal hominid, tentatively assigned the binomial *Orrorin tugenensis*, that inhabited the Tugen Hills about six million years ago. Current palaeontological thinking, subject to regular revision as new evidence emerges, is that our direct Homo ancestors coexisted with various *Australopithecus* species until the latter became extinct around 500,000 years ago, and that the two genera represent discrete evolutionary lines. Some scientists believe that the *Orrorin* fossils from Tugen represent a common ancestor of all hominids as well as modern-day chimpanzees.

East Africa entered the Stone Age at least one million years ago; indeed, there is some evidence to suggest that this oldest of human technologies arose in the region. The earliest recognisable human inhabitants of East Africa were 'Batwa' hunter-gatherers, similar in both culture and physique to the so-called Bushmen of southern Africa and Pygmies of the Congo Basin. These hunter-gatherers left an enduring memorial in the form of tens of thousands of rock paintings and engravings, most prolifically in South Africa and Zimbabwe, but also in parts of Kenya. Today, the Okiek people of the Mau Escarpment represent Kenya's only surviving hunter-gatherer culture.

Agriculture and pastoralism took root in East Africa over the course of the first millennium BC, and their spread is strongly associated with the arrival of Iron-Age technology and Bantu-speaking peoples from the present-day Congo Basin. Over the past 2,000 years, Kenya has been something of a cultural crossroads, as reflected today in its linguistic diversity. A variety of different Bantu-, Cushitic- and Nilotic-speaking tribes inhabit different parts of the country, and each of these language groups arrived via multiple migrations from elsewhere in the region.

The coast until 1500

The east coast of Africa has long attracted international maritime trade. Some 3,500 years ago, during the reign of Queen Hatshepsut, Egypt undertook at least one trade mission to a port called Punt, possibly in present-day Somalia or Kenya, while the ancient Phoenicians and Romans traded for ivory and tortoiseshell with a port called Rhapta, probably in today's Tanzania. The rise of Islam in Arabia marked the beginning of a more enduring Indian Ocean trade epoch, often referred to as the Shirazi or Swahili Era. The origins of this trade go undocumented, but the presence of 9th-century Islamic ruins in the Lamu Archipelago suggest it was firmly entrenched within a century or two of the Prophet Muhammad's lifetime.

From around AD1000, the main item of coastal trade was gold, mined in present-day Zimbabwe, transported by caravan to Sofala (Mozambique) and then shipped along to various more northerly ports for trade with boats from Arabia and, to a lesser extent, Asia. By the 13th century, the coast between Mogadishu and Sofala supported some 30 mercantile Swahili city-states, many of which were on islands and thus relatively easy to defend. Several of these city-states survive into the modern era, notably Mombasa, Malindi, Lamu and Pate in Kenya, but our best idea of their contemporary appearance comes from the ruins of those that haven't, for instance Gedi.

The ruins at Gedi, one of many Swahili medieval city-states along the East African coast (AZ)

The Islamic architectural influence at these coastal cities has led many popular accounts to treat them as Arabic implants, but historians believe there was significant integration between the Arab settlers and indigenous Africans, and that the latter were numerically dominant in most Swahili cities. Certainly KiSwahili, the main language of the coast, is fundamentally Bantu, both in terms of grammar and vocabulary, and where Arabic words have been adopted, this mainly occurred in the 18th century. Oddly, the early Swahili traders appear to have had little or no interest in the African interior, which remained largely unknown to outsiders until the 19th century.

The Portuguese and Omani eras

Portugal was the first European power to forge a maritime route to Asia via Africa, an epic of discovery that began with the capture of the Moroccan port of Ceuta in 1415 and culminated with Vasco da Gama's circumnavigation of the Cape of Good Hope in 1498. Before crossing the Indian Ocean to Goa, da Gama sailed up the east coast of Africa, and the hostile reception accorded to him at Mombasa, then the wealthiest port

The Vasco da Gama Pillar commemorates the Portuguese navigator's arrival in 1498. (AZ)

between Mogadishu and Kilwa, paved the way for the weaker Sultan of Malindi to forge an enduring alliance with Portugal. In 1505, Portugal captured Kilwa and Sofala, taking control of the gold trade at its source, and followed this up with vicious raids on several large ports further north, including Mombasa. Only Malindi was spared, to become Portugal's base on the northern part of the African coast.

By 1530, Portugal was entrenched as the dominant power in the Indian Ocean, having used its superior firepower to seize the Indian port of Goa and blockade the Persian Gulf to prevent boats from leaving Oman. However, while the spice trade with India boomed, the trade in gold was disappointing, not least because the Swahili merchants established clandestine routes that circumvented any Portuguese-held ports. In 1589, a rebellion against Portugal at Mombasa was quashed, and Portugal relocated there from Malindi, building Fort Jesus, its main East African stronghold over the next century.

In 1589 and 1596 respectively, the first British and Dutch boats sailed around the Cape, and Portuguese pre-eminence was threatened by the subsequent foundation of the British East India Company (BEIC) and Dutch East India Company. The BEIC blockaded Portugal's Indian stronghold at Goa, and combined forces with the Omani navy to evict Portugal from the entrance to the Persian Gulf in 1622, leading to the resumption of free trade between Oman and India, and to a tacit but enduring Anglo–Omani alliance. In 1698, Fort Jesus was captured by Oman, effectively ending the era of Portuguese influence on the coast north of present-day Mozambique.

Over the course of the 18th century, Britain asserted itself as the dominant European power in the Indian Ocean. By the start of the 19th century, its only significant rival was Oman, whose Sultan Seyyid Said radically reshaped the politics of the Indian Ocean during his lengthy rule (1804–54). In 1827, Said captured Mombasa from the upstart Mazrui dynasty, giving him full control over the coast north of Mozambique. Said selected Zanzibar as his East African base, due to its proximity to Bagamoyo (the terminus of a caravan route to Lake Tanganyika since 1823) and planted the island with cloves, giving scant regard to the land claims of the existing inhabitants. By 1840, the Omani dominated commerce on the island, and Sultan Said further consolidated his position by relocating his capital from Oman to Zanzibar.

Under Sultan Said, the slave trade out of East Africa, once negligible by comparison with West Africa, increased exponentially. By the 1830s, an estimated 50,000 slaves were sold annually on Zanzibar, and twice as many captives died on the long march from the interior to the coast, while many more met a brutal end in their villages at the hands of slave raiders. Britain made genuine efforts to stall this trade, encouraging Said to sign an 1822 treaty forbidding the sale of slaves to Christian countries, and an 1845 treaty outlawing the export of slaves south of Kilwa or north of Lamu. Neither treaty was easy to enforce, however, as it wasn't difficult for traders to use obscure ports to escape detection, and Britain had no influence over the Omani caravan routes through the interior to lakes Victoria, Tanganyika and Malawi.

European exploration of the interior

In 1850, Europe knew little more about the East African interior than it had when Portugal first landed on the coast 350 years earlier. Indeed, it was only in the 1840s that the German missionaries Rebmann and Krapf first reported the existence of Mount Kilimanjaro and Mount Kenya, and their

Livingstone and the slave trade

Remembered mainly as an explorer, Livingstone's greatest legacy was his role in the abolition of the slave trade, whose cruelties he had ample opportunity to witness first hand during his long wanderings. An outspoken critic of the trade, Livingstone believed it could be halted only by opening Africa up to the three Cs: Christianity, Commerce and Civilisation. His funeral at Westminster Abbey in 1872 catalysed the anti-

David Livingstone (1813–1873) (wc)

slaving efforts of several church institutions, industrialists and governments. But the biggest victory for anti-slavers came in 1873, when the British Navy blockaded Zanzibar, and the local British consul John Kirk, a former travel companion of Livingstone, offered Sultan Barghash (son of Said) full protection against foreign powers if he banned the slave trade. Barghash agreed. The slave market was closed and an Anglican church built over it. The trade continued on the mainland for some years, but at a much-reduced volume as most caravans reverted to ivory as their principal trade, while many coastal traders started rubber and sugar plantations.

descriptions of snow on the Equator met with open ridicule in Europe. Over the next 40 years, however, the likes of David Livingstone (see box, above), Sir Richard Burton, John Speke and Henry Stanley undertook a series of pioneering expeditions into the East African interior, prompted by a renewed obsession with a mystery that had tickled geographers since Roman times – the location of the source of the Nile. Over 1858–59, the continent's three largest lakes – Victoria, Tanganyika and Malawi – were all discovered, and Speke controversially nominated Lake Victoria as the Nile's source, an assertion that was confirmed by Stanley only in 1875.

With the exception of a German Mission founded in the Taita Hills in the 1840s, the Kenyan interior remained unexplored for several decades after Tanzania had been opened up. This is partly because the slave caravan routes followed by most European explorers left from ports south of the present-day border, and partly because of the renowned ferocity of the Maasai towards visitors. The first outside expedition into Maasailand was undertaken by the German explorer Gustav Fischer in 1883 and got as far as Lake Naivasha before being forced to turn back. Fischer was

Thomson's Falls are named after Joseph Thomson, the first European to travel through Maasailand. (AZ)

followed a few months later by Joseph Thomson, whose discoveries included lakes Bogoria and Baringo, as well as the waterfall outside Nyahururu that still bears his name. The more northerly Lake Turkana remained no more than a rumour until March 1888, when its eastern shore was mapped by the wealthy Hungarian aristocrat Count Teliki, a portly hedonist in his early 40s who shed more than 40kg during the course of an extraordinary expedition that also saw him become the first European to hike to altitudes of 5,350m on Mount Kilimanjaro and 4,725m on Mount Kenya. It would be another seven years before Donaldson-Smith became the first European to visit Marsabit Mountain. The last of Kenya's cartographic blanks was filled as recently as 1909, when Stigand crossed the Chalbi Desert between Marsabit and Lake Turkana.

Partition and colonisation

The foreign powers involved in the so-called Scramble for Africa entered into it with mixed motives – erratic enthusiasm, little premeditation and a combination of nonchalance and whimsy for which Africa is still paying. In the space of less than a decade, a handful of European bureaucrats contrived to divide up the continent into arbitrarily defined territories whose borders were formative to the African countries we know today. In many cases, these new boundaries bisected territories occupied by unified ethnic groups (the Maasai of Kenya and Tanzania, for instance) or made compatriots of neighbouring tribes with a long history of conflict.

The division of eastern Africa was particularly arbitrary. For much of the 19th century, Britain had held a degree of influence over Zanzibar that amounted to informal colonialism, and it was actively opposed to the direct acquisition of African colonies. Two events changed this. The first was the decision of King Leopold of Belgium to colonise the Congo Basin in 1878. The second, more immediately relevant to East Africa, was an unexpected German claim to several territories in present-day Tanzania that already formed part of the Sultanate of Zanzibar. In 1886, Britain and Germany negotiated a territorial partition identical to the modern border between Kenya and Tanzania. In 1890, German claims to Lamu and the northern Victoria hinterland led to a fresh round of negotiations in which Germany relinquished its claims to Zanzibar and much of present-day Kenya and Uganda in exchange for control over Heligoland, a strategic North Sea island less than 1km² in area.

In 1888, the fundaments of the pending colonial administration were set in place by Sir William MacKinnon and his Imperial British East Africa Company (IBEA), which established a series of fortified trading posts 80km apart between Mombasa and the fertile Lake Victoria basin. Several IBEA forts, notably Machakos and Mumias, have since developed into towns. The IBEA established treaties with several tribes, including the feared Maasai, who were at the time weakened by a combination of smallpox, rinderpest and drought. Other less suppliant tribes were quelled into submission using military force. Following the collapse of the IBEA in 1895, the British East African Protectorate was created, comprising present-day Kenya and Uganda (Kenya only became a Crown Colony in 1920). Between 1896 and 1901, Britain set about constructing the 'Uganda Railway' (a somewhat deceptive moniker to the modern reader, since the railway only reached Kisumu, part of Uganda until 1902), with the loss of thousands of lives to malaria and, with greater publicity, man-eating lions.

Decisive in shaping modern Kenya was Lord Elgin's pledge in 1907 that the fertile highlands around Mount Kenya and the Aberdares, traditional home of the Kikuyu, would be reserved for white settlers. As a result, the first militant anti-colonial action was centred upon these 'White Highlands' in the aftermath of World War II, when thousands upon thousands of African conscripts had been shipped around the world to fight for the freedom of their colonisers, only to return home and find

Officials of the Imperial British East Africa Company make a treaty with the Kikuyu people, 1897. (MEPL)

their own liberty as restricted as ever. Resentment rode particularly high in the central highlands north of Nairobi, where farmland owned by European settlers extended over an area six times larger than was allocated to the region's million-plus rural Kikuyu. So it was that in 1945 a group of dissidents, dominated by the Kikuyu, formed the anti-colonial Kenya African Union (KAU), leadership of which was assumed by Jomo Kenyatta, recently returned from a decade in the UK with a degree from the University of London, in 1947. An attack on a white farm near the Aberdares in 1952 prompted the colonial administration to declare a State of Emergency, to ban the KAU and to imprison Kenyatta and several other African leaders.

The Kikuyu response was the formation of the Mau-Mau, a Kikuyu-dominated guerrilla army that used the forests of Mount Kenya and the Aberdares as a base from which to attack government installations and settler farms. Portrayed as bloodthirsty savages by the colonial authorities and the international media, the Mau-Mau were responsible for the deaths of about 32 settlers and 60 British soldiers, less than 1% of the estimated 10,000–50,000 Kikuyu civilians who were either killed by the military or died in unsanitary concentration camps during the rebellion. Generally judged to be a military failure, this rebellion nevertheless did much to hasten the end of colonial rule, and it was a former Mau-Mau leader – Kenyatta – who eventually led Kenya to independence in 1963, and served as the country's first president.

Independence

Increasing internal pressure for self determination led to the Lancaster House talks in 1960, where it was agreed that a democratic election would be held in 1961 prior to the granting of independence in 1963. Shortly after this, the KAU split into two parties, KANU and KADU, the former officially led by Kenyatta who was at that time under house arrest. KANU won the 1961 election with 19 seats to KADU's 11, and it refused to assume power until Kenyatta was released. On 12 December 1963, Kenyatta became the first president of an independent Kenya, a position he held until his death in August 1978.

Contrary to the expectations of a great many doomsayers, the Kenyatta era was marked by a high degree of racial reconciliation and steady economic growth, the latter driven by the agricultural and tourist sectors (largely nullified by a correspondingly high birth rate which has seen Kenya's population quadruple since independence). Politically, the country rapidly became a one-party state, in effect if not in law, and Kenyatta's opponents tended to be jailed. In 1969, the assassination of Tom Mboya, the popular Luo vice president who was hotly tipped as

Prime Minister Kenyatta and the Duke of Edinburgh drive through cheering crowds in Nairobi during the independence day celebrations, 1963. (A/MEPL)

Kenyatta's successor, brought to the fore the tension between Kikuyu and Luo that has underscored Kenya's politics. Public faith in KANU was not improved in 1975 when the Kikuyu radical J M Kariuki called Kenya a nation of 'ten millionaires and ten million beggars'. He was arrested and weeks later found dead on the hills outside Nairobi.

Kenyatta's successor as president, Daniel arap Moi, gained some initial popularity by releasing all political prisoners and launching a campaign to stamp out corruption. It was all to be rather short-lived, however, as Moi realised that an atmosphere of open political debate was not entirely to his taste. The prominent Luo leader Oginga Odinga was expelled from KANU, academics and politicians were arrested, and in 1982 Kenya was officially declared a one-party state. Later that year, a failed coup attempt by the improbable combination of the air force and students resulted in 150 deaths and extensive looting in Nairobi. From this time up until the end of the Cold War, Moi ran Kenya as a 'benign' dictator on the lines of Malawi's Banda, and he profited greatly from the backing of Western governments and businesses.

During the 1990s, Moi came under increasing pressure to introduce political reform. After large amounts of Western aid were cut off in 1991, Moi held what was effectively the country's first multi party election in December 1992. Contrary to expectations, however, KANU won a comfortable majority of seats, a result that can be attributed to the combination of superior funding (banknotes totalling US$250 million in

Kenya shillings were printed just before the election for campaigning purposes), a hopelessly divided opposition (a mere 30% of the votes cast were actually for KANU) and some sophisticated gerrymandering. The 1992 election left Kenya in an uncomfortable political limbo, one that resulted in a great deal of ethnic violence, especially along the coast.

Kenya in the 21st century

Moi was returned to power for a second term in 1997, in equally controversial circumstances. However, under the terms of the new constitution, he was barred from seeking a third term in the election of 2002. And as that election loomed, a radical transformation of the political landscape occurred when the country's most prominent opposition parties merged under the leadership of the Kikuyu political veteran Mwai Kibaki to form the National Rainbow Coalition (NARC). The combination of Moi's resignation and newfound unity among the opposition finally put KANU's 40-year-long stranglehold on Kenyan politics to a meaningful test, and NARC emerged victorious, with Mwai Kibaki gaining a full 62% of the presidential vote in an election that was adjudged to be free and fair by local and international observers.

The next five years witnessed some complicated political machinations and infighting, starting with a split in NARC – always a coalition of convenience – that led to the sacking of all LDP (Liberal Democratic Party) parliamentarians. Non-LDP members of the NARC loyal to Kibaki founded a new party, NARC-Kenya, while the original NARC was left in under the leadership of chairperson Charity Ngilu. The LDP effectively became an opposition party and was soon revived as the Orange Democratic Movement (ODM), to receive the formal backing of Charity Ngilu and the original NARC for the December 2007 election. Meanwhile, President Kibaki and the newly formed NARC-Kenya entered into a coalition with several other parties, including its former rival, to contest the election as the Party of National Unity (PNU), with the backing of the retired former president Moi.

This messy electoral build-up was further complicated by an inflammatory element of tribalism when it emerged that Kibaki, of the politically and numerically dominant Kikuyu tribe, would be running against Raila Odinga, a member of the Luo, which – as Kenya's second-largest tribe – had long regarded itself to be politically sidelined. In the event, the election, held on 27 December 2007, was a disaster. A high level of polling irregularities was noted by international observers, and the result itself was bitterly contested, with early exit polls and initial Electoral Commission of Kenya (ECK) counts predicting a substantial ODM victory, but the final ECK count going in favour of the PNU by about 232,000 votes.

Kibaki was sworn in as president, but Odinga accused the ECK of rigging the result, claiming that at least 300,000 votes for Kibaki were falsified, and he called for a recount, declaring himself to be the People's President. And while the politicians strutted, the country was torn apart by the most extensive tribal violence in its history, sweeping through the slums around Nairobi and west through the Rift Valley to Naivasha, Nakuru and Kisumu, as anti-government rioters clashed with police, and members of differing tribes – in particular Luo and Kikuyu – set upon each other. In the weeks that followed, more than 1,500 people died in ethnic clashes, and another 300,000 were forced to flee their homes. The violence ended in February 2008, when an eminent persons group led by former UN secretary-general Kofi Annan brokered a power-sharing deal that effectively retained Kibaki as president but made Odinga prime minister in a grand coalition. So far, the coalition has held, but the events of early 2008 did much to tarnish Kenya's hard-earned reputation as being one of the most peaceful and stable of African nations, and it remains to be seen whether the spirit of reconciliation will carry on into the next election, scheduled for late 2012.

People

Kenya is an ethnically diverse country, with some 40 different tribes placed in three major linguistic groupings: Bantu, Cushitic and Nilotic. Of these, the Cushitic speakers, who originate further north in Ethiopia, have held tenure in Kenya the longest, probably about 3,000 years, though only the tiny Boni tribe are thought to be survivors of that earliest wave of arrivals, with the Somali and Rendille being more recent arrivals. Likewise, Nilotic-speakers have migrated into Kenya from the Sudanese Nile Valley on several unrelated occasions, with the earliest being the Kalenjin at least 2,000 years ago, and the most recent being the Maasai and Samburu within the last 300 years.

Maasai warrior draped in the customary red-checked blanket. (EL)

The origin of the various Bantu-speaking peoples is fuzzier. Linguistic and archaeological evidence indicates one extended migration of Bantu-speakers from the Congo Basin into eastern and southern Africa around 2,500–2,000 years ago. Simultaneously introducing Iron-Age technology to the region, these migrants fanned out in all directions to become the dominant linguistic group in most parts of sub-equatorial Africa through an undocumented process of absorption of and into the cultures of the existing inhabitants. (And, since it is difficult to say to what extent this process depended on intermarriage, political dominance, physical conquest and/or enslavement, the linguistic term 'Bantu-speaker' signifies no more about ethnicity than does the term 'English-speaker' in the USA.)

Bantu-speakers

Bantu-speakers account for more than 70% of Kenya's population, with the most significant individual tribes being the Kikuyu (21% of the total population), Luhya (14%), Akamba (11%), Gusii (6%), Ameru (5%), Embu (1.2%), Taita (1%) and Swahili (0.6%). It seems certain that these different tribes are the product of several different migrations into the region, as well as more localised movements, over the past two millennia. The most important of these involved the Kikuyu, Ameru, Akamba and Embu, all of whom live in and around the central highlands north and east of Nairobi, speak mutually understandable languages, and share varying degrees of cultural affinity. Oral traditions suggest that a common ancestor of all these tribes was a group of Bantu-speaking agriculturists that migrated from somewhere further north to the Nyambeni Hills (northeast of Mount Kenya) in the 13th century and expanded their influence all across the central highlands over the ensuing 300 years.

Kikuyu

The most populous tribe in Kenya, totalling an estimated eight million in 2010, is the Kikuyu, or more correctly Agikuyu ('Children of Gikuyu'). Oral tradition has it that the Kikuyu nation was founded in the 16th century by a man called Gikuyu, whose nine daughters married a group of nine men from a distant land. Kikuyu traditions centre upon a single deity called Ngai ('Provider'), who lives high on the glacial peaks of Mount Kenya (known to the Kikuyu as Kiriniaga). Their homesteads always face the sacred peaks, a custom referred to in the title of the late President Kenyatta's book *Facing Mount Kenya*. Predisposed to monotheism and heavily exposed to missionaries in the early colonial era, the Kikuyu are now predominantly Christian, and most shun traditional beliefs, which also placed a high premium on ancestral worship. As with most other Kenyan tribes, Kikuyu teenagers must traditionally undergo ceremonial initiation into adulthood,

with males being circumcised and females being subjected to female genital mutilation (FGM), a practice that is now illegal and in decline. The Kikuyu lifestyle, traditionally based around mixed agriculture, altered radically during the early 20th century, when most of the central highlands was carved up into settler farms, resulting in mass displacement and feudalistic dependency on colonial landlords. Ironically, this association led to the Kikuyu becoming the most educated and cosmopolitan of Kenya's peoples, and they have dominated business and politics affairs since independence.

Ameru and Embu

Linguistically and culturally affiliated to the Kikuyu, the Ameru and Embu people live on the eastern slopes of Mount Kenya, with populations centred respectively on the towns of Meru and Embu. While their language is clearly Bantu, the Ameru boast a complex and enigmatic oral tradition, rich in biblical overtones, stating that they migrated to their present homeland after being held as slaves on an island called Mbwa (possibly Manda or somewhere off the coast of Somalia or Yemen). Today, both the Ameru and the numerically less significant Embu practise mixed agriculture, and their fertile lands are the country's main producers of *miraa* (the mildly narcotic leaf also known as *khat*).

Akamba man with bow and arrow at his hut, Ngomongo
(AZ)

Akamba

The fifth-largest tribe in Kenya, the Akamba inhabit the dry hilly country northeast of Nairobi and west of Tsavo, a region known as Ukambani, centred on the towns of Machakos and Kitui. The Akamba served as intermediaries between the coastal traders and people of the central highlands during the 19th century, and many also worked as guides and porters, initially for the Omani trade caravans and then for the early European explorers and settlers. Traditionally renowned as skilled craftspeople, as well as for their business acumen, the Akamba produce many of the woodcarvings you see on sale at stalls in Nairobi and along the coast, and they are also very active in business and commerce. Their honey, produced from hives hung in baobab trees, is regarded to be the finest in Kenya.

Swahili

The Swahili, whose name derives from the Arabic *sawahil* (plural of *sahel*, meaning 'edge' or 'coast'), are a coastal people whose ethnicity and culture reflect more than a millennium of trade and cultural interchange between the Persian Gulf and East Africa, and the associated intermarriage between Arab settlers and indigenous Africans. Although the Swahili account for a mere 0.6%

Swahili girl wearing traditional *bui-bui* standing at a Zanzibar door in the Arab Fort, Lamu. (AZ)

of Kenya's population, they remain a dominant force in coastal trade, and their language KiSwahili – classified as Bantu, albeit with a relatively simplified grammar and a peppering of Arabic words – is the lingua franca of East Africa.

Culturally, the Swahili display a strong Arabian influence, most of all when it comes to religion, with Islam having been predominant along the coast for many centuries.

The Swahili stand alone from other Kenyans in many other aspects of their culture, from their distinctive urban architecture, which shows clear Islamic influences and is best seen today in Lamu, to their distinctive cuisine, which fuses Indian and Arabic spices with the trademark ingredient of grated coconut flesh or coconut milk. No records survive to tell us exactly when these exotic and indigenous elements first melded into

Music and literature

Swahili Taarab or Tarabu music fuses KiSwahili lyrics with Arabic-style melodies using traditional instruments such as the lute-like udi, darbuk drums and zither-like gannon alongside guitar, violin and keyboards. The oldest known Swahili document is *Utenzi wa Tambuka* ('Story of Tambuka'), an epic poem written in Arabic script in the town of Pate in 1728, but the Swahili literary tradition is much older than this, with the earliest works having been transmitted orally.

a distinct Afro-Islamic culture, but contemporary accounts and archaeological remains demonstrate that the East African coast was studded with stone-built Islamic city-states that are recognisably Swahili in character from the 12th century onwards.

Luhya and Gusii

The two main Bantu-speaking tribes of the western highlands, the Luhya and Gusii respectively comprise 14% and 6% of the national population, with the former being the second-largest ethnic group in the country. The two groups share many cultural affiliations, but their territories are separated by Winan Gulf, the arm of Lake Victoria that runs northeast to Kisumu. In the 19th century, the more northerly and centralised Luhya state ranked as the most important polity in this part of Kenya, with a territory that extended from the Ugandan border to Lake Naivasha. The Gusii, also known as the Kisii, inhabit the fertile hills southeast of Winan Gulf, an area surrounded on all sides by Nilotic-speakers, which led to them developing a rather warlike and insular mentality in pre-colonial times. The fertile highlands occupied by both tribes supports a natural cover of rainforest, most of which has been cleared for agriculture, the main pursuit in the region today. The area around Kericho and Kisii, the principal towns of the Gusii, supports the country's largest tea plantations and is renowned for the sculptures made from pink soapstone quarried at Tabaka.

Tea pickers on a large estate near Kericho (NP/C)

Taita and Mijikenda

Possibly the oldest Bantu-speaking tribe in Kenya, the Taita arrived in the Taita Hills and Taveta District from the south about 1,000 years ago.

Several subgroups exist, of which the Sagalla are linguistically closest to the Chagga of nearby Kilimanjaro District in Tanzania, while the Kasigau of the Taita Hills are strongly affiliated to the Mijikenda or Giriama, whose territory covers most non-urbanised stretches of coast in Kenya and northern Tanzania. Both the Taita and Mijikenda comprise several distinct tribal lineages, each with its own territories, traditions and leaders, and all traditionally place a greater emphasis on the worship of ancestors than of deities, though early exposure to missionaries (Taita was the site of the first inland mission in Kenya) means that Christianity now dominates.

Nilotic- and Cushitic-speakers

Although Nilotic- and Cushitic-speakers account for about 30% of Kenya's total population, the territory they inhabit comprises more than 70% of its surface area, including most areas that are neither suitable for agriculture nor set aside as national parks. The most numerically significant of these tribes, the Nilotic-speaking Luo and the Kalenjin, are the third- and fourth-largest in Kenya respectively, each accounting for slightly more than 12% of the total population. Most other Nilotic- and Cushitic-speaking tribes are pastoral nomads whose territories range across the vast arid badlands of the north and southeast. Although these tribes are mostly insignificant in numeric terms – indeed, none accounts for more than 1.5% of the total population – their adherence to traditional cultures and costumes makes them of considerable interest to visitors.

Luo

The main political rivals to the Kikuyu, the Luo inhabit the northeast Lake Victoria basin, and though their main population centre falls within Kenya it also spills across the border into parts of Tanzania and Uganda. The Luo are Nilotic-speakers who migrated southward from Sudan in the 15th century and came into conflict with the more centralised kingdoms of present-day Uganda before settling in the Lake Victoria region. Originally pastoralists, they announced their arrival here by making regular cattle raids on the existing residents, who either integrated into the Luo through war and intermarriage or else fled into the highlands around Kisii. Cattle herding still forms a part of traditional Luo lifestyle but the lake itself has long since become their main source of protein, though farming is also an important livelihood, and many Luo are active in business. Unlike most Kenyan tribes, the Luo have no tradition of ritual circumcision, but it had been traditional to remove the six lower front teeth as a form of initiation, a practice that has been discontinued today.

Following a series of decisive battles between 1896 and 1889, the Luo succumbed to colonial rule. This brought a significant benefit to the region in the form of the Uganda Railway, whose original terminus at Kisumu became the main port and economic hub of the Lake Victoria basin in the early 20th century. When independence came in 1963, the Luo enjoyed a high standard of education overall, and their political significance rivalled the Kikuyu. Indeed, KANU initially offered the presidency of Kenya to the Luo leader Oginga Odinga, who declined in favour of Jomo Kenyatta and became vice president instead. Odinga defected from KANU in 1966, since when the Luo have become increasingly politically marginalised, a circumstance that led to widespread rioting and killing when Raila Odinga (son of Oginga) lost the December 2007 election to Mwai Kibaki, a Kikuyu.

Kalenjin

A relict of the earliest-known wave of Nilotic-speaking migration into Kenya some 2,000 years ago, the Kalenjin inhabit the western Rift Valley and its escarpment and have an unverified oral history tracing their origin back to ancient Egypt. As might be expected of such long-standing inhabitants of Kenya, they are a culturally diverse lot, comprising about a dozen subgroups including the Kipsigis, Marakwet, Nandi, Pokot and Tugen. Indeed, the collective name Kalenjin, a Nandi greeting meaning 'I say', was first coined in the early 1950s, largely for political reasons, as it instantly transformed a cluster of small obscure tribes into one of the country's five major ethnic groups. Today, they are renowned for their prowess as long- and middle-distance runners; indeed, Kalenjin runners have won about 40% of the top honours available to men in international athletics at these distances since 1980, and the women have made an equally impressive showing in recent years. A great many of their runners, including Wilfred Bungei, Bernard Lagat, Peter Rono, Pamela Jalimo and Martin Lel, were born in or near the Nandi administrative capital of Kapsabet.

Pokot woman (EL)

Maasai hierarchy

Maasai men perform their traditional pogo-like dance, with plaudits going to he who jumps highest off the ground. (EL)

The central unit of Maasai society is the age-set. Every 15 years or so, a new generation of warriors or Ilmoran is named and every eligible boy must undergo circumcision, performed without anaesthetic, as entry into that group. Should the initiate cry out, his post-circumcision ceremony is cancelled and he will be rejected by his peers for several years before being forgiven. With the initiation of a new age-set, the existing age-set of Ilmoran become junior elders, responsible for all political and legislative decisions, and the junior elders graduate to become senior elders, a rank that means they are permitted to marry. Political decisions are made democratically, and the role of the Laibon (chief elder) is essentially spiritual and moral.

Maasai and Samburu

The most instantly recognisable of Kenya's peoples, the red-robed Maasai seem to embody popular perceptions of East Africa, yet oddly enough they are among the most recent arrivals to the region, having migrated southwards from the Sudanese Nile to settle in the Kenyan–Tanzanian border area in the 18th century. The warlike nature of the Maasai made life difficult for the existing inhabitants of this region, and it also ensured that their territory was studiously avoided by the slave caravans that started rolling into the interior in the early 19th century. Maasailand was one of the last parts of East Africa ventured into by Europeans, whose arrival triggered a rinderpest epidemic that killed more than 90% of Maasai cattle and caused much of their land to be recolonised by other tribes or incorporated into game reserves and settler farms.

Maasai culture and dress are similar to that of other related Nilotic-speaking pastoralists such as the Samburu, a northern offshoot who speak the same Maa language and inhabit the plains north of the central highlands. The Maasai men drape their body in a toga-like red blanket, dye their hair ochre, have decorated ear lobes cut away from the main part of the ear, and seldom go far without their trademark wooden poles and/or spears. Maasai women also usually dress traditionally, in loosely draped colourful cloths and, like the men, they wear lots of beaded jewellery. The illegal practice of FGM, often known euphemistically as female circumcision, is still practised widely among the Maasai and other pastoralist societies.

A Samburu courting dance in which young men and younger girls form future couples. (EL)

Maasai society is polygamous – an elder can take as many wives as he can afford. Arranged marriages are sometimes brokered before the female party is born, with a man 'booking' the next daughter produced by a friend for his son. The most important measures of wealth in Maasai society are cattle and children, and a man who has plenty of one but not the other is regarded to be poor. This rather anachronistic configuration means that many Maasai households live on the poverty line, despite being relatively wealthy – children are produced at an astonishing rate, and no self-respecting Maasai would demean his standing my converting cattle to cash!

The Maasai believe in a single deity with a dualistic nature: the benevolent Engai Narok ('Black God') and vengeful Engai Nanyokie ('Red God'). This deity lives in the crater of Ol Doinyo L'Engai ('Mountain of God'), a volcano on the Tanzanian shore of Lake Natron that most recently erupted in 2007. Traditionally, the Maasai feed almost exclusively off their cattle, shunning wildlife, vegetable matter or fish. Their main diet isn't meat but a blend of milk and blood (drained painlessly, it is said, from a nick in the cow's jugular vein), which is fermented in a calabash for several days before being drunk.

Gabbra women at a wedding dance (EL)

Northern nomads

The north of Kenya, like neighbouring parts of southern Ethiopia, is inhabited by some of the most traditional societies that remain in Africa.

For the most part, these tribes are Nilotic- or Cushitic-speakers who shun outside influences in favour of a pastoral lifestyle bequeathed to them by generations of stoic desert-dwelling ancestors. Traditionally, these people – the Borena, Turkana, Gabbra, Rendille and others – were true nomads, whose struggle to subsist in this merciless environment was mirrored by a perpetual state of territorial conflict. However, in the early 20th century, the new colonial administration imposed regional boundaries that served to entrench tribal territories as they happened to stand at the time, and today most of its inhabitants are semi-nomadic or sedentary. That aside, cultures, customs and dress codes throughout the region are staunchly traditional.

The most numerous people of the north are the Turkana, Nilotic-speakers who account

Turkana woman with traditional lip plug (AZ)

for about 1% of the total population. Superficially, the Turkana look quite similar to the Maasai and Samburu, and they dress with comparable flair, but their arrival in Kenya preceded that of the Maasai by several centuries, and their language is closer to Karamojong of northeast Uganda. They herd camels rather than cattle, and live in impermanent huts made of sticks and dried grass. Turkana women are often strikingly attired in beaten hides and beaded jewellery, with an ochre Mohican hairstyle and a goatee-like lower lip plug.

Among the most intriguing of the northern nomads are the Cushitic-speaking Gabbra and Borena, both small subsets of the Oromo of Ethiopia. The Gabbra, nomadic camel-herders of the Chalbi Desert, display an ancient Arabic influence in their vocabulary, in their complicated calendar (which has allowed them to maintain a very precise

oral history, albeit one that gets rather hazy regarding events prior to the 19th century), and in their dress of long, flowing colourful robes. The less nomadic Borena, whose main population centre is around Marsabit, are best known for their deep 'singing wells', some of which are thought to be almost a thousand years old. One of the cultural highlights of northern Kenya is the sight of dozens of Borena men chanting and singing as they line up to hoist buckets of water from the pool in the base of the well. Other Cushitic-speakers in northern Kenya include the Somali of the far northeast and the Rendille of the Maralal area.

Borena woman in the doorway of a traditionally painted house (EL)

2 The Natural World

Kenya's natural assets are legendary, and with good reason. Straddling the Equator, it boasts a remarkable natural variety, ranging from deserts to glacial peaks, lush rainforests to acacia-studded savanna, and palm-lined Indian Ocean beaches to vast inland seas such as Lakes Victoria and Turkana. As a result, it supports an incredible variety of life forms, most famously such safari favourites as lion, elephant, rhino, giraffe and leopard, though a better reflection of its biodiversity is the bird checklist of 1,136 species – more than any other African country other than the DRC, despite Kenya ranking a relatively lowly 22nd on the continent in terms of area. These wild places and their inhabitants are protected within a superb network of national park and reserves that include some of the finest safari destinations in the world.

Geography and climate

Kenya is a country of great geographic and climatic extremes. Simplistically, however, the country can be divided into a low-lying coastal belt in the southeast, which consists of 536km of tropical Indian Ocean frontage between the Somali and Tanzanian borders, and a more elevated interior. Much of the interior is volcanic in origin, with evidence of recent activity particularly visible in the vicinity of Tsavo West in the form of the 200-year-old Shetani Lava Flow and Chiamu Crater. The dominant geographic feature of Kenya is of course the Great Rift Valley, an ever-expanding chasm that formed as a result of tectonic activity some 20 million years ago, and which now bisects the country from Lake Turkana in the north to Lake Magadi in the south.

The highest part of Kenya is the southwest where the central highlands around Mount Kenya and Nairobi and the western highlands around Eldoret and Kitale are separated from each other by a dramatic stretch of the Rift Valley studded with lakes and dormant volcanoes. Set entirely within Kenya, the 5,199m Mount Kenya, an extinct volcano created by the same processes that formed the Rift Valley, is the second-highest mountain in Africa. It is exceeded in altitude only by the 5,891m Mount Kilimanjaro, which lies on the southern border of Kenya, dominating the landscape of Amboseli National Park, even though its volcanic peak actually lies within Tanzania. The highest peak in the western highlands is

View over the Rift Valley from the road between Nairobi and Naivasha (AZ)

Kenya's climate

Kenya is set entirely within the tropics; indeed, the Equator runs west from the Somali border to the Ugandan border via the towns of Meru, Nanyuki, Nyahururu and Kisumu. As such, altitude rather than latitude is the main determining factor in local climates. Broadly speaking, the coast of Kenya is very hot and moist, with temperatures and humidity levels peaking from December to March and rainfall figures peaking from April to June (and to a lesser extent October and November). The Lake Victoria basin is a bit cooler but has a similar rainfall pattern and humidity levels to the coast. Nairobi and the surrounding central highland areas are cooler than might be expected of a region straddling the Equator, and can often be quite chilly at night, with a main rainy season from March to May and another rainfall peak from late October to early December. The Rift Valley south of Nakuru is hot and relatively dry, as is the coastal hinterland protected within Tsavo and Amboseli national parks. The vast but thinly populated region north of Mount Kenya and the Tana River graduates from semi-desert to desert conditions, and typically has soaring midday temperatures, becoming a lot cooler overnight, and an average annual rainfall of well under 250mm.

the 4,321m Mount Elgon, which straddles the border with Uganda and is also volcanic in origin.

Some 11,227km^2 of Kenya comprises open water, accounting for 2.3% of its total surface area. This includes about 6% of Lake Victoria, at 68,800km^2 the largest body of water in Africa, with the other 94% being divided between Tanzania and Uganda. The largest expanse of water within Kenya's borders is the 6,405km^2 Lake Turkana, the northern tip of which extends into Ethiopia, where it is fed by the Omo River. Set in the arid base of the northern Rift Valley, Turkana is generally regarded to be the largest desert lake in the world. Other lakes set within the Kenyan Rift Valley include freshwater Naivasha and Baringo, and the more saline Nakuru, Bogoria, Elmenteita and Magadi. Kenya has few significant rivers. The largest are the Galana and the Tana, both of which rise in the central highlands and drain into the Indian Ocean. The Tana and various tributaries feed the country's largest artificial lake, the Masinga Reservoir, which lies northeast of Nairobi and is an important source of hydro-electric power and household water. Another important river is the Ewaso Nyiro, which rises on the western slopes of Mount Kenya, arcs west then north via Thomson's Falls and Samburu-Buffalo Springs, before flowing eastward into Somalia.

Habitats and vegetation

Kenya supports a rich diversity of habitats, and learning to identify the main ones can greatly enhance a safari, helping you to predict what wildlife might be seen in a given location, and assisting in the identification of similar-looking species. The term 'habitat' might refer to something quite small and specific, such as a lily-covered pool or isolated hill, or to a more generic landscape like the vast, semi-arid plains of the north. And some animals, like hippos, have very specific habitat requirements, whereas others, such as elephant and leopard, are relatively unspecialised in this respect.

Savanna

Savanna is a loosely defined term that can be used to describe any area of grassland or open canopy woodland. In Kenya, however, it is generally used to describe relatively moist grassland habitats studded with fire-resistant trees, including the famous 'short grass plains' and more densely wooded 'long grass plains', often given a burnished hue by the red oat grass *Themedatrianda*, characteristic of the Serengeti-Mara ecosystem. Savanna is probably the natural climax vegetation type in moist parts of Africa with defined dry and wet seasons, but it may also be the result of centuries of deliberate burning by pastoralists seeking to stimulate fresh growth to feed their cattle, aided and abetted by the tree-shredding activities of elephants.

Highly characteristic of the East African savanna are thorn trees of the genus *Acacia* (see box, opposite). Other savanna trees include the sausage

Lightly wooded moist savanna typical of the Masai Mara (VL)

Acacia

Kenya's savannas are home to a variety of acacia trees, including the tall flat-topped *A. tortilis* and *A. abyssinica*, the more shrub-like three-thorned *A. Senegal*

Umbrella thorn (*Acacia tortilis*) (WW/FLPA)

and hook thorn *A. mellitero*, the swamp-loving, jaundice-barked fever tree *A. xanthophloea*, and the scraggly whistling thorn *A. drepanolobrium* – the last so named for the low whistling sound created by the wind passing through ant galls fashioned around its twinned thorns. It is worth noting here that the African acacias were recently split from their Australian counterparts and controversially placed in a new genus *Vachellia*, but we have chosen to stick with the more familiar name until this debate is resolved.

tree *Kigalia africana*, which has a thick evergreen canopy and gigantic sausage-shaped pods eaten by elephants and used by the Maasai as gourds. The candelabra tree Euphorbia candelabra is a superficially cactus-like succulent with an inverted umbrella shape that grows to more than 10m in height.

The Kenyan savanna supports immense herds of grazing ungulates, most famously the wildebeest, zebra and gazelles that migrate annually across the Serengeti-Mara. Other large grazers associated with lightly wooded savanna include eland, hartebeest, topi, reedbuck and oribi, while more thickly wooded areas are preferred by impala, buffalo, giraffe and warthog. Predator populations are proportionately dense, particularly lion, spotted hyena and black-backed jackal. Open savanna tends to support a limited avifauna but is notable for the presence of heavyweights such as ostrich, kori bustards, secretary bird and ground hornbill alongside ground-dwelling plovers, larks, longclaws, ground barbets and cisticolas. More densely wooded savanna usually supports a greater avian variety, with conspicuous perching birds such as rollers, shrikes, bee-eaters and raptors occurring alongside the more active sunbirds, lovebirds, parrots, hornbills, starlings, and helmet-shrikes and relatively secretive bush-shrikes, owls, woodpeckers, cuckoos and batises.

The flightless common ostrich is the world's largest bird. (AZ)

View from Elephant Hill, Shimba Hills National Reserve (AZ)

Forest

Forest differs from woodland in having a closed canopy and dank jungle-like feel, often comprising several tall vertically layered sub-canopies that cast a permanent shadow over a tangle of undergrowth, epiphytes and vines. Indigenous forest accounts for less than 3% of Kenya's surface area, a figure that has declined greatly in recent decades, but it is the most biodiverse of the country's terrestrial habitats. It is of particular interest to birdwatchers as the main habitat of hundreds of localised species, including the hefty, conspicuous and noisy *Bycanistes* hornbills, the colourful turacos, and a miscellany of inconspicuous warblers, secretive thrushes and lookalike greenbuls. The invertebrate diversity of the forests is incalculable, with butterflies being very well represented.

Several different forest types are recognised in Kenya. The central highlands around Nairobi and Mau Escarpment support extensive patches of Afro-montane forests, most easily explored from one of the area's so-called tree hotels (such as Serena Mountain Lodge, see page 216). Kakamega in the west is a lowland forest with strong affiliation to its west-central Africa counterparts, while coastal forests include Arabuko-Sokoke near Watamu. Elsewhere, many watercourses and other wetland habitats sustain ribbons of riparian forest, often dominated by the fever tree and various leafy Ficus species, to provide a corridor supporting forest wildlife in non-forested habitats. A striking example of this is the Ewaso Nyiro River in Samburu-Buffalo Springs, whose forested banks provide refuge to the likes of bushbuck, waterbuck and elephant in an otherwise arid region. Likewise, forest-loving black-and-white colobus monkeys and turacos are frequently seen in the riparian forest that follows the Mara River through the Masai Mara.

Semi-desert

The northeastern two-thirds of Kenya are classified as semi-arid or arid, receiving an annual rainfall of below 500mm, which makes it too dry to support cultivation or commercial ranchland. These semi-arid areas vary greatly in soil type, from the red earthy plains of Tsavo East to the black stony expanses of Dida Galgalu, but generally they support a cover of scrubby acacia thicket that transforms into a short-lived blanket of flowering greenery after good rains. Other areas, such as the arid pans of the Chalbi Desert, are practically bereft of vegetation. Wildlife tends to be thinly distributed, and it comprises mainly desert-adapted creatures such as oryx, gerenuk, Grevy's zebra and ground squirrels. The arid north is, however, very productive for birds, supporting numerous dry-country specials, including the spectacular vulturine guineafowl, Somali ostrich, golden pipit, golden-breasted starling, and a few very localised endemic larks.

The long-necked gerenuk frequently stands on its back legs while feeding to improve its reach. (AZ)

Aquatic

From the sandy beaches of Lake Victoria to the shallow soda lakes of the Gregory Rift and mangrove-lined creeks of the coast, Kenya is richly endowed when it comes to wetlands, a term embracing any habitat that combines terrestrial and aquatic features. The significance of these wetlands is almost impossible to overstate, both as a self-sustaining

Marabou stork tries to claim a flamingo carcass from an African fish eagle, Lake Nakuru National Park. (YM & JE/FLPA)

ecosystem supporting fish, amphibians and other water-associated birds and mammals, and as a source of vital drinking water to most terrestrial creatures – including humans. Sadly, wetland habitats, more than any other, are frequently threatened by development, whether that be swamp drainage, industrial pollution, the disruption of riverine habitats to feed reservoirs or hydro-electric schemes or, in the case of Lake Victoria, the colonial-era introduction of the predatory Nile perch, which has guzzled many of its endemic cichlid species to extinction.

Mammals exclusive to aquatic habitats include hippo, sitatunga, marsh mongoose and otters, but elephant and buffalo also regularly take to water, and most other species need to drink daily. More than 100 Kenyan bird species are strongly associated with one or other aquatic habitat, ranging from the swallows and martins that feed above it, to aerial anglers such as the pied kingfisher and African fish eagle, to the waders that peck in its shallows. And while a few water-associated birds, such as the Egyptian goose or cattle egret, might inhabit almost any aquatic habitat, others have more specific requirements. The African finfoot and white-backed night heron, for instance, favour still or sluggish waters with overhanging vegetation, whereas African skimmer, white-crowned lapwing and many migrant waders are associated with exposed sandbanks, and quiet lily-covered pools are the haunt of the African jacana, pygmy goose and long-toed lapwing.

Mountains, hills and cliffs

The upper slopes of East Africa's taller mountains, including Mount Kenya and Mount Elgon, support some of the region's most rarefied habitats, an ethereal cover of pastel-shaded Afro-alpine moorland and grassland.

Neither is particularly diverse faunally, but montane grasslands often host a wealth of flowering perennials such as orchids, proteas, geraniums, lilies, aster daisies, spike leafed aloes and marsh-loving red-hot pokers, attracting prodigious numbers of colourful nectar-eating sunbirds. The Afro-alpine moorland belt, between the 3,000m and 4,000m contours, is generally accessible by foot only, and is characterised by grey-pink heathers studded with otherworldly giant forms of lobelia and senecio, sometimes growing up to 5m high. The moorland zone supports a low density of mammals, but rock hyrax and pairs of klipspringer are quite

Lobelia flower, Mount Kenya National Park (FL/FLPA)

Artificial habitats

A significant proportion of Kenya supports manmade habitats, from reservoirs and plantations to urban settlements and farmland. This isn't always bad news for wildlife. Artificial reservoirs create fresh habitats for aquatic creatures, urban settlements often sustain high densities of scavenging birds, and disturbed agricultural land is ideal for certain seedeaters and finches. But these examples are very much the exception, since all artificial habitats are created at the expense of an indigenous one: what used to be moist savanna is now cultivated monoculture, what used to be indigenous forest is now sterile plantation, what used to be an aloe-clumped grassy slope is now subsistence farm, and so on. And while arid regions are less overtly affected by human activity, many are eroded or denuded by the overgrazing of livestock.

A related threat to the ecological integrity of any given ecosystem is the spread of exotics (ie: species that don't occur there naturally). These might sometimes be animals, such as the Indian house crow that breed profusely in several coastal urban centres. More often, however, they are plants introduced deliberately for cropping, plantation or hedging purposes. Most such plants are poorly adapted to local conditions and cannot survive long or propagate without human intervention, but a small proportion will find local conditions to their liking, and these adaptable aliens – referred to as invasive species – often spread like the proverbial wildfire because here they aren't controlled by the natural enemies in their country of origin. Fortunately, Kenya is far less ecologically compromised than much of the world, which is why so much wildlife still remains there, but still, every year sees further deforestation and environmental degradation.

common on rocky outcrops, and eland and elephant range up from time to time. A limited range of birds includes lammergeyer, Verreaux's eagle, alpine chat, scarlet-tufted malachite sunbird, alpine swift and various crows.

Two other sloping habitats commonly found in Kenya are koppies (small rocky hills, from the Afrikaans/Dutch, meaning 'little heads') and the tall cliffs associated with parts of the Rift Valley escarpment. Both possess something of an island ecology, offering permanent or part-time refuge to a range of rock- and thicket-loving plants and animals that couldn't easily survive on surrounding plains. The most conspicuous cliff dwellers are bush and rock hyraxes, which often live alongside each other, with the former grazing around the rocks and the latter feeding mainly on acacia and other trees, which it climbs readily. An important part of the koppie

Olive baboon on the cliff, Hell's Gate National Park (AZ)

food chain, hyraxes are the main dietary constituent of the mighty Verreaux's eagle and other raptors that nest on the pinnacles, and are also preyed upon by leopards and smaller felids that take daytime refuge in the rocks, as well as the cobras and puff adders that live in the crevices between the giant granite slabs.

Koppies and cliffs are also favoured by baboons, which seem to be more skittish and vocal in this rocky environment than on the open plains. Antelope associated with this habitat are the rock-hopping klipspringers, which seldom leave the mid to upper slopes, and the diminutive dik-diks that lurk around the base. For birders, this is a good place to seek out nightjars (the spectacular pennant-winged nightjar often displays above koppies at dusk), while conspicuous diurnal species include the red-bellied mocking cliff-chat and duller tail-flicking familiar chat.

Wildlife

The overwhelming reason why most people choose Kenya as a holiday destination is for its wildlife, which ranks among the most diverse and prolific in the world, and is protected in a superb network of national parks, national reserves, marine reserves and other conservation areas. Individual reserves are covered in the main regional body of this guidebook, but the following section provides an overview of what you are likely to see where, focusing mainly on the larger mammals that are central to the safari experience, but also providing a brief introduction to the region's extraordinary avifauna (the second-most bird species of any African country), as well as its reptiles and amphibians.

Cats

For most visitors to Kenya, the success of a safari will rest largely on the quality of big cat encounters. Stealthy, secretive and inscrutable, the cats of the family Felidae are the most efficient of mammalian killers, the most strictly carnivorous, and they exude a singular fascination that might well be explained by the fact our ancestors expended so much time and effort on keeping out of their way.

The guaranteed showstopper on any first safari, the **lion**, *Panthera leo* is Africa's largest terrestrial predator, weighing up to 220kg, and it is common in several Kenyan reserves, nowhere more so than the Masai Mara. This is the most sociable and least secretive of the world's 36 cat species, typically living in prides of up to 15 individuals, and it is very unusual among felids in that it seldom takes to the trees, and a fully grown male sports a regal mane. It is mainly a nocturnal hunter, favouring large or medium antelope such as wildebeest and impala (though buffaloes form an important part of its diet in the Masai Mara). Most of the hunting is undertaken collaboratively by females, but dominant males normally feed first after a kill. Rivalry between males is intense and takeover battles are frequently fought to the death, so two or more males often form a coalition.

The Masai Mara is famed for its golden-maned lions. (AZ)

When not feeding or fighting, lions are profoundly indolent creatures, spending up to 23 hours of any given day at rest – your best chance of seeing action or interaction in is the cool of the early morning.

For experienced safari-goers, the black-on-gold spotted **leopard** *Panthera pardus* is generally the most prized carnivore. It is a powerful and stealthy creature, often getting to within metres of its prey before it pounces, and it habitually stores its kill in a tree to keep it from hyenas and lions. Its adaptability and intensely furtive nature has made the leopard the most successful of the big cats in modern Africa; it occurs in all habitats, favouring areas with plenty of cover such as riverine woodland and rocky slopes, and it often lives in close proximity to humans for years without being detected. Sightings are infrequent, except in Samburu-Buffalo Springs and the Masai Mara.

Superficially similar to the leopard, the **cheetah** *Acynonix jubatus* is the world's fastest land animal, attaining speeds of up to 110km/h in short bursts. A creature of the open plains, it can be distinguished from the thicket-loving leopard by its simple (as opposed to rosette) spots, streamlined greyhound-like build,

Cheetahs frequently use termite mounds as surveillance points. (AZ)

The serval is one of several seldom-seen 'small cats'. (AZ)

disproportionately small head and diagnostic black 'tearmarks' below the eyes. Within Kenya, it is most common in the Masai Mara, where solitary adults or small family groups might be seen pacing restlessly across the plains, often stopping to survey the surrounds from a termite mound or fallen tree. A diurnal hunter, it favours the same cool hours that are most popular for game drives, to adverse effect in busy game reserves that permit off road driving.

Three smaller cats are very occasionally seen in Kenya's reserves. The **serval** *Felis serval* has a similar build to a cheetah, with black on gold spots giving way to heavy streaking near the head, and it favours moist grassland and riverine habitats. Generally associated with more arid habitats, the **caracal** *Felis caracal* strongly resembles the European lynx with its uniform tan coat and tufted ears. The widespread **African wild cat** *Felis sylvestris* is similar in size and appearance to a household tabby, and is in fact ancestral to the domestic cat, with which it frequently interbreeds, causing some concern as to its long-term genetic integrity.

Other carnivores

Africa's second-largest carnivore, weighing around 70kg, the blotched brown **spotted hyena** *Crocuta crocuta*, is highly conspicuous in several reserves, including the Masai Mara. It is a highly sociable creature, living in loosely structured matriarchal clans, and safari-goers who stand vigil

The spotted hyena has a characteristic hunch-backed shape. (AZ)

The African hunting dog

Formerly abundant in most Kenyan reserves, the African hunting dog is now listed as endangered, partially due to its susceptibility to diseases spread by domestic dogs, partially as a result of human persecution. About 10% of the total wild population, estimated at 5,000, is resident in Kenya, centred on Laikipia.

(AZ)

outside a den entrance will often be rewarded with fascinating interaction and other behaviour. The smaller **striped hyena** *Hyaena hyaena*, pale brown with dark vertical streaks and a blackish mane, occurs alongside it in drier areas such as Samburu-Buffalo Springs. Both species have a characteristic sloping back, powerful jaws and dog like expression. Contrary to popular myth, hyenas are not exclusively scavengers – the spotted hyena in particular is an adept hunter capable of killing an animal as large as a wildebeest – while ancient charges of hermaphrodism stems from the false scrotum and penis covering the female's vagina. Much smaller than either of the above, the **aardwolf** *Proteles cristatus* is an insectivorous hyena that occurs in drier parts of the country such as Samburu-Buffalo Springs.

The most common dog is Kenya is the **black-backed jackal** *Canis mesomelas*, an adaptable and opportunistic feeder with an ochre coat and prominent black saddle flecked by a varying amount of white or gold. Also present in many parts of Kenya are the **side-striped jackal** *Canis adustus*, which has an indistinct pale vertical stripe on each flank and a white-tipped tail, and the more uniform **common** or **golden jackal** *Canis aureus*, which has a black tail tip. All three are generally seen singly or in pairs, and can often be very approachable at their dens.

Also known as the painted dog, the **African hunting dog** *Lycaon pictus* is easily distinguished from jackals by its larger size and cryptic black, brown and cream coat; see box above. The only other canid found in Kenya is the **bat eared fox** *Otocyon megalotis*, a small silver-grey insectivore, rendered unmistakable by its huge ears and black eye mask, and most common in arid country north of Mount Kenya.

The most conspicuous of Kenya's small nocturnal carnivores are the **small spotted genet** *Genetta genetta* and **large spotted genet** *G. tigrina*, slender and rather feline creatures whose grey to gold-brown coat is marked with black spots. Often seen scavenging around lodges after dark,

The banded mongoose is among the most sociable and common of Kenya's smaller carnivores. (AZ)

genets can be distinguished from all other carnivores by their exceptionally long ringed tails, and the colour of the tail tip (black for large-spotted, white for small-spotted) is the most reliable way to tell the two species apart. The related **African civet** *Civettictis civetta* is bulkier, shaggier and most likely to be seen along roads after dark, moving deliberately as it sniffs the ground.

Several species of mongoose occur in Kenya. The **dwarf mongoose** *Helogate parvula* is a diminutive and highly sociable light-brown mongoose often seen in the vicinity of the termite mounds where it dens. The larger and equally sociable **banded mongoose** *Mungos mungo*, uniform dark brown except for a dozen black stripes across its back, is a diurnal species associated with most wooded habitats. Also quite common is the large scruffy brown **marsh mongoose** *Atilax paludinosus*, while the nocturnal **white tailed ichneumon** *Ichneumia albicauda* is easily distinguished by its bulk, solitary habits, and bushy white tail.

The widespread but seldom observed **ratel** or **honey badger** *Mellivora capensis* is a large black mustelid with a puppyish face and grey white back. It is an opportunistic feeder, best known for its symbiotic relationship with a bird called the honeyguide which leads the ratel to a bee hive, waits for it to tear it open, then feeds on the scraps. Several other mustelids occur in the region, including the **striped polecat** *Ictonyx striatus*, a common but rarely seen nocturnal creature with black underparts and a bushy white back, and the similar but much scarcer **striped weasel** *Poecilogale albincha*. The **Cape clawless otter** *Aonyx capensis* a brown freshwater mustelid with a white collar, while the smaller **spotted necked otter** *Lutra maculicollis* is darker with light white spots on its throat, and is quite often seen in Lake Victoria.

Primates

Dominated by savanna habitats, Kenya lacks the primate diversity associated with the forests of western and central Africa, and none of the great apes occurs there naturally (though an introduced community of the unmistakable **common chimpanzee** *Pan troglodytes* can be visited at Sweetwaters on the Laikipia Plateau, page 222).

Three monkey species are characteristic of the Kenyan savanna. The most imposing of these, weighing up to 45kg, is the **olive baboon** *Papio anubis* (see page 38), which mostly lives west of the Rift Valley and is replaced by the more lightly built **yellow baboon** *P. cynocephalus* in the east. The two baboon species are both easily observed within their respective ranges, and they are easily distinguished from each other by their nominal coat colours, and from other monkeys by their far greater bulk, inverted 'U'-shaped tail, and distinctive dog-like head. Omnivorous and highly intelligent, baboons live in large troops whose complex social structure is dominated by rigid matriarchal lineages, and they are usually very entertaining to watch, whether it's youngsters trying to climb, adults bickering or females grooming.

Equally sociable but far smaller, the **vervet monkey** *Chlorocebus aethiops* is probably the world's most numerous primate (aside from humans). It inhabits savanna and woodland, spending a high proportion of its time on the ground, and its light grey coat, black face and white forehead band are diagnostic – as are the male's admirably gaudy blue genitals. In semi-arid parts of northwest Kenya, it might be confused with the localised **patas monkey** *Erythrocebus patas*, which is larger, spindlier, more strictly terrestrial, and has a distinctive orange-tinged coat and black forehead stripe.

Africa's most widespread forest primate, the **blue** or **Sykes monkey** *Cercopithecus mitis* occurs in most suitable habitats countrywide, including belts of riverine forest and suitable habitats in Mount Kenya and Aberdare national parks. It is common along the coast and in the central highlands, where the combination of dark blue-grey coat and white throat renders it

Sykes monkey with baby, Mount Kenya National Park (AZ)

Black-and-white colobus, Masai Mara National Reserve (AZ)

unmistakable. In the far west, it occurs alongside two other forest guenons: the **red-tailed monkey** *C. ascanius*, whose most distinguishing character is a bright white heart on its nose, and the more thickset white-bearded **DeBrazza's monkey** *C. neglectus*.

Another striking forest monkey is the **black-and-white colobus** *Colobus guereza* of the central highlands, which is replaced by the similar **Angola colobus** *C. angolensis* along the coast. Both are beautiful leaf-eating monkeys with jet-black coats punctuated by bold white facial markings, a long white tail, and white sides and shoulders in some races. These almost exclusively arboreal monkeys are capable of jumping up to 30m, a spectacular sight with the white tail streaming behind. Two endangered monkey species are endemic to the little-visited Tana River Primate Reserve, namely the **Tana River red colobus** *Procolobus rufomitratus* and the **Tana River mangabey** *Cercocebus galeritus*.

The **lesser bushbaby** *Galago senegalensis* is the most widespread and common of Kenya's prosimians, a group of diminutive nocturnal primates related to the lemurs of Madagascar. More often heard than seen, the lesser bushbaby is often very common in savanna habitats, and can sometimes be picked out by tracing a cry to a tree and shining a torch into its eyes. The much larger **greater bushbaby** *G. crassicaudatus*, which occurs alongside it in several parts of Kenya, produces a terrifying scream and is easily seen at night at Shimba Lodge in Shimba Hills (see page 183). The related **potto** *Perodicticus potto*, a sloth-like nocturnal prosimian of rainforest interiors, occurs in Kakamega Forest and can often be picked up there by spotlight.

Buffalo and antelopes

The widespread **Cape buffalo** *Syncerus caffer*, closely related to the similar-looking Indian water buffalo, is Africa's only wild ox and most powerful bovid, weighing up to 800kg. Its imposing bulk ensures it has few

Buffalo herd, Shimba Hills National Reserve (AZ)

natural enemies, though it is regularly preyed upon by lions in the Masai Mara, with the hunters occasionally coming off second best. Buffalo can adapt to most habitats, provided they are close to a reliable water source. Mixed-sex herds of 30–50 animals are typical, but older males often roam around in smaller bachelor groups, and herds of more than 1,000 are sometimes encountered. Good sightings can be had in most reserves, with large herds often seen in Tsavo East and Masai Mara.

Africa's most diverse group of bovids, the antelopes, are an unwavering feature of the Kenyan landscape, thriving in every habitat from rainforest to desert, except where they have been eliminated by human activity. Several of the region's most striking species belong to the tribe Tragelaphini (spiral-horned antelopes), among them the **common eland** *Taurotragus oryx*, the world's largest antelope, which stands up to 180cm tall and can weigh more than 900kg. It is light tan-brown with faint white vertical stripes, and a bovine appearance accentuated by its short horns and large dewlap. It is thinly but widely distributed in Kenya with the Masai Mara and Samburu-Buffalo Springs among the more reliable spots for sightings.

The magnificent **greater kudu** *Tragelaphus strepsiceros*, second in stature only to the eland, has a grey-brown coat and up to ten vertical white stripes on

Greater kudu male displaying his trademark spiral horns. (AZ)

each flank, but is most notable for the statuesque male's double-spiralled horns, which can grow to be 1.4m long. The Kenyan population has never recovered from the hammering it took during the rinderpest epidemic in the late 19th century, and it is only likely to be seen at Lake Bogoria. By contrast, the shy and more lightly built **lesser kudu** *T. imberbis* is quite often seen in Tsavo and Samburu-Buffalo Springs.

Related to the kudus, the widespread **bushbuck** *T. scriptus* is an endearingly Bambi-like medium-sized antelope that might occur in any non-arid habitat in Kenya, and is quite common outside of protected areas. Very attractive, the male is dark brown or chestnut, while the much smaller female is generally pale red-brown, and both sexes are marked with white spots and sometimes stripes. The similar but larger **sitatunga** *T. spekei*, a localised swamp-loving antelope with unique splayed hooves that assist it in manoeuvring through its watery home, is most readily observed in Saiwa Swamp. The **bongo** *T. euryceros* is a massive (up to 400kg) forest antelope whose deep russet coat is marked with around a dozen bold white vertical stripes. Its main centre of distribution is the lowland rainforests of west-central Africa, but the Aberdares supports a barely viable population of around 50 individuals, and there have been attempts to reintroduce zoo-bred specimens on Mount Kenya.

The **oryx** *Oryx gazella* is a powerfully built ash-grey antelope that stands 120cm high at the shoulder and has striking straight horns that grow to more than 1m in length, sweeping backwards at the same angle as the forehead and muzzle. Associated with arid environments, it can go without water for almost as long as a camel, obtaining all its needs from the plants it eats, and allowing its body temperature to rise as high as 45°C without perspiring. Two races are recognised in Kenya: the **Beisa oryx** is common

Beisa oryx, Samburu and Buffalo Springs National Reserve (AZ)

in Samburu-Buffalo Springs, while the **fringe-eared oryx** is most likely to be seen in Tsavo East. Built to similar proportions, the **sable antelope** *Hippotragus niger* and **roan antelope** *H. equinus* both have very restricted ranges in Kenya, the former occurring only in Shimba Hills, where it is common, and the latter in the remote Ruma National Park.

Common in Masai Mara and Amboseli, but mysteriously absent from the northern hemisphere, the **blue wildebeest** or **brindled gnu** *Connochaetes taurinus* looks a bit like a buffalo from a distance (wildebeest is Afrikaans/Dutch for 'wild ox'), but its slighter build, lighter coat and shaggy beard precludes confusion at close quarters. The related **kongoni** or **Coke's hartebeest** *Alcelaphus buselaphus* is similar in height but more

Blue wildebeest suckling on the Mara Plains. (AZ)

lightly built, with a light yellow-brown coat and an elongated face that gives it a somewhat morose demeanour. It is common in the Masai Mara, alongside the **topi** *Damaliscus lunatus*, a darker, glossier and more handsome variation on the same body plan. Near-endemic to Kenya, the critically endangered **hirola** *Beatragus hunteri*, a small brown hartebeest with impala-like horns and distinctive white 'spectacles', might be seen in Tsavo East, where herds were introduced in 1963 and 1996, a short distance south of their natural range.

Gazelles are graceful, relatively small-herd antelopes associated with arid and grassland habitats. The nippy **Thomson's gazelle** *Gazella thomsonii* (or 'Tommy') and **Grant's gazelle** *G. granti* are among the most characteristic grazers of the Masai Mara, where they are the favoured prey of cheetah, and can be told apart by the Tommy's smaller stature and bold black horizontal flank stripe. Common in Tsavo East and Samburu-Buffalo Springs, the striking **gerenuk** *Litocranius walleri* has an

Male Thomson's gazelles frequently lock horns to establish dominance, but seldom do each other serious damage. (AZ)

extraordinarily long neck, alluded to in the Swahili name *swalatwiga* ('gazelle giraffe'), and it habitually browses on acacias at full stretch (see page 35). Not a gazelle, but superficially similar, the **impala** *Aepyceros melampus* is a slender, medium-sized antelope whose chestnut coat displays diagnostic black-and-white rump stripes. It is highly gregarious and common in most savanna reserves, including Tsavo, Masai Mara and Amboseli, with the male's black annulated lyre-shaped horns being particularly magnificent in the north of its range.

The grizzle-grey **klipspringer** *Oreotragus oreotragus* is almost exclusively associated with mountains and rocky slopes (its name is Afrikaans for 'rock jumper') and boasts several unusual adaptations to this habitat, notably the unique capacity to walk on its hoof tips, coarse but hollow fur providing good insulation at high altitude, and binocular vision (a feature more normally associated with carnivores than herbivores) to help it gauge jumping distances accurately. It is common on the rockier upper slopes of Mount Kenya and in other suitable habitats throughout the country.

Many other antelopes occur in Kenya. Very common in Lake Nakuru National Park, the widespread **waterbuck** *Kobus ellipsiprymnus* has a shoulder height of up to 135cm, and is easily recognised by its shaggy grey-brown coat, pale rump, and the male's large lyre-shaped horns. By contrast, the **reedbucks** of the genus *Redunca* are lightly built grassland dwellers with few distinguishing features. The smaller **oribi** *Ourebia ourebi* is a localised grassland antelope with a sandy coat and a diagnostic black glandular patch below the ears. Among the smallest antelope in the region, the **dik-diks** of the genus *Madoqua* are dry-country dwellers with distinctive white eye-rings and a twitchy elongated nose. Similarly diminutive are the **duikers**, which include the savanna-dwelling grey duiker *Sylvicapra grimmia* and several forest dwellers of the genus *Cephalophus*.

Other large herbivores

The world's largest land animal, the **African elephant** *Loxodonta africana* (shoulder height 2.3–3.4m; weight up to 6,000kg) is intelligent, sociable and infinitely engaging, but also somewhat intimidating on account of its immense bulk, fierce trumpeting call and unpredictable temperament. Like humans, elephants are one of the few mammals capable of modifying their environment, and their  (EL)

habit of uprooting trees can cause serious deforestation and environmental degradation when populations are concentrated in restricted conservation areas. Elephants have two unique modifications in the form of a trunk and tusks, both of which have multiple uses. Female elephants live in close-knit clans in which the eldest member plays matriarch over her sisters, daughters and granddaughters, and mother–daughter bonds may last for up to 50 years. Males generally leave their birth group at around 12 years of age, to roam singly or form bachelor herds. The African elephant is widespread and common in habitats ranging from desert to rainforest, and populations within Kenya have largely recovered from the intense commercial poaching of the 1980s. Herds are likely to be seen on a daily basis in most of the region's larger national parks, but Amboseli stands out for its large tuskers and the opportunity to watch interaction at close quarters.

The pugnacious **black rhinoceros** *Diceros bicornis* (shoulder height 1.6m; weight 1,000kg) is the more widespread of Africa's two rhino species, and

Introduced from South Africa, white rhinoceros are now readily seen around Lake Nakuru National Park. (AZ)

the only one to occur naturally in Kenya. It was poached to extinction in most of its former range in the 1980s, since when numbers have recovered slightly, especially in Kenya and South Africa. The best places to look for it are Lake Nakuru, Meru and Laikipia, but it's generally more secretive than the bulkier **white rhinoceros** *Ceratotherium simum*, which has been introduced from southern Africa. There is, incidentally, no colour difference between the two: the misnomer 'white' derives from the Afrikaans *weit* (wide) and refers to its flattened mouth, an ideal shape for cropping grass. By contrast, the black rhino, a specialised browser, has a more rounded mouth and hooked upper lip.

The improbable-looking **giraffe** *Giraffa camelopardis* (shoulder height 2.5–3.5m; weight 1,000–1,400kg) is the world's tallest and longest-necked land animal, standing up to 5.5m high when fully grown. Quite unmistakable, it lives in loosely structured herds of up to 15 individuals. Three races occur in Kenya, with the **Maasai giraffe** being very common in southern reserves such as Amboseli, Masai Mara and Tsavo (see page 89), while the strikingly marked **reticulated giraffe**, near-endemic to northern Kenya, is most easily seen in Meru and Samburu-Buffalo Springs, and the very localised **Rothschild's giraffe** is represented by an introduced population in Lake Nakuru. Recent DNA testing suggests all these races should be treated as full species, in which case the latter two would both be IUCN listed as Vulnerable or Endangered.

The **plains zebra** *Equus burchelli* (shoulder height 1.3m; weight 300–340kg), also sometimes referred to as Burchell's zebra, is a charismatic striped equid that ranges throughout most of East and southern Africa, where it is often seen in large herds alongside wildebeest. It is common in most savanna reserves in Kenya, especially the Masai Mara, and still survives outside conservation areas in parts of the Rift Valley. Restricted to northern Kenya and a few parts of southern Ethiopia, **Grevy's zebra** *Equus grevyi* is bulkier than its plains counterpart, and can be distinguished from it by its much finer striping pattern. The two occur alongside each other in Samburu-Buffalo Springs, Laikipia and a few other more remote localities in the north.

Reticulated giraffe, Meru National Park (AZ)

The common hippopotamus is almost always seen in water. (AZ)

The **common hippopotamus** *Hippopotamus amphibious* (shoulder height 1.5m; weight 2,000kg) is the most characteristic large mammal of Kenya's large rivers and lakes, where it remains common, especially in freshwater Naivasha and Baringo. A bulky and lumbering animal, it spends most of the day submerged, but often ranges over long distances on land at night in search of food. Strongly territorial, herds of ten or more animals are presided over by a dominant male who will readily defend his patriarchy to the death. Hippos are abundant in most protected rivers and water bodies, and they are still quite common in suitable habitats outside of reserves, where they kill more people than any other African mammal.

Africa's only diurnal swine, the **warthog** *Phacochoreus africanus* (shoulder height 60–70cm; weight 100kg) is a widespread and often conspicuously abundant resident

Warthog, Hell's Gate National Park (AZ)

of Kenya's savanna reserves. It has a grey coat with a thin covering of hairs, wart like bumps on its face, rather large upward-curving tusks, and a habit of trotting off with its tail raised stiffly in the air. This last trait alone distinguishes it from the bulkier, hairier and browner **bushpig** *Potomochoerus larvatus*, which is as widespread as the warthog, but infrequently seen due to its nocturnal habits and preference for dense vegetation. Larger still, the 250kg **giant forest hog** *Hylochoerus meinertzhageni* is a localised species found in forest interiors, and generally very secretive (indeed, it eluded western science until as recently as 1904), though it is regularly observed at Mountain Lodge on the slopes of Mount Kenya, the best place to see it anywhere in Africa.

With the appearance of an oversized guinea pig but more closely related to elephants than to rodents, hyraxes (shoulder height 30–35cm; weight 4kg) are often seen sunning in rocky habitats and can become tame when used to people, as is the case at several lodges. The most commonly seen species is the diurnal **rock hyrax** *Procavia capensis*, but the nocturnal **tree hyrax** *Dendrohyrax arboreus* occurs in certain forested habitats, announcing its presence with an unforgettable banshee wail of a call. Like hyraxes, the **elephant-shrews** are a unique group of small rodent-like mammals that hop like miniature kangaroos and have absurdly elongated and perpetually twitching noses. Several small species are present in savanna reserves throughout Kenya, but none is so impressive as the **golden-rumped elephant-shrew** *Rhynchocyon chrysopygus*, which is endemic to Arabuko-Sokoke Forest.

Rock hyrax (AZ)

Surely the oddest of all African mammals, the **aardvark** *Orycteropus afer* is an exclusive insectivore that looks like a cross between a domestic pig, an anteater and a kangaroo. Widespread but strictly nocturnal and very seldom seen, one individual can snaffle up to 50,000 termites in one night with its long sticky tongue. Not so much similar to the aardvark as equally dissimilar to anything else, **pangolins** are unobtrusive and seldom observed nocturnal insectivores whose distinctive scaled armour plating bears a superficial resemblance to the American armadillos but this is probably a case of convergent evolution. The **ground pangolin** *Manis temmincki* is most widespread in East Africa, but sightings are an extremely rare event.

As many as 80% of Kenyan mammal species are bats or rodents of little interest to non-specialist safari-goers. One exception, represented in East Africa by two practically indistinguishable species, is the **porcupine**, among the largest of rodents at up to 27kg, and covered in long black-and-white quills that protect them from predators and also occasionally betray their presence by rattling as they walk. Another large and seldom-seen nocturnal oddity, the **springhare** *Pedetes capensis* is a rodent rather than a type of rabbit, whose distinctive kangaroo-like mode of locomotion means it is most often located when the spotlights pick out a pair of eyes bouncing up and down. Kenya also supports a wide diversity of squirrels, most commonly the **bush squirrel** *Paraxerus cepapi*. Also likely to be seen on safari is the endearing **unstriped ground squirrel** *Xerus rutilus*, a terrestrial dry-country creature with a grey-brown coat and prominent white eye-ring.

Sharpe's longclaw standing in an upland meadow (NB/FLPA)

Birds

Kenya is one of the world's great ornithological destinations, with 1,136 species recorded, a tally exceeded in Africa only by the much larger Democratic Republic of Congo. For dedicated birdwatchers, a well-planned two-week itinerary through Kenya is likely to result in a trip list of 350–400 species, a figure that compares favourably with anywhere in the world. It also offers the opportunity to seek out several birds that are endemic to Kenya (in other words, found nowhere else in the world) namely Williams' lark, Sharpe's longclaw, Aberdare cisticola, Tana River cisticola, Hinde's babbler, Taita thrush and Clarke's weaver, as well as near-endemics such as Jackson's francolin, Sokoke scops owl, Jackson's hornbill, grey-crested helmet-shrike, Abbott's starling, northern pied babbler, Sokoke pipit and Amani sunbird.

For safari-goers seeking an introduction to East Africa's commoner birds, the open savanna of southern Kenyan reserves such as Amboseli and the Masai Mara forms an excellent starting point, with the likes of superb starling, purple grenadier, lilac-breasted roller and African grey hornbill being conspicuous. The Rift Valley

Greater blue-eared starling, Aberdares National Park (AZ)

Seasonal birdwatching

Kenya offers excellent birdwatching throughout the year, but the prime season runs from September and April, when resident populations are boosted by Palaearctic migrants, refugees escaping the winter of the northern hemisphere. It's been estimated that as many as six billion individual birds undertake this trans-Sahara migration annually, ranging from the diminutive willow warbler and chiffchaff to the somewhat bulkier white stork, along with innumerable flocks of European (barn) swallow and various waders, wagtails, raptors and waterfowl. The European winter also broadly coincides with Kenya's rainy season, when several resident Ploceids (weavers and allies) undergo a startling 'ugly duckling'-style transformation, shedding their drab eclipse plumage in favour of bright yellow, black and red breeding colours.

Mixed waders at Ferguson's Gulf, Lake Turkana (JK/FLPA)

lakes are also superb for birds, and while Nakuru is rightly famed for its mind-boggling flamingo aggregations, the less celebrated Naivasha and Baringo are arguably even better for general birding, with water-associated species especially well represented.

For regular Africa safari-goers, a region of special ornithological interest is the arid north, where reserves such as Samburu-Buffalo Springs host a high quotient of dry-country species whose range is otherwise restricted to relatively inaccessible parts of Ethiopia and Somalia. Also worth singling out, especially for visitors with limited exposure to the rainforests of west-central Africa, are Kakamega Forest and Saiwa Swamp, which protect dozens of forest species at the very eastern extreme of their range.

A decent field guide is essential for anybody with more than a passing interest in birds, and they don't come any better than *Birds of Kenya and Northern Tanzania* by Dale Zimmerman et al.

Reptiles and amphibians

Reptiles receive a lot of bad press, not entirely without foundation in the case of crocodiles and certain venomous snakes, but most of Kenya's 300-odd species pose no threat to humans. Furthermore, the ecological value of reptiles cannot be overstated. A healthy snake population is vital to preventing plague-like outbreaks of rats and other fast-breeding rodents, while the lizards that skid around on hotel walls do much to control mosquito numbers, and crocodiles play a vulture-like role in devouring the carrion that might otherwise clog up lakes and rivers.

Nile crocodile on the Ewaso Nyiro River, Shaba National Reserve (AZ)

Africa's bulkiest and longest-lived predator is the **Nile crocodile**, which weighs up to 1,000kg and has a lifespan similar to humans. Crocodiles have inhabited the lakes and rivers of Africa for 150 million years, and they are more closely related to dinosaurs than to any other living creature. In Kenya, they occur in most freshwater habitats, and are often seen basking toothily on sandbanks. Lake Turkana harbours the world's densest crocodile population, with up to 15,000 individuals breeding on its islands. River-dwelling crocodiles are said to be responsible for more attacks on humans than their lake-dwelling counterparts, but bathing in any lake or river is risky.

Tortoises, **terrapins** and **turtles** are well represented in Kenya. Most visible is the leopard tortoise, which weighs up to 40kg, has a mottled gold-and-black shell, and is often seen motoring in the slow lane of game reserve roads. Flatter and plainer brown than terrestrial tortoises, terrapins occur in freshwater habitats, and are often seen sunning on partially submerged rocks or logs, or peering out from roadside puddles. The region's largest species, most likely to be seen around Lake Turkana, the Nile soft-shelled terrapin has a very wide shell and can reach a length of almost 1m. Five marine turtle species have been recorded off the coast; all are listed as endangered, and are much larger than any of the region's indigenous tortoises or terrapins.

The most numerous and conspicuous reptiles are **lizards**, with around 150 species present. The hefty **Nile monitor**, attaining a length of up to 3m, is common in aquatic habitats and sometimes mistaken for a small crocodile. **Agama lizards** are typically 20–30cm long and have bright blue, purple, orange or red scaling, with the flattened head generally a different colour from the torso. The most diverse lizard family is the **geckos**, whose unique adhesive toes enable them to run upside down on smooth surfaces – look out for the common house gecko, an endearing bug-eyed, translucent white lizard that scampers up lodge walls in pursuit of insects attracted to the lights.

The most charismatic of lizards, **chameleons** are known for their abrupt colour changes (a trait that's been exaggerated in popular literature), but

are no less remarkable for their protuberant eyes, which offer 180° vision and swivel independently of each other, and for the sticky body-length tongue they unleash in a blink-and-you'll-miss-it lunge at a selected item of prey. The flap-necked chameleon is the most common savanna and woodland species, while Jackson's chameleon, of the central highland forests, is the largest. Four species are endemic to Kenya.

Snakes are common but secretive. Of 45 venomous species known from East Africa, only 18 are on record as having caused a

The flap-necked chameleon is common in savanna habitats. (AZ)

Rock python adult coiled around a Nile crocodile. (FL/FLPA)

human fatality, and even these normally slither away unseen by approaching humans. Often seen on safari, the **rock python** is Africa's largest snake at up to 5–6m, and it kills by strangulation, wrapping its muscular body around its prey. The **puff adder**, a thickset resident of savanna and rocky habitats, is rightly considered the most dangerous of Kenya's venomous snakes, not because it is especially aggressive, but because its sluggish disposition means it is more often disturbed than other species. Other dangerous snakes include the **cobras and mambas**, while the **boomslang** – in theory the most toxic of Africa's snakes – is back-fanged and very non-aggressive, for which reason the only fatalities recorded have been snake handlers.

Kenya harbours almost 200 **frog** species, most nocturnal. Male frogs attract potential partners with mating calls, which are unique to each species, and often provide the most reliable clue to identification. Calling is most vigorous after rain, when safari-goers are often treated to an unforgettable evening medley of guttural croaks and ethereal whistles. The region's largest frog is the **African bullfrog**, which weighs up to 1kg and is generally associated with seasonal pools. Small and distinctively patterned, the diverse **'tree frogs'** have long broad-tipped toes adapted for climbing, and are associated with forest, woodland and reedy habitats. One of the region's most wondrous sounds is the ethereal popping chorus of the **bubbling kassina**, a 'tree frog' of marshes and moist grassland that is especially vocal over April–May.

The heavyweight African bullfrog often inhabits seasonal pools. (FL/FLPA)

3 Planning a Safari

Planning a holiday in Kenya needn't be daunting. This guide includes recommendations from some of the top safari operators, but a quick internet search will reveal any number of all-inclusive mid-range and upmarket safari companies offering packages suitable to anybody who possesses the wherewithal to stuff a change of clothes and toothbrush in a daypack, slip a passport in their top pocket, and stumble from a runway into the open passenger door of a waiting safari vehicle. However, there are a number of factors you might want to take into consideration before settling on an itinerary - from the best time of year to visit, to whether you want to fly or drive between reserves, sleep under canvas or in a lodge - and the following chapter runs through the most important planning aspects of a trip.

When to visit

Kenya can be visited at any time of the year, but several factors may influence the timing of a vacation, depending to some extent on your interests and preferences. An equatorial location means that Kenya doesn't experience the seasonal extremes associated with higher latitudes, and temperatures tend to be influenced as much by altitude as by time of year. That said, the few degrees that separate the hottest months of December to March from the coolest months of May to August make a tangible difference to comfort levels along the coast, and most people will find the cooler weather more tolerable. Unlike temperatures, precipitation in Kenya tends to be highly seasonal: approximately two-thirds of the annual rainfall comes during the long rains (late February to early June, peaking in April), which is a poor time to be at the coast or hiking on Mount Kenya, and there's usually also quite a bit of rainfall during the short rains (October and November). Other months are generally dry.

For most visitors, Kenya's main attraction is its wildlife, and here several seasonal factors come into play. In pure game-viewing terms, the main dry season, starting in late June, is the best time to be on safari. This is when the wildebeest migration is centred on the Masai Mara, usually crossing from the Serengeti in late July or August, and spending the next three months grazing the plains bare

The wildebeest migration is often a highlight of any trip to Kenya. (RC)

before they return southward in October. In other reserves, August to October is the toughest time of year for most large mammals, but it offers the best conditions for viewing them, as thirsty animals concentrate at lakes and other perennial sources of drinking water, most noticeably in Amboseli and Samburu-Buffalo Springs. Of course, the best game-viewing seasons are also the peak tourist seasons, so those seeking a more tranquil safari might prefer to visit at another time of year. For birdwatchers, the avian activity peaks during the northern winter (October to May), when many resident species shed their drab eclipse plumage to emerge in full breeding colours, and more than 100 species of Palaearctic migrants are present.

Public holidays

In addition to the following fixed holidays, the moveable holidays of Good Friday, Easter Monday and Eid al-Fitr are recognised as public holidays. When a public holiday falls on a Sunday, the Monday is normally taken as a holiday instead. The main effect of public holidays on tourists is that banks and some forex bureaux will be closed, as will many shops.

1 January	**New Year's Day**	20 October	**Kenyatta Day**
1 May	**Labour Day**	12 December	**Independence Day**
1 June	**Madaraka Day**	25 December	**Christmas Day**
10 October	**Moi Day**	26 December	**Boxing Day**

Types of safari

Several types of safari are on offer and the most suitable choice will depend on several factors, including your temperament, interests as well as budget.

Random group or private party?

The first thing to decide is whether to travel as part of a group put together arbitrarily by an operator, or to make bespoke arrangements as a private party. For most people, a **private safari** would be the preferred option, budget permitting, since it allows for a greater degree of autonomy and doesn't expose you to the risk of sharing your vehicle with disagreeable travel companions. In favour of **group safaris**, however, is that they do tend to be less costly, and the opportunity to share exciting sightings can be a bonus if the group gels, as can the social aspect round the campfire of an evening.

Accommodation

The next is to decide on the style of accommodation. The cheapest option in this regard is **budget camping**, which generally involves camping in a small two-person tent with basic bedding in a public campsite, and simple outdoor meals prepared by the operator's cook. Some companies offer semi-luxury or luxury camping safaris, which include larger tents, more comfortable bedding and more ceremonious meals. Budget aside, this sort of camping safari is the most hands-on and exciting option, and the one that brings you closest to the bush, especially at night, when clients are separated from the prowling wildlife by nothing but a sheet of flimsy canvas.

For unhappy campers, the best option is a **lodge-based safari**. Two broad types of accommodation are available: the large 'hotel-in-the-bush' lodges operated by several chains, and more intimate bush camps offering accommodation in standing tents. The former offer a roof over your head at night, restaurant food, and a far higher degree of comfort than you'd get on any camping safari, but they also tend to have a rather institutionalised mood that contrasts oddly with the wilderness outside. The packaged feel and physical solidity of these hotel-style lodges will be reassuring to nervous first-time safari-goers, but it undoubtedly diminishes the 'wow factor' of a safari by isolating guests from the immensity of the African night sounds and sky. On the whole, these lodges are aimed at the mid-range safari-goer and a considerable proportion of their custom derives from organised group safaris.

Safari experiences range from getting cosy at the campfire to luxury accommodation befitting a top-flight city hotel. (left: AZ & right: CK)

Bush camps, by contrast, tend to be smaller (anything from six to 20 units) and to blend into the surrounding bush in a manner that makes it difficult to forget that you are on safari. Most bush camps are surprisingly trendy in their style of décor, and many are genuinely luxurious, catering almost entirely to fly-in guests, for whom they provide all activities using their own experienced guides. Inevitably, this sort of experience comes with a substantial price tag, but for those who can afford it, there is no better way of experiencing Africa in the raw. Fortunately for those who can't, there are also a number of more rustic tented camps that combine a bush atmosphere with decent, but not luxurious facilities and rates comparable to the chain lodges – arguably the best of both worlds!

Travel between reserves

Another decision is how you travel between reserves: by air or by road or a bit of both. Flying between reserves will greatly reduce the time spent in transit, it places fewer geographic restrictions on the itinerary, and it is

Getting around: car hire and taxis

Relatively few visitors undertake **self-drive safaris** in a rented vehicle, since it is generally more straightforward to visit game reserves with a driver-guide who knows his way around the (mostly unsignposted) tracks and is experienced in African conditions. That said, self-drive is a perfectly viable option, provided that you have some experience of navigating along rough roads and tracks, and can adjust to the somewhat law-flaunting and reckless driving style that prevails in Kenya. Most safari companies offer car hire, but their vehicles are not always well maintained, so it's best to use a recognised international car-hire company such as Hertz (⌖ www.hertz.com) or Avis (⌖ www.avis.com). For safaris, you need a vehicle with high clearance and 4x4 is strongly recommended in the dry season and more or less mandatory during the rains.

Taxis are widely available in cities such as Nairobi and Mombasa, and from Jomo Kenyatta International and Wilson airports in Nairobi and Moi International Airport in Mombasa. In city centres, you won't usually wait longer than a minute or two to hail down a cab, but you can also ask your hotel reception to call one. Fares are cheap by international standards, but it is advisable to agree a fare in advance, as tourists tend to be overcharged unless they are prepared to negotiate.

considerably less likely to damage sensitive backs. Unfortunately, unless you are joining a group, flying between reserves also tends to increase the cost of a safari, as the operator must either book you into pricier bush camps that offer game drives as part of their package, or have different vehicles meet you at different reserves. The advantage of driving between reserves is that you get to see a lot more of the country, to get closer to the people of Kenya, and to build up an understanding with one driver-guide throughout. You could also look at combining the two options, for instance by visiting a few nearby reserves (Tsavo West and Amboseli, or Lake Nakuru, Samburu-Buffalo Springs and a tree hotel) by road, then flying into Laikipia or the Masai Mara.

Booking

A final choice is whether to book through a ground operator or a tour agency at home. By using an agent in your home country, you can plan an itinerary face-to-face, you may well get a cheaper flight to Kenya, payment is more straightforward, and (assuming the agent is bonded) you will have a significantly higher level of financial protection. Booking a package

Aardvark Safaris Ltd
📞 01980 849160
✉ mail@aardvarksafaris.com 🖱 www.aardvark
safaris.co.uk (UK) and www.aardvarksafaris.com (US)

Aardvark Safaris will work with you to tailor make your dream African holiday. With over 20 years' experience, we've slept in the beds, eaten the meals and walked with the guides. You can be confident that we have the knowledge and expertise to ensure that all your holiday wishes will be fulfilled. Offices in the UK and US.

Africa Sky
📞 0845 5432195 ✉ info@africasky.co.uk
🖱 www.africasky.co.uk

We cleverly negotiate deals to provide the best value and service your money can buy. Our service is personal and attentive – we take our time to ensure we build a bespoke holiday just for you. Having travelled extensively throughout Africa, we can be sure to create the trip of your dreams.

Lowis & Leakey
📞 +254 208 90316 ✉ inquiry@lowisandleakey.com
🖱 www.lowisandleakey.com

Ninian Lowis and his wife Lara Leakey founded this Kenya-based company, and their families have been involved in exploration and safaris here since the late 19th century. We provide privately guided safaris and do our best to escape the crowds. Largely US and South American clientele, some European customers. Non-bonded – guests are responsible for their own travel insurance.

through an unbonded Kenyan operator will usually be cheaper, but you will be less well protected in the event that something goes wrong and you will almost certainly need to buy additional travel insurance. However you book, the price of a safari is almost always inclusive of accommodation and/or camping gear, services of a vehicle and driver-guide, and all meals, park fees and pre-arranged activities – in short, everything except drinks, tips and other ad-hoc purchases. It is, however, advisable to have this specified in advance.

Rainbow Tours ✆ 0845 277 3330
✉ kenya@rainbowtours.co.uk
🖰 www.rainbowtours.co.uk

Consultants at W&O Travel Rainbow Tours are passionate about what they do – and it shows! Our specialist expertise is consistently recognised with four Best Tour Operator awards in the last six years. Clients appreciate our honesty, enthusiasm and extensive firsthand experience. We are committed to close, collaborative working relationships with our Kenyan partners.

Safari Consultants
✆ 01787 888590 ✉ info@safariconsultantuk.com
🖰 www.safari-consultants.co.uk

Safari Consultants, established in 1983, specialises in tailor-made safari holidays to Kenya and the rest of East and southern Africa. The hallmark of our success is our extensive knowledge of these areas, which allows our team of enthusiastic and dedicated specialists to provide ideal holidays created around our customers' individual requirements.

The Zambezi Safari and Travel Company
✆ 0845 2930513 ✉ bradt@zambezi.com
🖰 www.zambezi.com

Zambezi specialises in arranging safaris along the course of the mighty Zambezi River and well beyond into the remotest corners of East, central and southern Africa. From authentic safaris, to relaxing on pristine beaches – Zambezi serves adventurous spirits from all corners of the globe. Offices in the UK and the US.

Other UK-based safari operators

Audley 🖰 www.audleytravel.com. Tailor-made holidays.

Bridge and Wickers 🖰 www.bridgeandwickers.co.uk. Include coverage of Kenya.

Dragoman 🖰 www.dragoman.com. Overland trips; itineraries include Kenya.

Exodus 🖰 www.exodus.co.uk. Activity and adventure holidays.

Explore! 🖰 www.explore.co.uk. Small group adventures.

Imagine Africa 🖰 www.imagineafrica.co.uk. Bespoke holidays.

Journeys By Design www.journeysbydesign.com. Luxury trips. UK and US offices.

Naturetrek www.naturetrek.co.uk. Expert-led wildlife trips.

Somak Safaris www.somak.com. Also has US offices.

Steppes Travel www.steppestravel.co.uk. Tailor-made holidays.

Tribes Travel www.tribes.co.uk. Aims to offer inspiring trips.

Wildlife Worldwide www.wildlifeworldwide.com. Custom-designed wildlife tours.

US-based safari operators

Abercrombie & Kent www.abercrombiekent.com High-end packages; also UK-based offices.

African Travel www.africantravelinc.com. Mainstream Kenya packages.

Destinations and Adventures International www.daitravel.com. Top-end custom-designed packages.

Explore Africa www.exploreafrica.net. Customised packages. US and local offices.

Goway www.go-way.com. Selection of Kenyan safari holidays.

Micato Safaris www.micato.com. Various Kenya packages available.

Natural Habitat Adventures www.nathab.com. Focus on nature travel.

Your itinerary: 15 top attractions

The first step in planning an itinerary is deciding which places you absolutely must visit, perhaps starting with the brief synopsis of our 15 top attractions, below. Having done that, you will then have a basic route to discuss with your operator, who can help you sort out the logistics and add places along the way. One important decision irrespective of the actual places you visit is the broad divide between the 'bush' and 'beach' components of your trip – some visitors will favour an extended beach holiday punctuated by a two- to three-night safari to a major reserve such as Masai Mara, others would want to spend most of their trip on safari, with just a day or two reserved to chill on the beach at the end, while for others a 50/50 split would be ideal.

Kenya is blessed with a great many highlights, and during many months of exploration over the past two decades, it is my privilege to have visited most of them on several occasions. Allowing for an inevitable element of subjectivity, the following locations are those I would rate as the country's finest goals of their type for first-time (or repeat) visitors, depending of course on individual interests, budgets and available time.

Coast

1 Lamu

The most profoundly traditional Swahili town on the East African coast seduces most visitors, and is ideal for travellers seeking a holistic cultural experience rather than a beach resort. See page 203.

(AZ)

(AZ)

2 Mombasa

The largest coastal port in Kenya is the site of historic Fort Jesus and the gateway to superb and uncomplicated beach-holiday destinations such as Diani, Nyali and Bamburi. See page 179.

3 Watamu

This scenic resort overlooks superb coral gardens and is close to the jungle-clad Gedi ruins and endemic-rich Arabuko-Sokoke Forest. Perfect for nature-lovers who want to combine beachfront hedonism with snorkelling, diving and/or forest walks. See page 190.

Big Five

4 Aberdares/Mount Kenya National Park

A trio of 'tree hotels' where you can watch the elephant and rhino at close quarters alongside monkeys, giant forest hog and other forest creatures. See page 210.

(AZ)

5 Amboseli National Park

The best elephant viewing in Kenya, with Kilimanjaro providing a majestic backdrop. Plenty of other mammals and birds, too. See page 154.

(AZ)

6 Masai Mara National Reserve

This Kenyan extension of the Serengeti offers superlative big cat viewing and hosts the wildebeest migration from August to October. See page 119.

(AZ)

7 Laikipia Plateau

This vast network of contiguous private reserves north of Mount Kenya is studded with small exclusive lodges and supports a wealth of wildlife including the country's largest populations of black rhino, Grevy's zebra and African wild dog. See page 220.

(WW/FLPA)

8 Samburu and Buffalo Springs national reserves

Excellent cluster of semi-desert reserves notable for protecting many large mammal and bird species that are rare further south, including reticulated giraffe, gerenuk, oryx and vulturine guineafowl. See page 234.

(AZ)

9 Tsavo West and East national park

Kenya's largest national park has a dense elephant population, magnificent volcanic landscapes and great views towards Kilimanjaro. See pages 162 and 166.

Rift Valley lakes

10 Lakes Baringo and Bogoria Only 20km apart; Baringo is known for its varied birdlife, abundant hippo and crocodiles, and walking opportunities in every direction, while Bogoria offers a dramatic setting and searing hot springs alongside large flamingo flocks that sometimes outnumber Nakuru. See page 145.

(AZ)

(AZ)

11 Lake Naivasha Close to Nairobi, this a perfect first stop in Kenya, offering lovely scenery, plentiful birds and great walking opportunities at Hell's Gate and Longonot. See page 131.

12 Lake Nakuru National Park Up to two million flamingos on a good day, and the best place to see rhinos in Kenya. See page 141.

Off the beaten track

13 **Kakamega Forest** Kenya's finest birding spot, this isolated stand of west African-type rainforest protects primates, butterflies and birds rare elsewhere in Kenya. See page 149.

14 **Lake Turkana** The most remote and vast of the Rift Valley lakes, with a spectacular desert setting, populated by a rich cast of desert nomads. See page 245.

(SS)

(AZ)

15 **Meru National Park**

A remote and little-visited park with less wildlife than some, but worthwhile for the genuinely untainted wilderness atmosphere. See page 229.

Tourist information

Surprisingly, although Kenya is one of Africa's most-established and popular tourist destinations, there is no official tourist office in Nairobi, Mombasa or indeed anywhere else in the country. However, the **Kenya Tourist Board** does run a highly informative website (🖰 www.magicalkenya.com) and it is also well worth checking out the **Kenya Wildlife Service's** website (🖰 www.kws.org), which covers all the country's national parks and reserves.

Red tape

All visitors to Kenya require a **passport** valid for at least six months after the end of their stay. **Visas** are required by most nationalities, and can be issued on arrival at all land borders and international airports for a small fee, though it pays to check this is still the case with your operator and to buy a visa in advance if in doubt. A standard single-entry visa is valid for three months, can be extended to six months at any immigration office, and it remains valid if you cross into Tanzania (including Zanzibar) or Uganda during that period. Multiple-entry visas valid for up to 12 months are only available to certain nationalities and must be applied for in advance through a Kenyan embassy or high commission. See 🖰 www.kenyaadvisor. com/kenya-embassies for a list of embassies and commissions.

Technically visitors require a **return ticket** (or proof of sufficient funds to buy one) to enter the country. In practice this is seldom asked for, and a credit card will suffice as proof of sufficient funds. **Proof of yellow fever vaccination** may be required when crossing into Kenya from Tanzania or other countries where yellow fever is present, but not when arriving from Europe or North America.

Getting there

Nairobi is the focus point of travel within East Africa and Jomo Kenyatta Airport is among the busiest airports on the continent, handling more than four million passengers annually. Most major European, Asian and African airlines offer scheduled flights to Nairobi, among them British Airways (🖰 www.britishairways.com), KLM (🖰 www.klm.com), Emirates (🖰 www.emirates.com) and South African Airways (🖰 www.flysaa.com). The national carrier, Kenya Airways (🖰 www.kenya-airways.com), widely regarded to be one of the best airlines in Africa, operates an extensive network of flights to other African and European cities. There are no direct flights from the USA, but Kenya Airways flies there through various European cities in partnership with KLM and other European airlines, and it is also possible to fly via Johannesburg with Delta (⌂ www.delta.com) or South African Airways or via Addis Ababa with Ethiopian Airlines (⌂ www.ethiopianairlines.com). Once in Nairobi, domestic flights to most destinations in Kenya leave from Wilson Airport, which is closer to the city centre than Jomo Kenyatta. It is also possible to fly directly from Europe to **Mombasa's** Moi International Airport, an option offered mainly by specialist operators offering charter packages to the coast.

It is recommended to reconfirm your flights 72 hours before travelling both on your outbound and return leg.

Health and safety
with Dr Felicity Nicholson

Inoculations

The only international requirement is for yellow fever, valid for ten years. A certificate of proof of vaccination will usually be asked for if you arrive from another infected country such as Tanzania. The vaccine is not always recommended and where a certificate is required but the vaccine is not then an exemption certificate will be issued. It's important to be up to date on tetanus, polio and diphtheria, and hepatitis A. You might also consider immunisation against hepatitis B, rabies, typhoid, cholera and tuberculosis. See also *Rabies* page 84.

Travel clinics and health information

A full list of current travel clinic websites worldwide is available on ⌂ www.istm.org/. For other journey preparation information, consult ⌂ www.nathnac.org/ds/map_world.aspx. Information about various medications may be found on ⌂ www.netdoctor.co.uk/travel. Other useful sites include ⌂ www.fitfortravel.scot.nhs.uk (a useful source of general travel health information) and ⌂ wwwnc.cdc.gov/travel (includes updates on specific destinations and information for those with limited mobility and those travelling with children). Both the US State Department (⌂ http://travel.state.gov/) and the British Department of Health (⌂ www.nhs.uk/nhsengland/ Healthcareabroad) also provide dedicated travel health information.

Personal first-aid kit

Depending on where and how you travel, and for how long, a minimal kit might contain the following:
- A good drying antiseptic, eg: iodine or potassium permanganate
- A few small dressings (Band-Aids)
- Suncream
- Insect repellent
- Antimalarial tablets
- Antihistamine tablets and cream
- Aspirin or paracetamol
- Antifungal cream (eg: Canesten)
- Ciprofloxacin or norfloxacin, for severe diarrhoea
- Antibiotic eye drops
- A pair of fine-pointed tweezers
- Alcohol-based hand rub or a bar of soap in a plastic box
- Thermometer

Deep-vein thrombosis (DVT)

Prolonged immobility on long-haul flights can result in deep-vein thrombosis (DVT), which can be dangerous if the clot travels to the lungs to cause pulmonary embolus. The risk increases with age, and is higher in obese or pregnant travellers, heavy smokers, those taller than 6ft/1.8m or shorter than 5ft/1.5m, and anybody with a history of clots, recent major operation or varicose veins surgery, cancer, a stroke or heart disease. If any of these criteria apply, consult a doctor before you travel. Ensuring that you are well hydrated and try to move around during long periods of travel can help to reduce the risk.

Malaria

This mosquito-borne disease is the biggest single medical threat to visitors to Kenya. There is no vaccine, but several types of oral prophylactics are available, with Malarone (proguanil and atovaquone) being widely recommended for short trips, as it is very effective and has few side effects (though it is relatively expensive). Other possibilities include mefloquine and doxycycline, so visit a travel clinic for up-to-date advice about the most suitable option.

For on-the-ground advice on preventing malaria, plus other health issues to consider whilst on safari, see *Chapter 4*, page 82.

Women travellers

Women travelling alone in Kenya have little to fear on a gender-specific level. On an organised safari, guides and lodge staff are all highly professional and harassment of women safari-goers is practically unheard of. In other circumstances, an element of flirtation is inevitable, perhaps the odd direct proposition, but nothing that cannot be defused by a firm no – or that you wouldn't expect as a woman travelling alone in any Western country. That said, and at risk of stating the obvious, single women travellers might want to be particularly circumspect in terms of how they dress: wearing skimpy clothing might not only offend but be perceived – however unfairly – as provocative or an advertisement of availability.

The range of toiletries available in Kenya is not nearly as wide as in Western supermarkets, nor is there much of a selection when it comes to items such as sanitary towels and tampons. This is doubly so on safari, where the choice will be restricted to whatever is available in the lodge gift shop. It's therefore a good idea to make sure you arrive in Kenya fully equipped in terms of toiletries and other hygiene-related products, bearing in mind that travelling in the tropics can sometimes induce heavier or more regular periods than normal.

See also *Cultural etiquette*, *Chapter 4*, page 100.

Disabled travellers

with Gordon Rattray ⌐ www.able-travel.com

Kenya is one of Africa's more accessible destinations. Don't anticipate ubiquitous curb-cuts onto city streets and there's no guaranteed level entry into public buildings, but do expect a basic awareness of the needs of mobility-impaired travellers. Where help is required, Kenyans are naturally forthcoming and dignified solutions are usually found for even the most impractical situations.

All the major tourist destinations have at least one accommodation option with disability-adapted facilities and the situation is constantly improving. Mainstream operators will be able to arrange itineraries for most needs, but they do not have adapted vehicles, a useful knowledge of access in lodges or staff trained in the needs of people with disabilities. For this, it is highly recommended that you contact Go-Africa Safaris & Travel (✉ info@go-africa-safaris.com ⌐ www.go-africa-safaris.com), who are the recognised disability experts in East Africa, or Southern Cross Safaris (✉ reservations@southerncrosssafaris.com ⌐ www.southerncross safaris.com), who can reliably make itineraries for people with disabilities as long as no medical care is required.

Further information

Bradt's *Access Africa: Safaris for People with Limited Mobility* is packed with useful advice and resources for disabled and senior adventure travellers, and has detailed descriptions of access in safari accommodation.

What to take

Clothing

This will probably constitute the bulk of your luggage, dependent partly on the type of accommodation you opt for – you'll need a lot more spare clothing on a ten-day camping safari, for instance, than if you use small, exclusive lodges where anything you turf into the laundry basket is returned fresh and gleaming within 24 hours. The ideal safari clothing is loose-fitting, lightweight, informal and made of natural fibres. Bright colours are a definite no-no when tracking wildlife on foot; pale colours are less likely to attract tsetse flies but tend to show dust and dirt more conspicuously. Nairobi and the reserves of the central highlands are at high altitude, and nights are often cooler than one might expect, so bring a couple of sweatshirts and maybe a windbreaker, and something waterproof if you travel during the rainy season. From dusk onwards, it's advisable to wear closed shoes, socks and long trousers to protect against mosquito bites. Otherwise, vehicle-based safaris don't generally call for any special footwear, but decent walking shoes or boots are essential for foot safaris, forest walks and mountain ascents.

Photographic gear

Few people would consider going on safari without a camera and/or video recorder. It should be recognised, however, that wildlife photography and filming is a specialised field, and the fantastic footage and perfect still images that we're accustomed to seeing on television and in magazines are the product of patience, experience, planning, high-quality equipment and an element of luck. For decent results, an SLR camera is preferable to a 'point and shoot', and a high-magnification lens (200mm at the very least) is more or less essential. Zoom lenses (eg: 70–300mm) are generally more affordable and allow for greater compositional flexibility than fixed lenses, but they tend to lack the sharpness of the latter and lose at least one aperture stop at full magnification, making them less useful in low light conditions. Magnification can be increased by using a converter, but with some loss of clarity and a further loss of one or two aperture stops for a 1.4x/2x converter. The bottom line is, if you're serious about wildlife photography, buy the best long lens you can afford!

Binoculars

These are essential for viewing distant wildlife and obtaining close-up views of birds. For dedicated birdwatchers, 8x magnification is the minimal requirement, but 10x, 12x or (only for the steady of hand) 16x is even better. The trade-off between full-size binoculars (eg: 8x40, 10x50) and their compact counterparts (eg: 8x25, 10x30) is that the former have a wider field of vision and tend to show colours more brightly as a result of capturing more light, while the latter are considerably more portable and steady to hold, and they tend to be cheaper. On the whole, you will get what you pay for when it comes to binoculars: common problems with cheap or obscure brands include poor focusing or lens alignment, a distorting or prismatic effect, and dull or inaccurate rendition of colours. If your budget runs to it, it's worth paying a bit more and sticking with a recognised brand. Avoid gimmicky binoculars (with features like zoom or universal focus) at all costs.

If you use a digital camera, make sure you have all the batteries, plugs, connectors and storage devices you need, as well as a universal adaptor. If you use film, this may not be readily available once you're on safari, so bring as many rolls as you are likely to need. Most first-time safari-goers and many experienced amateur photographers underestimate the importance of proper support in obtaining sharp wildlife shots: a beanbag is the most flexible and stable option for shooting out of a vehicle, and is easy enough to make yourself, ideally with a zip so you can fly with it empty and fill it up with whatever is available (beans, rice, dried corn) at the start of your safari. Make sure your camera bag is well insulated against the insidious dust associated with most African safari circuits.

Other essentials

Don't forget to bring sunscreen, a hat and sunglasses, a day pack to carry binoculars and field guides et al, a toilet bag containing razors, deodorant, tampons, lip salve and whatever other accessories you might need, a basic medical kit (see above, page 74), and a penknife, torch and possibly an alarm clock. Contact-lens users with sensitive eyes might be glad of a pair of old-fashioned glasses in the dusty conditions that often prevail on safari. Travel guides and field guides, though available in Nairobi and some lodges, are best bought in advance, if only to forestall Sod's Law that the particular book you want is universally out of stock when you arrive. (See also *Women travellers*, page 75.)

Electricity

Mains electricity is at 220-240V 60Hz. Round or square three-pin British-style plugs are in the widest use, so if you are carrying electrical equipment with two-pin or other plugs, be sure to bring a travel adaptor or two. The electricity supply in most cities and towns is reasonably reliable, and upmarket hotels will almost always have a generator that kicks in during power cuts. Most game lodges and camps are not on the mains grid but depend on generators, solar power or a combination of both, and it may only be possible to charge camera gear and other devices at certain hours, so check the situation at reception and try to avoid letting batteries run down so low that they require urgent charging.

It is advisable to take photocopies of passports and any other important travel documents and to store them separately from the originals in case anything is lost or stolen.

Finally, don't leave home without adequate **travel insurance**. This should include both medical insurance (specifically one that will fly you home in the event of an emergency) and a travel protection plan which would cover non-reimbursed travel expenses if an emergency occurs before or during your trip causing it to be cancelled, interrupted or delayed. Check out www.worldtravelcenter.com and www.globaltravelinsurance.com for more information.

Organising your finances

People who visit Kenya on a pre-paid tour or safari generally don't need to carry a great deal of money on their person, as most costs will have been built into the package, including airport and other transfers, ground transport, services of a driver and/or guide as specified, pre-booked domestic flights, national park and other entrance fees, and accommodation. With meals, the most common arrangement is for city hotels to be booked on a bed-and-breakfast basis, beach lodges on half-board (breakfast and dinner) and safari lodges and tented camps full board. However, some tours are booked on a full-board basis throughout, so check the arrangements with your specific operator. Certain exclusive lodges also include all drinks in the accommodation rate, but that is the exception not the rule.

Assuming that you are paid up in advance, then you will only need enough cash to cover **day-to-day expenses** such as drinks, tips (see page 86) and curios, which are unlikely to tally up to much more than US$500. The simplest way to carry this sort of sum is the form of hard currency, ideally US dollars, British pounds, or euros, which will be accepted at most game lodges, curio shops and recipients of tips, and can also be converted to local currency at forex bureaux in Nairobi, Mombasa and most other small towns. It's worth carrying a few Kenyan shillings with you at Wilson Airport as dollars and sterling may not be accepted. However, it is easy to change money at Kenyatta so there is no need to buy your shillings before you arrive. If you need to carry more money than this, you might want to protect against theft by carrying the bulk in **travellers' cheques**, even though cash is more widely accepted at forex bureaux, etc. Note that US dollar bills printed before 2002, particularly larger denominations such as US$50 and US$100, may be refused by banks and foreign exchange bureaux. Also, larger denominations get a better exchange rate than smaller bills.

Without being overly dependent on a **credit or debit card** it, it is definitely worth carrying one as a back-up. Most large towns have at least one 24-hour ATM (auto-teller) where local currency can be drawn against an international credit card, but there is always a risk of the machine being out of commission or temperamental, and this could enforce unwanted delays on any itineraries that focus on safari destinations rather than towns. Cards can be used to pay extras at most upmarket lodges and hotels, but they are less often accepted at shops, craft stalls and restaurants. Visa is far and away the most widely accepted card brand in Kenya, the likes of Maestro, MasterCard and American Express have more limited use, and most other brands will simply not be recognised.

For more on money and advice on tipping, see *Chapter 4*, page 85.

Visiting parks and reserves

An entrance fee is charged by all national parks and reserves in Kenya, ranging from US$50 per person per 24 hours at the ever popular Amboseli National Park and Masai Mara National Reserve to US$10 per person per 24 hours at certain more obscure ones. In practice, these fees are almost always built into rates quoted by safari operators and are handled on the ground by the driver-guide. However, self-drive safari-goers will need to familiarise themselves with the current situation regarding fees and deal with payment themselves. For most parks, the fees are payable in US dollars or local Kenyan currency, but certain more popular parks now operate to a smart card system instead of taking cash payments. Details are available at the **Kenya Wildlife Service** website (🖰 www.kws.org).

WOODLEY RD.

WILD ANIMALS HAVE
RIGHT OF WAY

NAISHI SUB HQS 8.5KM
MAKALIA FALLS 13KM
PICNIC & CAMPSITES

16

MAIN GATE EXIT 19KM
BABOON CLIFF LOOKOUT 16KM

4 On the Ground

Those visiting Kenya on an organised safari will usually find that the ground operator and/or their appointed guide handles most day-to-day practicalities, whether it be checking into a hotel, paying park entrance fees, or locating a suitable place to eat, or to change or draw money. Nevertheless, it can be useful have some advance knowledge about how things work on the ground, and this chapter will take you through the most important points, from health and safety, to foreign exchange and telecommunications. It may seem like a lot to absorb, but don't be daunted – local guides are generally very helpful and will quickly help you deal with anything that requires local savvy.

Health and safety in Kenya
with Dr Felicity Nicholson

Kenya is not an especially hazardous country to visit, and the overwhelming majority of safaris there pass without negative incident, but it is certainly worth being alert to the commoner health risks – whether that be sunburn or malaria – and the other aspects of health and safety discussed briefly below.

Malaria

No prophylactic is 100% effective, so take all reasonable precautions against being bitten by the nocturnal *Anopheles* mosquitoes that transmit the disease. These including donning a long sleeved shirt, trousers and socks in the evening, and applying a DEET-based insect repellent to any exposed flesh, and sleeping under an impregnated mosquito net – or, failing that, in an air-conditioned room, under a fan, or with a mosquito coil burning. Malaria normally manifests within two weeks of being bitten, but it can take as little as seven days and as long as 12 months, so if you display possible symptoms after you get home, get to a doctor immediately, and ask to be tested.

Sunstroke and dehydration

Overexposure to the sun can lead to short-term sunburn or sunstroke, and increases the long-term risk of skin cancer. Wear a T-shirt and waterproof sunscreen when swimming. On safari or walking in the direct sun, cover up with long, loose clothes, wear a hat, and use sunscreen (at least factor 30). The glare and the dust can be hard on the eyes, so bring UV-protecting sunglasses. A less direct effect of the tropical heat is dehydration, so drink more fluids than you would at home.

Travellers' diarrhoea

Many visitors to unfamiliar destinations suffer a dose of travellers' diarrhoea, and Kenya is no exception. By taking precautions against travellers' diarrhoea you will also avoid rarer but more serious sanitation-related diseases such as typhoid, cholera, hepatitis, dysentery, worms, etc. The maxim to remind you what you can safely eat is:

PEEL IT, BOIL IT, COOK IT OR FORGET IT.

This means that fruit you have washed and peeled yourself, and hot foods, should be safe, but raw foods, cold cooked foods, salads, fruit salads prepared by others, ice cream and ice are all risky. It is more rare to get sick from drinking contaminated water but it happens, so stick to bottled water. If you suffer a bout of diarrhoea, it is dehydration that makes you feel awful, so drink lots of clear fluids, ideally infused with sachets of oral rehydration salts, but any dilute mixture of sugar and salt in water will do you good, for instance a bottled soda with a pinch of salt added. If you have a fever, or have slime or blood with diarrhoea you may have dysentery. Always seek medical help as soon as possible.

Bilharzia

Also known as schistosomiasis, bilharzia is an unpleasant parasitic disease transmitted by freshwater snails in lakes and rivers. It cannot be caught in hotel swimming pools or the ocean. If you do swim in a lake or river, you can test for bilharzia at specialist travel clinics, ideally six weeks or longer after exposure, and it is easy to treat at present.

HIV/AIDS

Kenya has one of the world's highest rates of HIV infection, and other sexually transmitted diseases are rife, so if you do indulge, use condoms or femidoms to reduce the risk of transmission.

Skin infections

Any mosquito bite or small nick is an opportunity for a skin infection in warm humid climates, so clean and cover the slightest wound in a good drying antiseptic such as dilute iodine, potassium permanganate or crystal (or gentian) violet. Prickly heat, most likely to be contracted at the humid coast, is a fine pimply rash that can be alleviated by cool showers, dabbing (not rubbing) dry and talc, and sleeping naked under a fan or in an air-conditioned room. Fungal infections also get a hold easily in hot moist climates so wear 100% cotton socks and underwear and shower frequently.

Wild animals

Don't confuse habituation with domestication. East Africa's wildlife is genuinely wild: the lions that lie docilely in front of your Land Rover would almost certainly run away from or turn on anybody fool enough to disembark in their presence, and elephant, hippo, rhino and buffalo might all bulldoze a

Though habituated to vehicles, wildlife in Kenya remains genuinely wild, and should be treated with respect. (AZ)

pedestrian given the right set of circumstances. Such attacks are rare, however, and they almost always stem from a combination of poor judgement and poorer luck. A few rules of thumb: never approach wildlife on foot except in the company of a trustworthy guide; never swim in lakes or rivers without first seeking local advice about the presence of crocodiles or hippos; never get between a hippo and water; never leave food in the tent where you'll sleep; and be aware that running away from a predator can trigger its instinct to give chase. See below for advice on rabies.

Rabies

You should assume that all warm-blooded mammals can carry rabies (even a village dog or habituated monkey). So if you are bitten, scratched or licked over broken skin then scrub the wound with soap and running water and get to medical help as soon as possible. Ideally anyone travelling to Kenya should get pre-exposure (Prep) doses of rabies vaccine. Three doses over a minimum of 21 days are advised. Prep will change the need for the expensive and hard-to-come-by rabies immunoglobulin, thus making treatment so much easier.

Tickbite fever and quick tick removal

Ticks in Africa are not the rampant disease transmitters they are in the Americas, but they may spread tickbite fever and a few dangerous rarities. Tickbite fever is a flu-like illness that can easily be treated with doxycycline, but as there can be some serious complications it is very important to visit a doctor.

Ticks should ideally be removed as soon as possible as leaving them on the body increases the chance of infection. They should be removed with special tick tweezers that can be bought in good travel shops. Failing that you can use your finger nails: grasp the tick as close to your body as possible and pull steadily and firmly away at right angles to your skin. The tick will then come away complete, as long as you do not jerk or twist. If possible douse the wound with alcohol (any spirit will do) or iodine. Irritants (eg: Olbas oil) or lit cigarettes are to be discouraged since they can cause the ticks to regurgitate and therefore increase the risk of disease. It is best to get a travelling companion to check you for ticks; if you are travelling with small children, remember to check their heads, and particularly behind the ears.

Spreading redness around the bite and/or fever and/or aching joints after a tick bite imply that you have an infection that requires antibiotic treatment, so seek advice.

Snake and other bites

Snakes are very secretive and bites are a genuine rarity, but certain spiders and scorpions can also deliver nasty bites. In all cases, the risk is minimised by wearing closed shoes and trousers when walking in the bush, and watching where you put your hands and feet, especially in rocky areas or when gathering firewood. Only a small fraction of snakebites deliver enough venom to be life threatening, but it is important to keep the victim calm and inactive, and to seek urgent medical attention. Mosquitoes aside, the most annoying biting insects are tsetse flies and horseflies, which are harmless to tourists. Check yourself closely for ticks after walking in grassy places – they are usually easy to remove within an hour or two of clambering on board. For tips on tick removal, see opposite.

Car accidents

After malaria, dangerous driving is the biggest threat to life and limb in East Africa. On a self-drive safari, drive defensively, being especially wary of stray livestock, pot-holes and imbecilic or bullying overtaking manoeuvres. Many vehicles lack headlights and most local drivers are reluctant headlight users, so avoid driving at night and pull over in heavy storms. On a chauffeured safari, don't be afraid to tell the driver to slow or calm down if you think he is too fast or reckless. (See also *Getting around*, page 63.)

Banking and foreign exchange

The Kenya shilling (Ksh) currently trades at around US$1 = Ksh81, £1 = Ksh125 and €1 = Ksh103. Most upmarket hotels will accept any international currency for payments, but other craft stalls, restaurants and the like more usually work in the local currency. Foreign currency can be changed into Kenya shillings at any bank or bureau de change (known locally as forex bureaux), though the latter often deal in cash only and refuse to take travellers' cheques. All banks are open 09.00–14.00 on weekdays and in the cities they often stay open until 16.30 and open briefly on Saturday mornings. Private forex bureaux keep longer and more variable hours, but are often closed on Sundays. The foreign exchange desk at Jomo Kenyatta Airport stays open until midnight every day.

Generally, private forex bureaux offer a better rate of exchange than banks, but this often varies so it's worth shopping around before a major transaction. The private bureaux are almost always far quicker for cash transactions than the banks, which might be a more important consideration than a minor discrepancy in the rate they offer. The

Tipping

Knowing when to tip, and by how much, is frequently a source of stress in a foreign country, particularly so when there's such a glaring gap in wealth between visitors and most locals. In Kenya, the rules of thumb are fairly straightforward. At the sort of restaurants frequented by tourists, a 10% tip would be standard, depending on how good the service has been, but tipping would be more discretional at local restaurants. Most game lodges and camps operate on a full-board basis, and it's usually easier to sign drinks to the room than to pay cash, but you could always leave a tip for an individual waiter or barperson if you feel they deserve it, or add one to the bill. In both cases, however, we have heard so many stories of tips charged to credit cards here and elsewhere in Africa not reaching the intended person that we would always recommend a direct cash tip rather than signing it onto the rest of the bill.

At most lodges, there's a tip box at reception where you can leave cash to be distributed amongst all the staff, a system that seems fairer on backroom workers in a country where hotel staff are very poorly paid. It is also customary to tip your guide at the end of a safari, as well as any cook and porter who accompanies you. Expectations in both the above cases will vary from one company to the next, and will also depend on the size and quality of the lodge or camp, so while we would recommend as a very general guideline figures of around US$10-20 per guide or per room per day, it is worth discussing this with your operator before you travel.

legalisation of private forex bureaux has killed off the black market that previously thrived in Kenya, and anybody who approaches you in the street to change money is most likely a con artist, so stay well clear. Visa and to a lesser extent MasterCard are accepted by many tourist hotels, and can also be used to draw local currency at ATMs in most towns and cities.

On safari: locating wildlife

Television documentaries can create unrealistic expectations of an African safari. A top-notch wildlife film might be the product of years spent following one semi-habituated animal, and the high-speed chases and intimate wildlife interaction laid on for armchair safarigoers is seldom observed so easily in the flesh. It's a gap comparable to watching a sporting highlights package on TV and being present at a live match – the former is all action, punctuated with thrilling close-ups and slow motion replays, but it lacks the immediacy and atmosphere of actually being there as events unfold.

Game drives

Most driver-guides will do all they can to ensure a safari runs smoothly, but the onus is also on you to take a proactive role in game spotting, route planning, bird identification, deciding on photographic stops et al.

Timing

Typically, a day on safari is structured around a four- to five-hour morning game drive and a shorter afternoon drive, returning to camp in between for a leisurely lunch and siesta. Where possible, embark on your morning game drive shortly before sunrise (most lodges can provide a packed breakfast on request) and time your afternoon drive to return to camp at the latest hour permitted by park regulations. The first and last hours of daylight are when you are most likely to encounter secretive predators, and to witness action and interaction. In addition, temperatures are cooler, tourist traffic is lower, avian activity is higher, and light is best for photography.

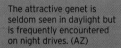
The attractive genet is seldom seen in daylight but is frequently encountered on night drives. (AZ)

If your lodge offers night drives, don't miss out the opportunity to look for a host of unusual creatures seldom seen in daylight – for instance, bushbabies, elephant shrews, genets, civets and rarities such as striped hyena, aardwolf and aardvark. Even if you see very little in terms of wildlife, the African bush possesses an unforgettable haunted quality after dark, and the night sky can be mesmerising.

Where to look

Even the most experienced driver-guide can miss seeing a roadside lion if he is looking the other way or focussing on a difficult stretch of road, so don't leave all the wildlife spotting to him. Except in the early morning and late afternoon, most animals prefer to lie or stand in the shade, so scan the ground below isolated trees in open country, and try to look into thicker bush rather than letting your eyes follow openings through it. In an open-topped vehicle, you'll stay more alert if you stand rather than sit, and the extra altitude will allow you to see further into the bush than a seated driver or passenger. Be conscious of a 'ticking' mentality that informs the way some drivers conduct game drives – if you've seen and photographed one giraffe, for instance, your driver might well decide not to stop for any other giraffes, no matter how distant or static that initial sighting was, or how photogenic a subsequent one is.

It's always worth stopping at any accessible river, reservoir or other watering point. Most animals drink at least once daily, so perennial water bodies tend to attract a steady trickle of thirsty elephant, buffalo, zebra, giraffe and other ungulates from mid-morning onwards, especially during the dry season. Should elephants be hovering at the water's edge, stick around to see whether they actually get into the water and start playing.

Vegetated riverbanks attract fewer transient drinkers than isolated reservoirs, but switch off the engine and sit for ten minutes at an apparently deserted riverbank scene, and you'll be surprised at what you see – a crocodile or hippo surfacing, a flash of brilliant colour as a kingfisher or bee-eater swoops from its perch, a bushbuck or kudu emerging from the tangled undergrowth, or a troop of monkeys erupting into treetop activity.

Tracks and signs

Even where large mammals seem to be uncommon, the bush is littered with their faecal spoor: the gigantic steaming pats deposited by elephant and rhino, the sausage-shaped scats of carnivores such as lion and jackal, the chalky white calcium rich droppings of bone-chomping hyenas, and the neat piles of pellets that mark the territorial boundaries of a dik-dik or duiker.

Giraffe front footprint (C&TS/FLPA)

Sandy trails or dirt roads are often criss-crossed by all sorts of animal tracks. Most numerous are the near-symmetrical cloven-hoof marks of antelopes, a pair of teardrop-shaped segments that look like an elongated inverted heart split lengthwise down the middle. Most antelope prints are too similar to be identified by shape alone, but the possibilities can be narrowed down when factors such as size, number of prints and environment are taken into account. The print of a duiker or dik-dik is only 2cm long, an eland is up to 14cm, and intermediate species tend to have proportionally sized spoor, with reedbuck, bushbuck and impala prints measuring about 6cm long, and wildebeest, oryx and hartebeest 11-12cm.

Of the other cloven-hoofed ungulates, a buffalo print is larger and more rounded than that of any antelope, while the giraffe's is squarer, more

Maasai giraffes crossing the Mara River. (MS)

elongated, and can be up to 20cm long. The print of a zebra comprises a large horseshoe in front of a pair of small antelope-like teardrops, while a hippo print looks like a gigantic four-pronged fig leaf. Larger still, rhino prints look a bit like squashed heads with outsized ears, while oval elephant prints, up to 70cm long, are recognisable by size alone.

Look closely, and you may pick up the spoor of a carnivore, typically an inverted heart-shaped pad print below a quartet of oblong or circular toe marks. When trying to identify what made the print, look for a row of triangular claw marks above the toes – this is lacking in the case of genets and all cats other than the (non-retractably clawed) cheetah. As with antelope, print size is generally

Leopard print (NB/FLPA)

proportionate to the animal. A clawless cat-like print of 10cm or longer is almost certainly the spoor of a lion, while a similar-sized print with doglike claw marks would have been made by a spotted hyena. The print of a leopard, cheetah or African wild dog is typically 7–9cm long, and at the other end of the spectrum, that of a dwarf mongoose is only 2cm. Two deceptively proportioned carnivore prints are those of the Cape clawless otter and honey badger, both up to 8cm long. It would be possible to confuse primate and carnivore prints, but the former almost always resemble a human footprint in general shape, and have five clearly defined toes – baboon prints can measure up to 16cm from heel to tip, but most other monkey prints are 4–6cm long.

A female leopard and her cubs make their way along a manmade track in the Masai Mara. (PS/FLPA)

Following clues

Look for indirect signs of predator and 'Big Five' activity. Circling or roosting vultures will often point towards a recent kill, while vociferous agitation amongst an arboreal baboon troop or guineafowl flock might well be in response to a prowling predator.

Many animals follow manmade roads in the same way that they would follow established wildlife tracks, so a trail of fresh paw prints laid on a muddy or sandy road, especially when located in the early morning, will often lead an experienced guide to the predator that made them, while a few steaming piles of roadside dung combined with torn-off branches and other destroyed vegetation is a sure sign that elephants passed through recently. Ironically, however, the most frequent and overt indirect evidence of an interesting sighting in the more popular Kenyan parks requires no specialist bush knowledge to interpret, consisting as it does of a huddle of 4x4s and/or minibuses further along the road.

Guided walks

In most non-forested, non-montane national parks, visitors are confined to their vehicles except at lodges, rest camps, entrance gates and other designated spots (a notable exception being Hell's Gate). However, there is no more exciting way of seeing wildlife than on foot, and many private reserves and game reserves that fall outside the national park system offer morning game walks led by an armed local guide.

Responsible wildlife watching

Avoid any activity that needlessly disturbs the wildlife or has a negative impact on the environment, and be prepared to discourage your driver/guide from doing so too. Desist from littering, especially from throwing matches or cigarette butts into the bush, which could instigate an uncontrolled fire. Discourage your driver from off-road driving where it is forbidden, and from the moronic practice of hurtling along behind predators while they are on the hunt. Hooting or yelling at wildlife to gain its attention is another no-no, and allowing your driver to provoke an elephant into mock charge is plain daft. Never feed the wildlife: monkeys and baboons in particular will quickly learn to associate humans with food and are often shot as vermin once they do.

Wilderness walks are more involving than game drives, frequently transforming a relatively mundane sighting into something altogether more immediate and inspirational – and lending a real edge to any encounter with elephant, buffalo, rhino or lion. No less important, you are far more conscious of sounds, smells and physical textures on foot – and have the opportunity to concentrate on smaller creatures such as birds, bugs and butterflies, and to examine all manner of environmental minutiae, from animal tracks to spider webs.

Animals habituated to vehicles are often less relaxed when they encounter human pedestrians. Blend in by wearing neutral colours such as green, grey or khaki, removing conspicuous accessories such as brightly coloured caps or scarves, and desist from dousing yourself in perfume or any other non-functional artificial scents. Lightweight long trousers, socks and solid shoes provide better protection against thorns and biting insects than shorts and open shoes, and a sunhat and sunblock will protect against direct sunlight.

Depending on the duration of the walk, you might also want to carry drinking water, a snack of some sort (avoiding fruit or meat), and a raincoat and/or sweatshirt just in case the weather turns nasty. As a rule, it is more difficult to approach wildlife closely on foot, so you are less likely to make use of a camera and more likely to require binoculars.

Even more so than on a game drive, noisy chatter is likely to scare off animals and to spoil the excursion for other guests, so talk as softly as possible, or better still keep silent. As for safety, the risk of being attacked by a wild animal is very small, but it is vital to pay attention during your pre-walk briefing and to listen to your guide, especially in the presence of a potentially dangerous animal.

A walk with a knowledgeable guide will greatly enhance your understanding of the bush. You'll be shown how to identify the more common and interesting trees, and may have their traditional medicinal uses explained. Especially in the early morning, the volume and variety of birdsong can be quite overwhelming, and a bush walk offers the opportunity to seek out mixed bird parties comprised of inconspicuous sunbirds, warblers, bush-shrikes and other species.

Butterflies, generally most active from mid-morning onwards, are often abundant near water and forest edges, while large webs made by colourful

Guided walk through the Selenkay Wildlife Conservancy. (AP)

spiders dangle in the treetops, and creepy-crawlies such as dung beetles and millipedes creep and crawl along the ground. You'll probably want to look out for lizards and tortoises, and while snakes are unlikely to be observed, you may well see the odd series of S-shaped ripples created by their undulating method of locomotion on sandy soil.

Boat trips

Boat trip on Lake Turkana (AZ)

Wildlife viewing from a boat makes a welcome change from the standard safari regime of two daily game drives, but in Kenya it is only an option at certain Rift Valley lakes, where you are likely to see plenty of hippos and birds, and possibly a few crocodiles, but little in the way of terrestrial wildlife. Bear in mind that the intensity of the sun is amplified when reflected by water, so you'll burn more quickly than on foot or in a vehicle. Wear a hat (ideally tied around your neck) and douse yourself liberally with sunscreen. Crocodiles pose no real threat unless your boat capsizes, in which case swim directly to the closest shore. There is always a risk of being drenched by a storm or by choppy waters, so carry all valuables and damageable goods in a waterproof bag.

If you carry a long photographic lens, bear in mind that the constant rocking of a boat makes it too unstable to be a useful support: you'll need to handhold the camera and may have to sacrifice depth of field in order to maximise shutter speed and probable sharpness. Boats provide a superb platform for snapping water-associated birds, and a skilful pilot will often be able to get in very close to herons, storks and other large wading birds.

Camps and lodges

After a long day driving in or between reserves, it is easy (and for many, desirable perhaps) to perceive time in camp or a lodge as an opportunity to catch a quick nap or to settle down at the poolside bar with a book and drink. But lodge gardens often offer an opportunity to seek out lizards, frogs, hyraxes, squirrels and other small animals, and can be relied upon to provide good birdwatching, especially in the early morning and late afternoon, when fruiting *Ficus* trees and flowering *Aloe* shrubs often attract species that are less easily seen from a fast-moving vehicle.

Many lodges are built alongside excellent natural viewpoints, from where you can scan the surrounding bush for passing wildlife, while others overlook rivers or lakes that attract a steady trickle of transient wildlife.

Lodges situated near water can provide ample opportunity for wildlife watching. (SC)

Such aquatic viewpoints are especially worth your time too if they are spotlighted after dark, when they may be visited by hyenas, bushpigs, genets and other small predators. The lodge-as-hide concept is taken to its logical conclusion at the so-called 'tree hotels' in the central highlands (Treetops, The Ark and Mountain Lodge – see *Chapter 9*, pages 212 and 216), where game drives are forsaken entirely in favour of long afternoons and nights watching what comes to the waterholes.

Urban habitats

At first glance, Kenya's cities don't hold out much promise for viewing wildlife. And it's true enough that you're unlikely to see an elephant or lion wandering through the urban heart of Nairobi or Mombasa. But cities can be surprisingly rewarding when it comes to birds and other medium to small vertebrates. The compellingly ungainly marabou stork, for instance, often nests atop office blocks, while hotel grounds set in the leafy suburbia of Nairobi are home to a hoist of birds and elusive chameleons. Almost every urban wall below an altitude of around 1,500m is likely to host a few bug-eyed, insect-chomping gecko lizards, and the eerie nocturnal call of the bushbaby is often heard in suburban Nairobi and Mombasa. More dramatically, the forested Karen Hills fringing Nairobi still support a population of elusive leopards, while Nairobi National Park is famed for its improbable juxtaposition of giraffes, gazelles and even big cats against a heat-hazed backdrop of shimmering skyscrapers (see page 110). In short, should your itinerary enforce upon you a stray morning or afternoon in urban surrounds, odds are that with a little forethought and initiative, it will present a great opportunity for some low-key wildlife watching.

A tripod is vital for supporting long lenses when photographing outside the vehicle. (WD)

Photography

Game drives are better than boat trips or walks for wildlife photography, because the vehicle doubles as a hide and a stabilising device for your camera. Some drivers are more skilled at lining up vehicles than others, so some direction might be necessary. As a rule, it's best to approach along a line that places you between the animal and the sun, whilst avoiding placing any distracting vegetation between subject and lens. You'll develop a feel for the right speed of approach: too fast and direct and you might scare off the animal, too slow or stop-start and it might feel like it's being stalked. If the animal is getting twitchy, stop for a minute or two, and if it still doesn't settle, leave it in peace.

Photographers using a long lens will improve its stability (and increase the odds of a sharp result) if they use the car as a support, by resting the camera on a beanbag or even some bunched up clothing. Be aware, however, that the vibration of a running engine will almost certainly result in a blurred image, as will the shuffling of an antsy-pants driver or any other slight movement that affects the car while the shutter is open. Finally, in an open-top vehicle, don't always shoot from the roof – the elevation may provide a better vantage point for distant animals and perched birds, but where the subject is at ground level close to the car, you'll get a more pleasing perspective shooting square on from the window.

Eating and drinking

Food

On safari, it's customary to eat all meals at your lodge or camp, if for no other reason than there is generally no alternative within a reasonable driving distance, and most such places offer full-board packages. Meals provided by lodges are generally of a high standard and you are unlikely to go hungry. Smaller camps generally do set menus comprising three or four courses, with a choice of at least two dishes for each course, while larger lodges typically serve expansive buffet meals. Vegetarians and others with special dietary requirements should specify this to their tour operator in advance, and – bearing mind the long chain of communications that links a desk in London or New York to a lodge in the remote Kenyan bush – are strongly advised to confirm (or ask their driver-guide to confirm) arrangements upon arrival at each lodge.

Most lodges and camps offer the option of a packaged breakfast and/or lunch box, so that their guests can eat on the trot rather than having to base their game-viewing hours around set mealtimes. The standard of the packed lunches is rather variable (and in some cases pretty awful) but if your first priority is to see wildlife, then taking a breakfast box in particular allows you to be out immediately after sunrise, when wildlife is most active and

The Kenyan coast is renowned for its fresh seafood. (AZ)

photogenic. In both cases, ask your driver-guide to make arrangements at reception the night before.

In cities and beach resorts, many tourists will also eat at their hotel either for convenience sake, or because they have been booked in full-board. However, Nairobi and Mombasa in particular are blessed with an

Local cuisine

If you want to sample the local cuisine, it usually consists of a lightly spiced stew eaten with the main local staple *ugali* (stiff maize porridge) or with rice *orchapatti* (a flat Indian-style bread). The most common stews are chicken, beef, goat and beans, and the meat is often rather tough. In coastal towns and around the great lakes, whole fried fish is a welcome change. The distinctive Swahili cuisine of the coast makes generous use of coconut milk and is far spicier than other Kenyan food. For the sweeter toothed, *mandaazi*, the local equivalent of doughnuts, are tasty when freshly cooked. Note that KiSwahili names for various foods are given on page 252.

excellent and cosmopolitan selection of stand-alone restaurants that collectively represent most global cuisines. Seafood is particularly recommended on the coast, while Nairobi excels when it comes to meat dishes and Indian restaurants, the latter usually offering a good vegetarian selection. If you want to explore beyond the selections listed in this book, ask your operator or hotel for local recommendations, and to arrange a taxi to drop and collect you.

Drinks

Ideally suited to the warm, dry conditions that prevail on safari, locally bottled lager beer is ubiquitous, with the most popular brands being Tusker, White Cap, Castle and Pilsner, which come in 500ml and/or 330ml bottles, chilled or warm (locals tend to prefer the latter). Local beers are very cheap in supermarkets and local eateries, but places aimed at tourists tend to charge accordingly. Bars at most tourist lodges also stock a selection of imported spirits and South African wines, the latter generally of a high quality and quite reasonably priced by international standards. Sodas such as Coke, Pepsi, Sprite and Fanta are widely available, but the most widely drunk beverage is *chai*, a sweet tea where all ingredients are boiled together in a pot, sometimes flavoured with spices such as ginger. In Kenyan hotels, tea is served in the more familiar way, and is generally preferable to filter coffee, which for some reason always tends to be pretty abysmal – if it's not burnt or over-stewed, it tends to be insipid. On the coast and in some parts of the interior, the most refreshing, healthy and inexpensive drink is coconut milk, sold by street vendors who will decapitate the young coconut of your choice to create a natural cup, from which the juice can be sipped. Tap water cannot be recommended but mineral water is widely available.

Shopping

Nairobi and to a lesser extent Mombasa and Malindi boast an excellent selection of shops, at least by African standards, though the reality is that few tourists on organised safaris will have much opportunity to browse

Shela village market, Lamu (JB)

them. Shops in smaller towns are less varied and more poorly stocked, but most items likely to be required by tourists will be available in the likes of

Buying local crafts

Craftshops generally charge fixed prices, though there may be some slight wiggle room for negotiation, and are generally more expensive than craft stalls, though bargaining is essential at the latter. What should be understood, however, is that the fact a stall owner is open to negotiation does not mean that you were initially being overcharged. Indeed, the seller will generally quote an initial price in the expectation that it will be bargained down, so it is not necessary to respond aggressively or in an accusatory manner; just suggest a lower price and then see where both parties meet. There are no fixed rules about this: some people say that you should offer half the asking price and be prepared to settle at around two-thirds, but my experience is that curio sellers are far more whimsical than such advice allows for. The sensible approach, if you want to get a feel for prices, is to ask the price of similar items at a few different stalls before you actually contemplate buying anything.

Nakuru, Nanyuki, Nyika and Kisumu. Toilet rolls, soap, toothpaste, pens, batteries and locally produced food are widely available at *dukas* (stalls) in pretty much every settlement countrywide. However, once in the game reserves that form the centrepiece of most tours to Kenya, the only shops are usually the gift shops in lodges and camps, which generally stock a fair selection of basic toiletries, books about Kenya, expensive touristy clothing, handicrafts and a few packaged goods such as chocolate bars, crisps and chewing gum.

The opportunities for **craftshopping** in Kenya are practically endless: there are handicraft shops and stalls dotted all around Nairobi and the various coastal resorts, as well as along several of the more widely used trunk roads and outside game reserves and national parks. In addition to an almost limitless choice of tacky identikit wildlife carvings and paintings, a range of more interesting and individualistic items is available, including intricate Makonde carvings and fantastically stylised Tingatinga paintings, from neighbouring Tanzania, inventive batiks, traditional musical instruments, Akamba basketwork, Gusii soapstone carvings, malachite knick-knacks, Maasai beadwork and other tribal items, as well as toys made inventively from wire, wood or whatever other materials the creator found to hand.

(JB)

Media and communications

Internet

The internet is widely available in Kenya, though it is largely restricted to towns and servers tend to be very slow by North American or European standards. Most upmarket city hotels have an in-house internet centre, and many also offer Wi-Fi in public areas. Cheaper than hotels, public internet cafés are prolific and affordable in most major urban tourist centres. Internet access is not available in most game reserves and national parks, however, and lodges that do offer browsing or email services tend to charge very high rates.

Telephones

Mobile (cell) phones dominate in Kenya. If you bring one with you from home, it's probably worth the minor investment in a local SIM card, as international text messages and calls are very affordable. By contrast, you'll rack up a hefty bill if you use your normal mobile number to make/receive calls and/or messages in Kenya, since in most instances these are charged double the international rates out of your home country. The most popular service provider in Kenya is Safaricom, which serves more than eight million subscribers and has the widest network coverage within the country. Its main rival Zain is less popular in Kenya, but has the advantage of a cross-border network extending across 12 African countries including Tanzania. Be aware that while reception can be guaranteed in most towns and their immediate environs, the network is spotty or absent in most national parks and reserves.

Media

Kenya has a relatively free **press**, dominated by the Nation Media Group, whose popular *Daily Nation* is a balanced English-language newspaper providing good local and international coverage. It also publishes the *East African*, an excellent weekly newspaper whose coverage is focused on Kenya, Tanzania, Uganda and Rwanda, and has a very good news website (www.nation.co.ke). Other **English-language dailies** include the *East African Standard* and *Kenya Times*, the latter a state-owned paper with a clear pro-government bias. In Nairobi and Mombasa, it is also easy to pick up *Time*, *Newsweek* and international newspapers, usually a day or two after publication. **Televisions** are provided in most city hotels rooms and many beach resorts, but usually not in game lodges. The state-owned Kenya Broadcasting Service (KBC www.kbc.co.ke) has a single channel, supplemented in most hotels by DSTV, a South African satellite broadcast service whose bouquet includes BBC News, CNN and several

Language

The official languages are English and KiSwahili. English is spoken to a medium-to-high standard by most people working in the tourism industry, and visitors on organised tours are unlikely to ever hit a situation where any other language is required. KiSwahili is the most widely spoken language in the country, and it is worth learning a few greeting and phrases (see page 250) for politeness's sake if nothing else.

sports and entertainment channels. KBC is also responsible for the state radio services that compete with an ever-increasing number of private regional broadcasters, notably Capital 98.4 FM and Kiss.

Business and time

Opening hours

Business hours are broadly similar to those in Europe or North America. Shops, museums and offices in upcountry towns generally open between 08.00 and 09.00 and close sometime between 17.00 and 18.00 Monday to Friday, and most shops and museums are also open over similar (or slightly shortened hours) on Saturdays and in some cases Sundays. Along the hotter and more humid coast, many places close for a two-hour siesta at sometime during 12.00 and 14.00, and stay open later in the evenings. In villages and small towns, the notion of fixed opening hours is often quite meaningless.

Time

Kenya, as with all of its neighbours, operates on East Africa Time, three hours ahead of GMT/UTC and eight hours ahead of US Eastern Standard Time. There is no daylight saving in place, as the country's equatorial location means that sunrise and sunset stay within about 30 minutes either side of 06.30 and 18.30 throughout the year. Note that while most Westernised and tourist-oriented institutions use the familiar 24-hour clock, most local people use and think in Swahili time, which runs six hours behind (see page 251 for a more detailed explanation). As a result, Kenyans will sometimes absent-mindedly say '9 o'clock', for instance, when they actually mean '3 o'clock'. Best thing to do is, when in doubt, check whether the person means Swahili time or Mzungu (European) time.

Cultural etiquette

On the whole, Kenya is a very relaxed and friendly country, and people won't easily take offence at a minor *faux pas*. That said, like anywhere else, it does have its rules of etiquette, and while allowances will be made for tourists, there is some value in ensuring that mistakes are not made too frequently. Probably the most important single custom that needs to be absorbed by visitors is the importance of formal greetings. Kenyans usually greet each other elaborately, and while tourists aren't expected to do the same, it would be very rude to blunder into conversation or interrogative mode without first exchanging greetings – a simple 'How are you?' or '*Jambo!*' delivered with a smile will be adequate.

The public display of certain emotions is regarded to be in poor taste, most obviously any informal public show of affection – such as holding hands, kissing or embracing – between males and females. It is also considered bad form to show anger publicly, and losing your temper will almost certainly be counterproductive when dealing with obtuse officials, dopey waiters and hotel employees, or unco-operative safari drivers.

Homosexuality is illegal in Kenya, a law that is currently seldom enforced, though that may well change in the puerile atmosphere of overt homophobia gripping East Africa. Gay travellers are advised to exercise discretion. Oddly, at least to us, Kenyans regard it to be normal for two friends of the same sex to walk around hand-in-hand, and male travellers who get into a long discussion with a Kenyan male shouldn't be surprised if that person clasps them by the hand and retains a firm grip on it for several minutes – this is a warm gesture, one that is particularly appropriate when the person wants to make a point with which you might disagree.

There is a strong Islamic presence, particularly along the coast, and while local Muslims live peacefully alongside Christians and are mostly used to tourists, it cannot hurt to comply with certain Islamic codes of conduct. For instance, Muslims reserve the left hand for ablutions, and may take offence if you use this hand to pass/receive something, or offer it when shaking hands, or when eating with your fingers. Even those who are naturally right-handed will occasionally need to remind themselves of this (for example, you are carrying something in your right hand and give money to a shopkeeper with your left); left-handed travellers must make a constant effort.

In traditional Muslim societies it is offensive for women to expose their knees or shoulders, and for men to bare their chests publicly, customs that ought to be heeded along parts of the coast where tourists remain a relative novelty. As a rule, however, you can wear what you like in game reserves and on recognised tourist beaches (although topless bathing is not considered acceptable!).

Kenya HIGHLIGHTS

5 Nairobi and Surrounds

The capital of Kenya, Nairobi is the largest city in East Africa, and the site of its busiest international and domestic airports. Set at an elevation of 1,800m in the central highlands, it provides a pleasant climatic introduction to Africa, except perhaps if you are greeted by one of the flash storms that characterise the rainy season. The city centre lacks discernable character, unsurprisingly perhaps when you consider it was founded as recently as 1899, and the con artists, safari touts and curio sellers that prowl the streets can be a little overwhelming. By contrast, parts of suburban Nairobi can be very tranquil and attractive, studded with plush hotels whose verdant gardens are interspersed with relict patches of indigenous highland forest. And for those who have the time to settle in, Nairobi can be a very likeable city, vibrantly good humoured and endowed with limitless opportunities for shopping, eating out and other urban pursuits.

History

Nairobi has a somewhat compressed sense of history, founded as it was in the last year of the 19th century, initially as a supply depot at Mile 327 during the construction of the Uganda Railway. As suggested by its name, a corruption of the Maa phrase *ewaso nyarobi* (cold water), the location was perhaps too swampy to be the ideal choice for a capital city. Nevertheless, with its temperate malaria-free highland climate, Nairobi proved attractive to European settlers, and by 1905 it was sufficiently well established to replace coastal Mombasa as the administrative capital of British East Africa. A few buildings dating to its first decade of existence survive, among them the Norfolk Hotel and National Archives, but otherwise central Nairobi is rather bland and modern in appearance, reflecting its immense growth since independence, from around 300,000 people in the early 1960s to more than four million today.

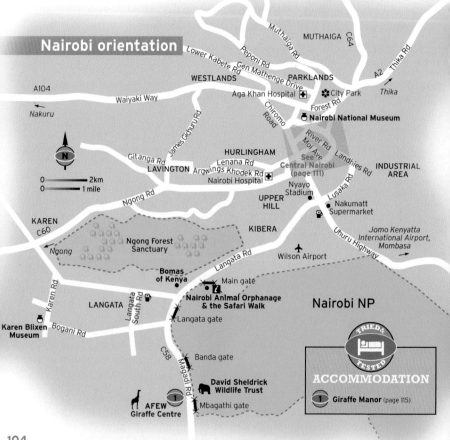

Nairobi highlights

Suburban Nairobi

Nairobi National Museum

☎ 020 3742161-4 ⌨ www.museums.or.ke
🕐 09.30-18.00

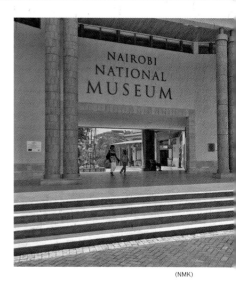

(NMK)

Established in 1910 and relocated to its present site on **Museum Hill** in 1929, this exceptional museum reopened in 2008 following an extensive programme of expansion and modernisation. It has a good prehistory section, with displays dedicated to human evolution in East Africa and the reproductions of rock art shelters from Kolo (northern Tanzania) and further afield. Ethnographic displays include a gallery of paintings by Joy Adamson, while the Lamu Gallery explores coastal history from the 9th to the 19th century. The natural history section is less absorbing, though it includes decent sections on marine life and birds. The museum gardens are dotted with contemporary Kenyan sculptures, and a respected snake park, established in 1959, is attached.

Nairobbery

Nairobi - often referred to as 'Nairobbery' - has a long-standing reputation as a crime hotspot, one that is largely justified, though a little bit of commonsense goes a long way to avoiding becoming a victim. Upmarket hotels, even in the city centre, are as safe as anywhere in the world, and you can further reduce your exposure to crime by staying at a suburban hotel, since crime targeted at tourists is mostly associated with the city centre. By day, the dodgiest part of town is the triangle of streets between Moi Avenue and River Road, an area that attracts plenty of backpackers but is seldom visited by package tourists. However, nowhere in Nairobi can be considered safe at night. As a rule, it's advisable to use taxis to get around, even for walkable distances, especially after dark or when you are carrying valuables or large sums of money. If you want to go sightseeing in the city centre, there is much to be said for arranging a local guide, either through your tour operator or your hotel.

Practicalities

All international and some domestic **flights** land at Jomo Kenyatta International Airport, some 10km southeast of the city centre off the Mombasa road. However, the light aircraft flights that connect Nairobi to the Masai Mara, Laikipia and other game reserves leave from Wilson Airport, on Langata Road only 2km south of the city centre. At either airport, people on organised safaris will normally be met by a hotel shuttle or ground operator, but if that doesn't happen, taxis are plentiful and fares quite cheap by international standards. The main hubs for terrestrial **public transport** are the railway station, at the southeast end of the city centre, and the cluster of bus operators in the River Road area.

Few African cities surpass Nairobi when it comes **tourist facilities and amenities**. Banks, ATMs and foreign exchange bureaux can be found at the international airport, in a plethora of suburban shopping malls, and throughout the city centre (though the crime issue discussed on page 105 makes it advisable to discuss your options with your safari guide or hotel reception before you enter the fray with hard currency, cash or credit card in hand). There are also plenty of internet cafés, safari companies, book and handicraft shops dotted around town, with the main concentration being along Kenyatta Avenue. Nairobi is also home to East Africa's most

Accommodation

For full details of tour-operator recommended accommodation, see page 115. Here follows a few further suggestions from the author.

Exclusive
Ngong House ⌂ www.ngonghouse.com
Norfolk Hotel ⌂ www.fairmont.com
Palacina Residence & Suites ⌂ www.palacina.com
Shompole Lodge ⌂ www.shompole.com

Upmarket
Fairview Hotel ⌂ www.fairviewkenya.com
Hilton Nairobi ⌂ www.hilton.com
InterContinental Nairobi ⌂ www.ichotelsgroup.com
Karen Blixen Coffee House & Cottages ⌂ www.blixencoffeegarden.co.ke
Nairobi Serena Hotel ⌂ www.serenahotels.com
Sarova Stanley Hotel ⌂ www.sarovahotels.com

cosmopolitan dining-out scene, boasting a profusion of restaurants that collectively represent most global cuisines, none more legendary than The Carnivore, a perennially popular out-of-town venue for a post-safari binge. For a more central drink or meal break, head to the balcony of the iconic Norfolk Hotel (Harry Thuku Road), the city's oldest and arguably grandest hostelry.

Shops along River Road, Nairobi (SS)

Moderate
Blue Posts Hotel ☎ 067 22241/22181
Hotel Boulevard ⌂ www.sentrim-hotels.com
Meridian Court Hotel ⌂ www.meridianhotelkenya.com
Silver Springs Hotel ⌂ www.silversprings-hotel.com

Budget
Karen Camp ⌂ www.karencamp.com
Olorgesailie Bandas ⌂ www.museums.or.ke
Upper Hill Campsite & Backpackers ⌂ www.upperhillcampsite.com

Eating out

Alan Bobbe's Bistro (French) Riverside Dr, Westlands ☎ 020 4446325
Bhandini (Indian) InterContinental Hotel, City Hall Way ☎ 020 3200000
Carnivore (Grilled meat) Langata Rd ☎ 020 609441
Tamarind (Fresh seafood) Haile Selassie Av ☎ 020 251811
Trattoria (Italian) Cnr Kaunda & Wabera sts ☎ 020 340855

Central Nairobi landmarks

Nairobi is not overly endowed when it comes to 'must see' tourist attractions, and most visitors spend only one night there before they move on to the wildlife reserves and beaches for which Kenya is famed. However, those who spend longer in Nairobi have plenty to keep them busy, whether it's a half-day safari to look for lions and rhinos in the underrated Nairobi National Park, a tour of the recently revitalised

Nairobi's skyline from Uhuru Park (SS)

National Museum or suburban Karen Blixen Museum, or a visit to one of the private wildlife orphanages that lie south of the city centre. But Nairobi's high-rise city centre also hosts several notable landmarks, and the risk of trouble can be minimised by leaving behind all valuables in your hotel room. Some of the places worth visiting are as follows:

Central Market

Situated off Koinange Street, this offers some great handicraft shopping opportunities. There are also plenty of good shops two blocks further south, on and around Kenyatta Avenue.

(NMK)

Karen Blixen Museum
☎ 020 880021 🖱 www.museums.or.ke
🕘 09.30–18.00
Situated 10km from the city centre in the forested suburb of Karen, this impressive 1912 colonial homestead was the dwelling place of the Danish baroness Karen Blixen from 1918 to 1931. Probably the most famous personage associated with colonial East Africa, Blixen published an account of her time in Kenya called *Out of Africa* in 1937 (under the pseudonym Isak Dinesen), and was the subject of the eponymous Oscar-winning 1985 movie starring Meryl Streep. The house was restored and furnished in period style for the filming, and it opened as a national

Nairobi Gallery

Uhuru Av ⌁ www.museums.or.ke ⌚ 09.30-18.00

A recent addition to the centre's limited range of tourist attractions, this gallery is housed in a former police commissioner's residence built in 1913, and it hosts a variety of temporary fine art and photographic exhibitions relating to Kenya past and present.

National Archives

Moi Av ☎ 020 2228959 ⌁ www.kenyarchives.go.ke ⌚ 08.15-16.15 Mon-Fri

An impressive collection of paintings, books and historic artefacts relating to Kenya is housed in the former Bank of India building, which was built in 1906 and is one of the city's finest colonial relicts with its columned façade.

Railway Museum

Station Rd ☎ 020 2049169 ⌚ 08.30-17.00

Although it is mainly of interest to rail buffs, this small and rather quirky museum has some interesting displays relating to the construction of the 'Lunatic Line' to Uganda c1900 and the associated dramas with man-eating lions in present-day Tsavo.

August 7th Memorial Park

Moi Av ☎ 020 341062 ⌚ 07.00-18.00

This simple memorial stands on the site of the former US Embassy, which was destroyed in the tragic 1998 terrorist attack in which 218 people were killed and thousands injured.

museum in 1986, with attached gift shop and coffeeshop, and a nature trail running through the forested gardens.

AFEW Giraffe Centre

☎ 020 891658 ⌁ www.giraffecenter.org ⌚ 09.00-17.30

The African Fund for Endangered Wildlife (AFEW) is an NGO established in 1979 to conserve the endangered Rothschild's giraffe, an endangered five-horned race whose range is restricted to northern Uganda and western Kenya. At the time of AFEW's foundation, a mere 130 wild Rothschild's giraffes survived in Kenya, largely as a result of habitat loss, and the Ugandan population, centred on Murchison Falls, was probably even smaller. AFEW tackled this problem on two fronts, firstly by raising funds to translocate four herds of Rothschild's giraffe from unprotected areas to national parks or reserves, including Lake Nakuru, and secondly with the establishment of this Giraffe Centre in Karen. A popular tourist attraction, the AFEW Giraffe Centre offers visitors the opportunity to eyeball a giraffe from an elevated viewing platform, but it also serves the more serious purpose of breeding Rothschild's giraffes for release in the wild – youngsters born here have been translocated to four reserves and ranches countrywide, and the national population now stands at around 300. Also on site is a superb boutique lodge called Giraffe Manor (see page 115), a bird sanctuary and a 1.5km self-guided walking trail.

Nairobi National Park

☎ 020 600800 🌐 www.kws.org ◷ 06.00-19.00

The premier tourist attraction in the vicinity of Nairobi, this remarkable 117km² national park lies a mere 7km south of the city centre, where it frequently offers the unique spectacle of lion or rhino below a background of shimmering skyscrapers. Despite its proximity to the capital, there is nothing artificial or contrived about the park, which is fenced on the city side for obvious reasons, but not along its other designated boundaries, allowing for free movement of wildlife between the park and surrounding areas such as the Athi Plains.

Secretary birds are often seen in Nairobi National Park. (AZ)

Almost every species of plains wildlife associated with southern Kenya occurs here, the only notable exception being elephant, and it is one of the best parks in Kenya for seeing lion kills and black rhino. The park is especially worthwhile between July and August, when its permanent pools attract a mini-migration of wildebeest, plains zebra and gazelle from the adjacent Athi Plains. Despite its small size, the park can be highly rewarding to birdwatchers, with more than 400 species recorded, and it's a good place to look for larger ground birds such as ostrich, secretary bird, southern ground hornbill and various bustards. Roads within the park are well maintained, so it can be explored in any rental car, and it is easy to arrange half-day tours through any Nairobi operator.

The main entrance to the park is at the Kenya Wildlife Service (KWS) headquarters on Langata Road, 7km southwest of the city centre. Popular with children, the animal orphanage here, founded in 1964, provides sanctuary to an ever-changing variety of young animals, most of which are eventually re-released into the wild. Also at the main gate is the

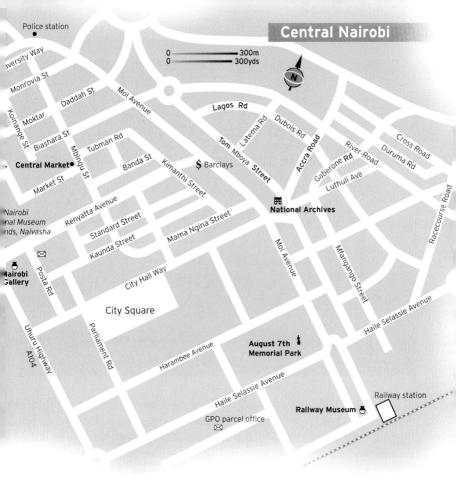

exciting safari walk, which opened in 2006 and offers good views into a series of large modern enclosures harbouring everything from the rare bongo antelope to lion and leopard. Within the park proper, allow four hours to cover all the main road loops, longer if you plan on stopping for birds, and try to time things to take advantage of peak wildlife activity in the early morning and late afternoon.

David Sheldrick Wildlife Trust

☎ 020 891996 www.sheldrickwildlifetrust.org ☉ 11.00-12.00

Guided tours at this wildlife orphanage near the Mbagathi Gate to Nairobi National Park offer a unique opportunity to interact with orphaned elephant and occasionally rhino babies that are hand-reared for eventual release into the wild – so far more than 80 orphans raised here have been released into Tsavo. The trust was established in 1977 by Daphne Sheldrick, whose achievements, depicted in the recent BBC documentary *Elephant Diaries*, earned her an MBE in 1989 and a

A resident at the David Sheldrick Wildlife Trust (SS)

damehood in 2006. The trust also funds a mobile veterinary unit and de-snaring activities in Tsavo and Amboseli. It is named after her late husband David Sheldrick MBE, the legendary founder warden of Tsavo East National Park. Daily tours are offered but by appointment only, and donations are encouraged.

Bomas of Kenya

☏ 020 891391 ⌨ www.bomasofkenya.co.ke ⏱ 14.30–16.00 Mon–Fri, 15.30–17.15 Sat, Sun & public holidays

Established by the Kenyan government back in 1971, this popular cultural centre in Langata comprises 11 life-size homesteads (*bomas*) representing different traditional construction styles from around the country. Daily performances include some vibrant drumming and dancing representing traditions from all around the country.

Further afield

Ngong Hills

Situated to the southwest of the city centre, these hills – whose name is a Maa word meaning 'knuckles' – form part of the Rift Valley escarpment, and while the highest peak (2,459m) is not a great deal higher than Nairobi itself, it towers more than 1,000m above the Rift Valley floor to its west.

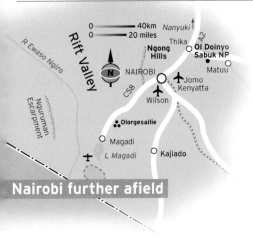

0 ————— 40km *Nanyuki*
0 ————— 20 miles
R Ewaso Ngiro
Rift Valley
Thika
Ngong ○ **Ol Doinyo**
Hills **Sabuk NP**
● **NAIROBI** ○ *Matuu*
N ↑Jomo
C58 Kenyatta
Wilson
Nguruman Escarpment
● **Olorgesailie**
○ *Magadi*
✝ *L Magadi* ○ *Kajiado*

Nairobi further afield

In addition to offering great views (all the way to Kilimanjaro on a clear day), the easily reached peaks support patches of indigenous forest inhabited by buffalo, bushbuck, leopard and an interesting selection of birds. Mugging has been a problem in the area for some years, so it is inadvisable to hike here unescorted, but guides can be arranged for a small fee at the KWS office in Ngong village, which lies about 15km from central Nairobi along the old Narok road.

Olorgesailie prehistoric site

☎ 020 3742161-4 🖥 www.museums.or.ke
🕐 08.00-18.00

Flanking the Magadi road some 65km south of Nairobi, this underrated site lies in an untrammelled part of the Rift Valley that remains very sparsely settled, aside from a few traditional Maasai villages, and that still holds significant populations of large mammals, most conspicuously

(NMK)

giraffe. The prehistoric site overlooks what, 500,000 years ago, would have been a large shallow lake that supported plenty of aquatic wildlife. Excavations undertaken in the 1940s by Richard and Mary Leakey unearthed many fossils, including extinct species of giant elephant and hippo, along with a wealth of Stone-Age tools used by the *Homo erectus* hunter-gatherers that lived around the shore. Most of the key finds are kept on site and can be viewed along a short, guided walking trail. This is also a great spot for dry-country birds such as red-and-yellow barbet, slaty-coloured boubou, chestnut sparrow, cutthroat finch, African silverbill, purple grenadier and Somali golden-breasted bunting.

Lake Magadi

The Rift Valley lake that makes the fewest concessions to tourism is, oddly enough, the one closest to Nairobi. Lake Magadi forms the terminus of a

The soda-encrusted shores of Lake Magadi in the Rift Valley, south of Nairobi (IP/A)

110km surfaced road that runs south from the capital through a starkly beautiful stretch of the Rift Valley reminiscent of the remote Turkana hinterland. In truth, the bizarre and inhospitable apparition known as Magadi is not a lake in the conventional sense, but a 105km^2 sludge bed of blindingly white salt and soda deposits that have been commercially exploited by the Magadi Soda Company (MSC) since 1911. Host to large flocks of flamingos and other waterbirds, the lake is most easily explored along the various causeways that lead out from the small eponymous town that serves as the MSC headquarters.

Nguruman Escarpment

⌐ www.shompole.com

Set on the Tanzania border 30km southwest of Magadi, this remote part of Kenya was once the exclusive reserve of hardy 4x4 expeditioneers, but today part of it is formally protected within the Shompole Conservancy, a private venture undertaken in collaboration with local Maasai communities. The Ewaso Nyiro River runs through the area and supports a similar range of large mammals to other reserves in southern Kenya and northern Tanzania, and while wildlife densities are lower, it possesses an aura of untrammelled exclusivity, with just three small upmarket camps scattered around the property.

Thika

Linked to the capital by 45km of nippy dual carriageway, Thika today is practically a satellite of Nairobi, one whose aspirations are summed up in the less than enticing motto 'Your Industrial Town' – which somewhat oversells the scattering of a dozen or so textile, cigarette and food processing factories around its periphery. The town's more rustic Edwardian incarnation is evoked in Elspeth Huxley's novelistic account of her colonial childhood *The Flame Trees of Thika*, adapted for television in the 1980s. The only surviving relict of Thika's early days, founded in 1908, is the Blue Posts Hotel, with its ivy-clad period architecture, pretty flowering grounds overlooking a pair of attractive waterfalls, and small zoo.

Ol Doinyo Sabuk National Park

☎ 020 2062503 ᐦ www.kws.org ☉ 06.00–19.00

Situated about 15km from Thika on the Garissa road, this scenic but little-visited national park protects the isolated 2,145m Ol Doinyo Sabuk (Maa for 'Big Mountain', a name that seems unduly hyperbolic given its proximity to Mount Kenya). The grassy summit can be reached by 4x4 or on foot, following a steep 10km dirt road that leads through forested slopes inhabited by buffalo, leopard, blue monkey, bushbuck and various highland birds. Assuming it isn't too misty, the views from the top are worth the effort, even though the pristine setting is undermined by a cluster of hilltop communications towers. On the way up, you'll pass the grave of Sir William McMillan, an obese wealthy settler whose heavy coffin was carried up the mountain by a tractor that packed up some 3km before it could reach the summit. Only 2km from the base of the mountain, but outside the national park, Fourteen Falls is formed by the Athi River as it splits into several small streams before tumbling over a wide rock lip, most impressively in April and December. A hippo pool lies five minutes' walk upriver.

THE ZAMBEZI SAFARI & TRAVEL CO. LTD

Giraffe Manor

ᐦ www.giraffemanor.com

Original, quirky, but above all, fabulous, Giraffe Manor remains one of our favourites in Nairobi – and it's the only place where you can feed giraffe food pellets from your bedroom window. It is ideal for easing into or out of a safari, with six en-suite bedrooms set in 40 acres of parkland just outside the city. The old manor house oozes romance from every chandelier and with an exceptionally warm welcome it's no wonder people keep coming back.

6 Southwest Safari Circuit

The southwest offers some of the country's finest wildlife viewing. Here you will find the country's most prominent safari destination, the peerless Masai Mara, whose dense resident wildlife populations are boosted every August by the million-plus herds of wildebeest and zebra on their cross-border migration from the Serengeti Plains. Further north, the basaltic cliffs of the southern Rift Valley hem in a classic East African landscape of open savanna studded with jagged volcanic outcrops and beautiful lakes famed for their birdlife – in particular the immense flocks of flamingos associated with Lake Nakuru, also known for its concentrations of white rhino. There are also paleontological sites recording the presence of our earliest hominid ancestors, while modern African cultures are represented by the Maasai, whose adherence to their traditional pastoralist lifestyle and colourful costumes lend a compelling aura of authenticity to proceedings.

Southwest safari circuit

KITALE

Saiwa Swamp NP

A1

B2

R Kerio

A104

Bungoma

ELDORET

C51

Kampi Ya Samaki

16

R Ewaso Ngiro

R Nzoia

Kakamega Forest NR

Kapsabet

Marigat

Lake Baringo

R Ewaso Ngiro

Kakamega

C39

A104

B4

Lake Bogoria NR

50km

25 miles

KISUMU

Kericho

Menengai Crater

NAKURU

Hyrax Hill

B5

Lake Victoria

15

Kendu Bay

Lake Nakuru NP

Lake Elmentaita

A104

Kariandusi

Gilgil

19

Kigio Wildlife Conservancy

R Tana

Homa Bay

Kisii

B3

Narok

NAIVASHA

Lake Naivasha

(see page 131)

R Athi

R Gori

A1

B3

B3

R Mara

RIFT VALLEY

R Athi

NAIROBI

A3

Tanzania

ACCOMMODATION

Masai Mara National Reserve

Mt Kipeko

Ngerende

C13

Ngorongore

4

11

17

Aitong

Loita Plains

10

18

2

MARA NORTH CONSERVANCY

MOTOROGI CONSERVANCY

R Olare Orok

Koyiaki

Narok

10km

6 miles

Leopard Gorge

12

OLARE OROK CONSERVANCY

NABOISHO CONSERVANCY

8

Musiara gate

13

Musiara Swamp

7

3

R Siana

5

Ballooning point

Talek gate

R Talek

Paradise Plain

1

Sekenani gate

Ololaimutie gate

Ballooning point

Park HQ

R Mara

Wildebeest crossing

6

Wildebeest crossing

Ngama Hills

14

Wildebeest crossing

Oloololo Escarpment

Wildebeest crossing

9

Mara Triangle (Mara Conservancy)

Ballooning point

R Sand

MASAI MARA NATIONAL RESERVE

Hippo pools

Mara Bridge

Sand River gate (closed)

Tanzania

Masai Mara National Reserve

☎ 050 22068 🖰 www.masai-mara.com 🕓 06.00-19.00

Gazetted in its present form in 1968, the 1,510km² Masai Mara National Reserve is easily the most famous and popular safari destination in Kenya, and with good reason. The 'Mara', as it's known locally, hosts a volume and variety of African plains wildlife rivalled only by Tanzania's Serengeti National Park, to which it forms an unfenced northern extension. Game viewing is excellent at any time of year, particularly when it comes to lion and other large predators, but it is truly outstanding between August and October, when the hilly grassland is host to one of the world's most awe-invoking wildlife spectacles, the legendary wildebeest migration that streams across the Mara River from the Serengeti Plains.

Masai Mara highlights

Ecologically, the reserve is dominated by open grassland, but as implied by its Maa name (Mara means 'spotted') the landscape is anything but uniform, rather a mosaic of plains, koppies, patches of acacia woodland, swamps, riparian forest and thicketed slopes. An excellent way to get an aerial overview of this patchwork is to book onto one of the dawn balloon safaris that are offered – at a considerable price – by almost all the lodges. The hilliest part of the Masai Mara is in the far east, where the quartzite Ngama Hills south of Sekenani Gate include four peaks that top the

A hot air balloon offers a vulture's-eye perspective on the moist Mara plains. (KTB)

Practicalities

A **packaged fly-in safari from Nairobi** is the easiest and most comfortable option, and it can be arranged through any reputable operator. **Road safaris** from Nairobi are also popular, and will generally work out to be quite a bit cheaper than flying, though do bear in mind, especially for stays of under three nights, that a significant proportion of your time and energy will be consumed by the drive there and back. The main Sekenani Gate lies about 265km west of Nairobi along a road that starts out promisingly enough, but deteriorates once you turn west from the Old Naivasha Road. The drive takes about six hours, depending on current conditions, and it is literally spine-jarring in parts, torturously so to anybody with back problems. A second, more circuitous route, only viable in good weather, connects the Masai Mara to Kisii in western Kenya via the Mau Escarpment.

En route from Nairobi by road, the last town you pass through is **Narok**, which lies about 65km before the main entrance gate and will be your last opportunity to do any grocery shopping, to go online affordably, or to draw money before you pass back through on the return trip – though in all instances you'd be better off dealing with things of this sort while you're still in Nairobi. Narok has a few adequate restaurants and small local guesthouses, and self-drivers should ideally fill up their tank here (some lodges within the park sell fuel, but generally at an inflated price). Worth a quick look if you want to stretch your legs in Narok is the Maa Museum, which includes displays relating to traditional and contemporary Maasai culture, and a fascinating gallery of recent photos of day-to-day life taken by Maasai women with disposable cameras.

Accommodation

For full details of tour-operator recommended accommodation, see page 125. Here follows a few further suggestions from the author.

Exclusive

Elephant Pepper Camp ⌁ www.elephantpepper.com
Il Moran ⌁ www.governorscamp.com
Mara Explorer ⌁ www.heritage-eastafrica.com
Mara Simba Lodge ⌁ www.marasimba.com

When booking your safari, the **location of your lodge** is paramount. The Masai Mara has a reputation for being too touristy and overcrowded, and it's certainly not unusual to find yourself jogging for space with half a dozen other vehicles circling a lion pride or a pacing cheetah. This might happen anywhere in the reserve, but it is most extreme in the sector southeast of the Talek River and its confluence with the Mara which hosts, or is bordered by, most of the larger lodges and the camping sites used by budget safaris. By comparison, the central sector, cupped between the Talek and Mara rivers north of their confluence, hosts relatively few camps, and the far west, flanked by the Mara River and Oloolo Escarpment, is less developed still.

The Mara's cheetah are very habituated to vehicles. (EN/FLPA)

Additionally, an *ipso facto* fourth sector comprises the large tract of unfenced Maasai community land immediate north of the national reserve and east of the Mara River. These are in the process of being gazetted as community conservancies that effectively function as private reserves and are relatively quiet in terms of tourist traffic. The Maasai conservancies here include Olare Orok, Motorogi, Mara North, Naibosho, Olkinyei and Enonkishu, not all of which are yet formally gazetted or fully up and running.

There's not much to choose between these sectors in terms of game viewing, and the paucity of bridges means that game drives are generally confined to the same sector as one's lodge or campsite. So, assuming that your budget runs to it, it is emphatically worth booking into one of the lodges in the central or western sectors, or in the northern conservancies.

Upmarket
Fig Tree Camp ᐯᕕ www.madahotels.com
Governor's Camp ᐯᕕ www.governorscamp.com
Keekorok Lodge ᐯᕕ www.wildernesslodges.co.ke
Kichwa Tembo Tented Camp ᐯᕕ www.andbeyond.com
Mara Serena Lodge ᐯᕕ www.serenahotels.com
Masai Mara Sopa Lodge ᐯᕕ www.sopalodges.com
Sarova Mara Game Camp ᐯᕕ www.sarovahotels.com
Siana Springs ᐯᕕ www.heritage-eastafrica.com

Budget
Mara Springs Safari Camp ᐯᕕ www.mountainrockkenya.com

Mara River crossings

The drama of the wildebeest migration is encapsulated by the multiple river crossings that punctuate the great herds' three-month tenure in the northern part of the Serengeti-Mara. The river crossings usually start in August, when the wildebeest disperse into the plains surrounding the Mara River, after which herds of a few hundred or thousand regularly cross back and forth – whether in blind adherence to the 'grass is greener' philosophy or in response to fresh rainfalls, it's difficult to say – using a few favoured crossing points. There are eight such sites in the Masai Mara, and the four that are used with greatest regularity lie along a 5km stretch of the Mara upriver of its confluence with the Talek.

(KTB)

1,800m mark, but the most prominent montane landmark is the Oloololo Escarpment running along the western boundary. The main watercourse is the perennial Mara River, which flows through the reserve from north to south before crossing into Tanzania, eventually to drain into Lake Victoria. The Mara is joined in the centre of the reserve by the Talek, a perennial river that flows in a westerly direction, along with several smaller seasonal tributaries. These two main rivers divide the reserve into three distinct sectors, which are connected only by three bridges: one across the Mara immediately before it flows into Tanzania, another crossing the Mara about 3km north of the reserve boundary, and one across the Talek alongside the eponymous entrance gate.

The Masai Mara is the best public reserve in Kenya for Big Five sightings. Elephant are very common, as are buffalo, the latter being the favoured prey of the unusually large lion prides characteristic of the

The build-up to a crossing is tense and unpredictable. Thousands of wildebeest might congregate over several days, teasing themselves as much as the spectator as a few individuals peer over the edge of the riverbank or make their way to the water's edge, dithery and indecisive. More often than not, they'll then withdraw back into the bush, milling around aimlessly it seems, or slowly making their way to another crossing point a kilometre or two away. The level of agitation within the herd rises and falls, regularly manifesting itself in a pitched outbreak of plaintive and hysterical communal braying that ends as suddenly as it starts.

Then, finally, after several false starts, an unidentifiable trigger or moment of madness will compel one or two individuals to leap from the bank and hurtle blindly into the water. The rest of the herd will follow, charging shoulder high through the river to erupt thunderously onto the opposite bank. For the human spectator it is breathtaking and utterly unforgettable: visually three-dimensional, aurally magnificent, infused with infectious chaos and confusion, and tangibly charged with adrenalin!

For the wildebeest themselves, it's a somewhat more perilous enterprise. Outsized crocodiles weave gape-mouthed through the crossing herd, ready to snatch down any individual that make a false move, while lions frequently lurk in wait on the opposite shore, killing as many emerging wildebeests as they can lay their paws on. Misjudged high-water crossings sweep away and drown many wildebeest. In total, an estimated 3,000 wildebeest perish in river crossings every year, most of them trampled or trapped in deep water, but numbers are readily replenished by the average 400,000 calves born in the Serengeti every January/February.

reserve. Numbers of black rhino dropped alarmingly in the late 20th century, but an estimated three dozen individuals still survive, and are most likely to be seen in thickets associated with the Ngama Hills. Other ungulates are well represented, too, with impala and gazelle being most numerous, except when the migrating wildebeest and zebra pass through.

There's no better place for close-up views of the normally skittish eland, the world's largest antelope, and you can

A topi surveys the plain from the top of a termite mound. (AZ)

The black-backed jackal is the commonest canid in Kenya. (AZ)

also rely on seeing giraffe, topi, Coke's hartebeest, reedbuck, Defassa waterbuck, hippo and warthog. Relatively small numbers of wildebeest and plains zebra are resident, but populations are boosted to the nth degree in late July, when the migrant Serengeti herds cross into Kenya, dispersing across the Mara plains until it is time to return south in October.

An estimated 250–300 lions have territories within the reserve's boundaries, one of the highest population densities anywhere in Africa, and good sightings are practically guaranteed, with a high chance of encountering prides comprising a dozen or more individuals on a kill. It's one of the best reserves in Africa for cheetah, supporting an estimated population of 50, which are frequently seen pacing the plains, or surveying the surroundings from fallen branches or termite mounds. The reserve's 400-plus spotted hyenas are frequently observed interacting around their clan dens, leopards are elusive but more easily spotted than in most reserves, and smaller predators include bat-eared fox, black-backed jackal, banded mongoose, serval, caracal and striped hyena. The formerly abundant African hunting dog became extinct throughout the Serengeti-Mara ecosystem in the 1980s, though recent reports of breeding packs in the northern Serengeti and regular sightings in the Aitong Hills on the north edge of the Mara Plains suggest gradual recolonisation is underway.

The Mara provides a fine introduction to East Africa's savanna birdlife, with more than 500 species recorded in and around its borders,

The southern ground hornbill is one of the largest and most striking birds of the plains. (AZ)

including such conspicuous perennial favourites as the lilac-breasted roller, superb starling and little bee-eater. It is particularly good for large ground birds such as ostrich, southern ground hornbill, secretary bird, kori bustard and localised Denham's bustard, and raptors are also very well represented, in particular vultures. The riparian forest along the Mara and Talek rivers is an important niche habitat for certain species, including Ross's turaco, Schalow's turaco, grey kestrel and black-and-white casqued hornbill, while the Musaria Swamp near the eponymous entrance gate is generally good for storks, plovers and wading birds, and it is the only site in Kenya where rufous-bellied heron is regularly seen.

rainbow tours

Basecamp Explorer
www.basecampexplorer.com

Basecamp Explorer, a gold-rated eco-lodge, commends itself to anyone committed to responsible travel. You'll be in good company – the Obamas chose it! The 12 spacious, canvas tents are mounted on fixed structures under cooling thatch, and most overlook the Talek River, providing a ringside seat for watching river life and serene views across the savanna. Game is prolific, but we like Basecamp because it's as much about the people and their culture as it is the wildlife.

Karen Blixen Camp
www.karenblixencamp.com

Affordable, eco-friendly and well located on the Mara River, this camp ticks all the boxes for a Kenyan safari and consistently good reviews keep it top of our list. Travellers who may be unsure about sleeping under canvas love that the 22 elegant tents are set on raised decks, while the pool is a rare plus in the area. The commitment to low-impact tourism is coupled with a strong involvement in the Mara North Conservancy in which the camp is based.

Kicheche Bush Camp
www.kicheche.com

This small, unpretentious camp is second to none for value and is one of our favourites. Six classic safari tents are well located in prime wilderness just outside the main reserve,

and the game is consistently good year-round. Life in camp is flexible – 'go mobile' for the day, with ample provisions on-board to cover all eventualities, or get back to basics with a brilliant walking safari and overnight fly camping. Long-serving, committed staff provide exceptional guiding and a personal service.

Kicheche Mara Camp
www.kicheche.com

Located north of the reserve, this camp has to be one of the best-value properties available. 22 guests are accommodated in spacious, en-

suite living tents – the ethos here is to provide an exceptional wildlife experience at affordable prices. Specially designed vehicles offer great viewing – the camp is sought after by photographers. We like that the camp exudes a traditional safari atmosphere with drinks around the campfire, alfresco communal dining and traditional safari bucket showers.

Little Governors' Camp
www.governorscamp.com

This is *Big Cat Diary* territory. Located in the Masai Mara, for us Little Governors' epitomises the classic, timeless safari experience of a bygone era. 17 very comfortable, canvas, Hemmingway-style tents are set in an unfenced horseshoe overlooking a busy waterhole. Getting there is an adventure in itself as the camp is reached by boat across the Mara River. It is one of the few to offer three daily game drives and is situated near the hot-air balloon launch pad.

Mara Intrepids
www.heritage-eastafrica.com/
tented-camps/mara-intrepids/

Each of the 30 luxuriously furnished tents is raised on stilts and has a private veranda overlooking the Talek River providing guests with *the* signature view over the Mara plains. Set in the heart of *Big Cat Diary* country, you are sure to see more wildlife up close than you could ever imagine. Families are also made welcome with two interconnecting family tents. The permanently structured bar and restaurant add that extra bit of luxury to your stay.

Mara Plains
www.maraplains.com

Perhaps the best camp for a 'full-on' exclusive Masai Mara experience – you are almost certain to be alone with the wildlife. Seven huge, octagonal tented rooms stand on raised decks along the river, ideal for watching game from your bed or private veranda. It's the wildlife that takes priority as game drives can turn into all-day excursions, and the lodge brings lunch to you. Your safari contributes to the future of the Mara as commitment to the community is integral.

Mara Porini Camp
www.porini.com

The Mara Porini is set in 24km^2 of private conservancy covering some of the most beautiful wilderness areas in the Serengeti-Mara eco-system. Great care is taken over the preservation of the natural surroundings to ensure that as little environmental impact as possible occurs as a result of your stay. With just six spacious tents, this exclusive safari experience offers a personal and attentive service in simple yet luxurious surroundings, which is why so many Africa Sky customers keep coming back.

Naibor

🖱 www.naibor.com

Naibor's seven palatial tents, generous king-sized beds and shaded veranda complete with comfy sofa and plump cushions, set a romantic tone. We love the quirky furniture

made from fallen fig trees and the tent sides that open up so that you can lie in bed to watch wildlife. Set beside the Talek River, the lodge is near the main wildebeest migration crossings which run from August to October. Dine alfresco, at the banquet table or in the privacy of your own tented retreat.

rainbow tours

LOWIS & LEAKE
Privately guided safar

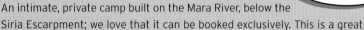

Ngare Serian

🖱 www.serian.net/serian/ngareserian.htm

An intimate, private camp built on the Mara River, below the Siria Escarpment; we love that it can be booked exclusively. This is a great

base from which to explore the new Mara North Conservancy. The four tents are built on wooden decks under the canopy of African greenheart trees. From your sunken bathtub, watch hippos wallow and be entertained by a cacophony of noises. For birders there are wonderful species to be found in the riverine forest.

Nomadic Encounters

🖱 www.nomadicencounters.com

We've worked with Rekero Camp for many years and their latest venture, three private houses in the heart of the Mara, has got us

really excited. Each three-bedroom house comes with a private guide and vehicle, cook and house staff so guests are free to decide their own schedule of activities. The local Maasai guides are wonderfully skilled at seeking out game in the more remote parts of the busy park. A perfect choice for families or friends travelling together.

Aardvark
SAFARIS L

Offbeat Mara
🖰 www.offbeatsafaris.com

Set within a forested location on the edge of the OlareOrok River just north of the reserve, Offbeat is a seasonal camp catering for just 12 guests in comfortable, en-suite living tents. Game viewing within the Mara ecosystem is the finest in the world, but what we like about this small camp is the personal service, flexible daily routine geared around the wildlife on show, and the traditional safari-camp atmosphere – evenings around the campfire, safari bucket showers, and convivial conversation.

Porini Lion Camp
🖰 www.porini.com

Set in the 20,000-acre Olare Orok Conservancy bordering the Masai Mara, this eco-friendly exclusive ten-tented camp offers you the ultimate safari experience. The camp is aptly named as several lion prides tend to frequent the area, so expect exclusive, unhurried viewing from your purpose-built 4x4 safari vehicle – a truly mind-blowing experience. As with all the Porini camps, the local community benefit from and participate in the guests' experience and wildlife conservation.

Rekero Camp
🖰 www.rekero.com

This classic tented safari camp is always near the top of our Mara list. Set in a remote corner of the reserve, eight tents overlook the Talek River and plains beyond – there's an almost ceaseless procession of game to watch. Superb Maasai guides offer their encyclopaedic knowledge of the fauna, flora and culture of this spectacular area and will inspire anyone, whether a safari first timer or old hand. For an all-round game experience it is one of the best there is.

129

Saruni Mara Camp
🖱 www.sarunicamp.com

Six cottages in a remote valley in a private
conservation area just outside the Mara provide the setting for
this intimate and luxurious lodge. It's a perfect choice for stunning

accommodation without losing the chance to sleep close to nature. Game drives with knowledgeable guides allow guests to experience the incredible Mara wildlife, while walking safaris with local Maasai guides afford the opportunity to appreciate the sights and smells of the surrounding plains and bush in more detail.

Serian Camp
🖱 www.serian.net

Serian, owned by professional guide Alex Walker, is built on
a rocky outcrop above the Mara River. The seven luxurious tents have
wooden decks to the fore and private bathroom facilities a few steps away

in thatched chalets. Every booking is granted a private guide and vehicle, and walks are taken in a private concession across the river. Mobile camping within the reserve and adventurous tree-house 'sleep-outs' are also available. We love the homely atmosphere, private guiding and variety of experiences available.

Lake Naivasha

Situated at an altitude of 1,890m on the Rift Valley floor 90km northwest of Nairobi, scenic Lake Naivasha is a shallow near-circular freshwater body fringed by spectral fever tree forests and low mountains. Naivasha's proximity to Nairobi makes it an ideal first stop in Kenya, particularly for those seeking to break up the long, rough drive to the Masai Mara. The lake hinterland offers a exceptional selection of excursions and activities, among them the pedestrian-friendly Hell's Gate National Park, the lovely Green Crater Lake, and the steep ascent to the vast caldera atop Mount Longonot, whose distinctive volcanic outline is visible for miles around.

One of only two freshwater lakes in the Kenyan Rift Valley, Naivasha is fed by the Gilgil and Malewa rivers, which flow into its swampy northern

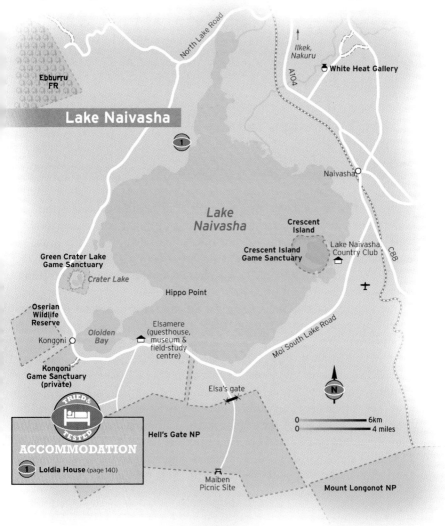

Practicalities

The gateway to the lake is the pleasant small town of **Naivasha**, which lies about 90 minutes' drive from Nairobi along a (mostly good) surfaced road, though it may take longer in heavy traffic. Boasting several filling stations, supermarkets, banks, ATMs and internet cafés, Naivasha feels very relaxed compared with Nairobi, and it's a good place to deal with any outstanding practicalities before heading on to the lake. You might also want to stop at the veteran La Belle Inn for a drink or meal on the shaded balcony.

Accommodation

For full details of tour-operator recommended accommodation, see page 140. Here follows a few further suggestions from the author.

Exclusive
Chui Lodge ^Ů www.oserianwildlife.com
Great Rift Valley Lodge ^Ů www.heritage-eastafrica.com
Malewa Wildlife Lodge ^Ů www.kigio.com

shore. It has no known surface outlet, but scientists believe that an underground outlet, resurfacing at Lake Magadi, might explanation its non-salinity. Naivasha normally extends over some 130km^2, but it is prone to unexplained fluctuations in water level, almost drying out completely in the late 1940s, and the nature of the lakeshore is forever changing, sometimes open, sometimes fringed by dense stands of papyrus. The name 'Naivasha' is a corruption of the Maa *enaiposha*, which loosely translates as 'restless water', in reference to the rough waves that sweep across the surface on windy afternoons.

In 1883, Gustav Fisher became the first outsider to reach Naivasha, followed a year later by Joseph Thomson. In the 1930s, the Lake Naivasha Country Club (now a hotel) on the southern shore was built as a staging post for the flying boat service from the UK to South Africa. The Naivasha area was a focal point of the hedonistic colonial social scene depicted in the film *White Mischief*, and former lakeshore residents include Lady Diana Delamere and Joy Adamson. Tourism is important to the local economy, but the main industry is floriculture, with large plantations growing roses

Leading southwest out of Naivasha town, the Moi South Lake Road runs parallel to the southern lake shore for about 30km, offering access to numerous lodges as well as Hell's Gate National Park and Elsamere. It is surfaced for most of its length, though the first short stretch out of Naivasha town is very dusty, and serviced by regular public transport. The tarmac ends at Kongoni Junction, near the entrance gate to Oserian Wildlife Reserve, where the road veers northwards, becomes more erratic in standard, and is used by relatively little traffic, though it does offer access to the Green Crater Lake.

Upmarket
Crater Lake Sanctuary ⌃ www.prideofsafaris.com
Lake Naivasha Sopa Resort ⌃ www.sopalodges.com

Moderate
Elsamere ⌃ www.elsatrust.org
Lake Elmentaita Lodge ⌃ www.jacarandahotels.com
Lake Naivasha Country Club ⌃ www.kenyahotelsltd.com

Budget
Fisherman's Camp ⌃ www.fishermanscampkenya.com

and other exotic flowers for sale to the European market. Sadly, the inflow of pesticides from this lucrative but ecologically frivolous industry poses a threat to the environmental integrity of the lake, which is a Ramsar wetland but is otherwise completely unprotected, as does the presence of introduced species ranging from the beaver-like South American coypu to the tilapia-gobbling Nile perch.

For all that, the Naivasha still supports a fair amount of indigenous wildlife, most of it concentrated in private sanctuaries such as Green Crater Lake, Oserian Wildlife Reserve and Crescent Island. Giraffe, hippo and various antelope might be seen almost anywhere on the lakeshore, while Hell's Gate National Park offers a rare opportunity to cycle or hike unguided in an unfenced safari setting. Naivasha also provides the ideal ornithological primer for first-time visitors to East Africa: resident birders talk glibly of clocking up 100+

The white-fronted bee-eater nests in tall sandbanks. (NB/FLPA)

species before breakfast, and while neophytes should set their sights lower, it's a great place to get to grips with the region's savanna and wetland avifauna. Water-associated species are especially well represented, most visibly African fish eagle and great white pelican, while the incessantly noisy and brightly coloured Fischer's and yellow-collared lovebirds are characteristic of the surrounding woodland, along with the likes of white-fronted bee-eater, purple grenadier and grey-capped warbler.

Lake Naivasha highlights

Crescent Island

Situated opposite Lake Naivasha Country Club, 5km from Naivasha Town along the Moi South Lake Road, this aptly named island comprises the western rim of an extinct volcanic caldera whose submerged floor forms the deepest part of the lake. Large herbivores such as giraffe, buffalo and waterbuck inhabit the island, which also supports a diverse birdlife, and can be explored freely on foot. Although it is linked to the mainland by a marshy causeway that occasionally allows direct foot access, the island may only be visited as an organised motorboat excursion, which can be organised through any hotel.

Hell's Gate National Park

\ 020 600800 🖱 www.kws.org
🕐 06.00–19.00

Named after the twin basaltic cliffs that guard its northern entrance, Hell's Gate National Park, gazetted in 1984, protects a geologically dramatic 68km² landscape whose ancient lava plugs, sulphuric water vents, glossy black obsidian outcrops and dormant volcanoes pay testament to the region's ongoing tectonic instability. However, the central valley that runs through the park, hemmed in by 120m-tall cliffs that glow golden in the early morning light, is not volcanic in origin, but a dead riverine valley carved by a former outlet of Lake Naivasha.

Hell's Gate offers the unique opportunity to cycle through herds of plains game. (AZ)

Near the north entrance, Fisher's Tower is a striking 25m-tall volcanic plug named after the German explorer who climbed it in 1883. A local legend, recalling the biblical story of Sodom and Gomorrah, is that this monolith is actually the petrified figure of a Maasai bride who defied custom by turning around to take one last look at her family home *en route* to her wedding. Other volcanic landmarks include the similar but larger Central Tower about 12km further southwest, the glassy obsidian caves at the end of Twiga Loop, and the searing steam vents that erupt from the floor of Ol Njorowa Gorge outside the southern park boundary.

For most visitors, the main attraction of Hell's Gate is not so much the geology as the opportunity to walk or bicycle unguided through seasonally impressive herds of big game. Encountering wildlife without the protection of a vehicle adds a

Rüppell's griffon vulture has a distinctive horn-coloured beak. (AZ)

new and exhilarating dimension to game viewing, and buffalo, giraffe, zebra, wildebeest, impala, Thomson's gazelle, Grant's gazelle and eland are almost certain to be seen along the main road through the park. Scarcer but also resident are leopard, cheetah and spotted hyena, and – just to keep things interesting – elephant and lion also pass through from time to time. The cliffs support klipspringer, Chanler's reedbuck, rock hyrax and olive baboon (see page 52 and 38), and although the endangered pair of lammergeyers – magnificent cliff-dwelling vultures with a 2.8m wingspan – that once bred here haven't been seen in years, the likes of Verreaux's eagle, Egyptian vulture, Rüppell's griffon vulture and augur buzzard are all present.

The easiest point of access is Elsa's Gate, which lies about 3km south of the Moi South Lake Road along a dirt track signposted 16km from Naivasha town. Bicycles can be hired on the spot from a kiosk at the junction for Elsa's Gate. The most rewarding route for wildlife is the flattish 12km road between Elsa's Gate and Maiben picnic site – allow three hours in either direction on foot, or about an hour if you're cycling. A dawn start is recommended, as wildlife is most active in the cooler hours, and the valley becomes very hot and exposed in the middle of the day. Carry a hat, sunscreen and plenty of drinking water. For those with a vehicle, is possible to continue to the little-visited western part of the park, site of the Ol Koria Geothermal Power station, and to explore Twiga Loop in the east.

Elsamere

☎ 050 2021055 ✉ info@elsamere.com 🖥 www.elsamere.com ⏰ 10.00-18.00

Situated 22km from town along the Moi South Lake Road, Elsamere, named after the lioness 'Elsa' of *Born Free* fame, was the home of Joy Adamson from 1966 until her death in 1980. It is now a field study centre, and the proceeds from tourist visits go towards creating environmental education opportunities for locals and promoting ecological awareness at a grass-roots level. Joy Adamson's old house is maintained as a museum and low-key guesthouse; the walls are hung with her finely observed paintings of wildlife and local tribespeople, and many of her personal possessions are also on display, including first editions of her books in various languages. A lavish all-day tea buffet is included in the entrance fee, and guided nature trails through the lakeshore garden and surrounding fever trees forest offer the opportunity to see some of the 200 bird species recorded in the immediate vicinity, as well as the troop of handsome black-and-white colobus monkeys that pass by daily. Hippos regularly graze the lawn at night.

Oserian Wildlife Reserve

☎ 050 2020792 🖥 www.oserianwildlife.com

Established in 1996, this 100km² private reserve lies below the impressive Mau Escarpment on the west side of the Moi South Lake Road about 30km from Naivasha town. Traversing rights are limited to guests at the ultra-exclusive Chui Lodge and Kiangazi House, which lie within the reserve and offer all-inclusive packages including expertly guided game drives and bush walks. Oserian protects a striking landscape of fever trees and euphorbia forests, and it forms a busy wildlife corridor between Hell's Gate and Lake Naivasha, frequented by leopard, cheetah, spotted hyena, buffalo, greater kudu and topi, alongside introduced white rhinoceros, Grevy's zebra and Beisa oryx. For bird enthusiasts, it's the best place to seek out the localised grey-crested helmet-shrike, and the full checklist exceeds 300 species. Although day visitors are not permitted, quite a bit of wildlife can be seen along the bordering stretch of the Moi South Lake Road, most commonly giraffe, plains zebra and various antelopes.

Green Crater Lake Sanctuary

☎ 050 2020613 ⏰ 06.00-18.00

Accessed from the Moi South Road about 6km north of Kongoni, this small private sanctuary once formed part of the estate of Lady Diana Delamere, who was buried there in 1987 alongside her third and fourth husbands. The reserve's centrepiece, overlooked by a very pleasant tented camp, is the alkaline Songasoi Crater Lake, whose Maa name means 'sterile bull', alluding to its inability to support fish or any other sub-aquatic fauna (it has a pH of 11.5). Nowhere more than 5m deep, the 8ha lake is cast green by a dense concentration of Spirulina algae, which attracts aggregations of lesser flamingo, especially over June to August. The crater also supports lush forests, a rich birdlife, several troops of black-and-white colobus monkey, and other wildlife such as buffalo, eland, waterbuck and bushbuck. Guided game walks are on offer, as are bird walks around the crater rim, horseback excursions, and diurnal and nocturnal game drives. Day visitors are welcome.

Longonot National Park

⌖ www.kws.org ⌚ 09.00-18.00

Mount Longonot – a name derived from the Maa Ol Nong'ot, meaning 'Mountain of Spurs' – is the distinctive ragged-edged volcano that dominates the southern skyline from the Moi South Lake Road and parts of Hell's Gate. Protected within the 52km² national park, it rises steeply from the Rift Valley floor to an altitude of 2,776m, and there are fantastic views from the peak in all directions. Assuming you're reasonably fit, it is well worth climbing to the rim of Longonot's perfect volcanic caldera, which last erupted in the 1860s, depositing a layer of fine ashy soil on the starkly vegetated outer slopes, and whose forested floor is still pockmarked with steam vents. The entrance and starting point for climbs is the village of Longonot, which straddles the old Nairobi road about 20km from Naivasha town. Guides are available at the KWS office here. The ascent usually takes about 90 minutes, the descent is slightly quicker, and its possible to the walk around the crater rim over three to four hours, so allow plenty of time – ideally starting at dawn to avoid overexposure to the sun. The informal path to the crater floor is rather more treacherous.

The lava-ravaged slopes and crater of Longonot are evidence of its volcanic origin. (YAB/C)

White Heat Art Gallery

📞 050 2020829 🕐 09.00-17.00

Signposted from the Nakuru road about 5km north of Naivasha town, this exceptional craftshop stocks items made on site from recycled metal, along with pottery, beadwork, paintings, prints, cards and carved Swahili furniture. The shady balcony is a nice spot for a coffee or snack, and full four-course meals are served by prior arrangement.

Kigio Wildlife Conservancy

📞 020 3742435 🖥 www.malewaranch.com

Situated off the Nakuru road about 20km from Naivasha town, this fenced private reserve consists of a former ranchland bordering the perennial Malewa River before it empties into Lake Naivasha. The acacia scrub and open grassland supports zebra, gazelle, warthog, eland, and a breeding herd of endangered Rothschild's giraffes translocated from Lake Nakuru in 2003. The absence of dangerous wildlife makes game drives seem rather tame, but it also means that guided walks are available to guests at Malewa Wildlife Lodge, an attractive new boutique lodge on the eponymous river.

Lake Elmentaita

Situated near Gilgil some 30km north of Naivasha, this small alkaline lake has a primeval setting amongst evocatively shaped volcanic plugs, including the formation known to the Maasai as Elngirigata Ol Morani ('Sleeping Warrior') and to the colonials as Lord Delamere's Nose (after the British aristocrat who settled there in 1906). The main road to Nakuru offers distant views over the lake, but there is no public access as it lies entirely within the Delamere Estate. The best viewpoint over the lake, whose shallows are frequently tinged pink by flamingos, is obtained from a conspicuous hilltop cairn erected in memory of the 4th Earl of Enniskillen in 1929 some 2km west of the main Nakuru road. Close by, the former Enniskillen homestead is now the Lake Elmentaita Lodge, the only place to stay or eat near the lake.

Volcanic outcrops encircle Lake Elmentaita. (AZ)

The Great Rift Valley

The single largest geographical feature on earth, Africa's Great Rift Valley exists on such an immense scale that it was the only such entity recognisable to the first lunar astronauts. The rift stretches for about 6,000km from the Red Sea to the Zambezi Valley, following the juncture of the Arabian and African tectonic plates, which started to separate some 20 to 30 million years ago. Its expansion has been accompanied by much geological violence: the floor is studded with dormant volcanoes, and several massifs outside the main valley, including Africa's two tallest mountains, Kilimanjaro and Kenya, are by-products of the rifting process. Eventually – several million years from now – the Rift Valley is likely to flood completely, and Africa as we know it will split into two or three discrete land masses, much as happened when present-day India and Madagascar were separated from the African mainland.

The Rift Valley consists of two discrete branches, which diverge in a northerly 'Y 'shape in southern Tanzania. The westerly branch, often referred to as the Albertine Rift, runs along the Congolese borders with Tanzania, Burundi, Rwanda and Uganda. Kenya, meanwhile, is bisected by the easterly branch, which also runs through Tanzania, Ethiopia and the Red Sea, and is sometimes referred to as the Gregory Rift (after the geologist John Gregory, who coined the term 'Rift Valley' in 1893). Few parts of the Rift are quite so dramatic as the stretch that cuts through the highlands west of Nairobi: the scintillating descent road to Naivasha and the Masai Mara offers views over several of the two dozen dormant volcanoes that rise from the valley floor, which also supports the beautiful lakes Naivasha, Nakuru, Bogoria and Baringo.

Kariandusi prehistoric site

📞 020 2021682 🖱 www.museums.or.ke 🕐 09.00-18.00

Some 700,000 years ago, Kariandusi was the site of a Stone-Age village on the shore of a lake that encompassed present-day Naivasha, Elmentaita and Nakuru. It is thought that this village was a factory for the production of Stone-Age tools, which have been unearthed there by the hundred, made either from local lava rocks or from glassy obsidian sourced at nearby Mount Eburu. Excavated by Louis Leakey between 1928 and 1931, Kariandusi lies on the outskirts of Gilgil, and offers a 30-minute guided tour concluding at the small site museum. A neighbouring mine extracts diatomite – a crumbly white silica-based rock composed of compressed shelled algae from the floor of the extinct lake – for use as a water filter and insecticide.

Loldia House

🖱 www.governorscamp.com

Situated on the shores of Naivasha, this homestead-style lodge accommodates 16 guests in simple but comfortable rooms located in the main house or in cottages within the gardens. One of the cottages is a short drive away on top of a ridge and is ideal for two couples sharing or a family. We like the range of Rift Valley experiences, with activities centred around Lake Naivasha as well as Lake Nakuru. Peter Njoroge, manager extraordinaire, also hosts a fine table.

SAFAR
CONSULTAN

Sunbird Lodge

🖱 www.sunbirdkenya.com

THE ZAMBEZI SAFARI
& TRAVEL CO. LTD

Sunbird Lodge is a real Kenyan bolt hole, popular with locals and visitors alike, affording stunning views over Lake Elementaita and its legendary pink flamingos. Just over 1¹/₂ hours' drive from Nairobi, the lodge is a peaceful spot to unwind, soak up the sunset, or walk along the shore of the lake. Small, exclusive, personally hosted and affordable, Sunbird offers excellent food and an idyllic setting. The 14 spacious cottages have king-sized beds and large verandas – your own peaceful haven.

Lake Nakuru National Park

☎ 051 2217151 🖰 www.kws.org 🕐 09.00-18.00

Extending southward from Kenya's fourth-largest town, also called Nakuru, this is a relatively small national park at 188km^2, but its rich biodiversity makes it an enduringly popular fixture on the safari circuit. Its centrepiece is Lake Nakuru, famed for its immense concentrations of flamingos, a phenomenon that the renowned American ornithologist Roger Tory Peterson once proclaimed to be 'the most fabulous bird spectacle in the world'. Like an avian counterpart to the Serengeti-Mara wildebeest migration, the flamingos of Nakuru are a mesmerising sight, especially when a flock of several hundred birds takes graceful flight, revealing bright pink-and-black under-wings.

Lake Nakuru is essentially a shallow sump, encircled by majestic mountains and hills, and fed by three modest rivers, underground springs, treated sewage water and untreated urban effluent. With no known outlet and a relatively small catchment area, the lake is unusually prone to fluctuations in water level; covering a maximum area of 62km^2, it contracted to an all-time low of 5km^2 in the mid-1990s, but water levels have been consistently higher since the El Niño flooding of 1998, though large swathes of soda-encrusted flats are usually exposed during the dry seasons (July to October and January to February). Flamingo numbers are strongly associated with water level: an almost complete exodus to lakes Bogoria and Elmentaita occurred when the lake almost dried up in the mid-1990s, since then the count has seldom dropped below 500,000, and peaks of up to 1.5 million have been estimated seasonally.

The highly alkaline water supports high concentrations of the algae *Spirulina platensis*, which give the lake its distinctive turquoise-green cast, as well as being the main fodder for its trademark flamingos. No fish occur naturally, but the introduction of an alkali-tolerant tilapia from Lake Magadi in 1953, mainly to control mosquitoes, has significantly affected the local ecology by attracting an influx of fish-eating birds, including some 50,000 great white pelicans. Nakuru attracts a varied selection of other birds, including some rare migrant waterfowl, but it is less satisfying for general birding than the other Rift Valley lakes, because walking is forbidden and the lake mostly lies too far from the road for easy identification of smaller waterbirds.

One of the few Kenyan parks to be fenced in its entirety, Nakuru now forms a stronghold for endangered species such as black and white rhino, and Rothschild's giraffe. The park's last naturally occurring pair of black rhinos were joined by 20 translocated black rhino and a dozen white rhino in the mid-1990s. Today, rhinos are more easily seen here than anywhere

Practicalities

Some 160km from Nairobi along a surfaced road, Lake Nakuru is arguably the most accessible of all Kenya's major wildlife reserves, with its main entrance gate situated on the southern outskirts of Nakuru, only 2km from the town centre. Most people visit as part of an **organised safari** from Nairobi (often as an overnight stop *en route* between the Masai Mara and Central Highlands) but it is also a straightforward **self-drive destination**, and day trips can be arranged with local operators or taxi drivers in Nakuru town. The two lodges set within the park form the most attractive bases for exploration, both in terms of facilities and location. If they are full, however, there is no shortage of cheaper accommodation in Nakuru town, though nothing that meets the standard of the lodges. Most other practicalities are best dealt with in the town, which has several banks, ATMs, internet cafés, restaurants, supermarkets and filling stations.

Accommodation

Upmarket
Lake Nakuru Lodge ⏱ www.lakenakurulodge.com
Sarova Lion Hill Lodge ⏱ www.sarovahotels.com

Moderate
Midland Hotel ☏ 037 212155

else in East Africa, with a total population of each species estimated at around 50 (another 40 individuals were relocated to Meru National Park in 2007). The white rhino is common on the lake floodplain, while the more secretive black rhino prefers the denser southern bush. Also present are lion, leopard, buffalo, waterbuck, impala, gazelle, eland, baboon, vervet monkey, warthog and buffalo.

Lake Nakuru highlights

Nakuru game drives

The best but busiest game-viewing loop is the well-maintained 35km dirt road that encircles Lake Nakuru in its entirety. This requires about two hours, longer if you're serious about birds, and while game viewing is best in the early morning or late afternoon, traffic congestion is lowest during breakfast hours. The lodges lie in the east of the circuit, where the road is too densely wooded to offer clear views over the lake, but buffalo and waterbuck are common here, and a striking euphorbia forest covers the slopes between the two lodges. Emerging from the eastern slopes onto the southern floodplain, the open grassland is a prime spot for white rhino and other grazers, while Muya's Causeway is a good place to look for waterfowl and waders, and the lakeshore immediately west of the Enderit River mouth often offers close-up views of flamingos and pelicans. An all-but-mandatory diversion on the west side of the lake is the short but steep ascent road to Baboon Cliff, from where the full scale of the flamingo phenomenon is most apparent, with tens of thousands of birds forming a shimmering pink band along the bleached lakeshore.

Flamingos

Flamingos have long exerted a fascination over humans. The ancient Egyptian hieroglyph for the colour red was a flamingo, while in Mediterranean Europe these distinctive pink-tinged birds are depicted in cave paintings dating back 7,000 years. More contentiously, it has been suggested that the resurrecting phoenix of ancient folklore is based on mangled reports of flamingos breeding in the ash-strewn volcanic Natron area of northern

(WD)

Tanzania. Even if this is fanciful, there's no doubt that this brightly coloured bird forms East Africa's most popular avian attraction. Two species are present, the greater flamingo *Phoenicopterus ruber* and lesser flamingo *P. minor*, and they are often seen alongside each other in their thousands, feeding on algae and microscopic fauna sifted through filters contained within their unique down-turned bills. Highly sensitive to the water level and chemical composition of the shallow lakes wherein they feed, the birds will readily relocate when conditions change, which means that a site that hosts large numbers one month might be abandoned the next, but still, it is rare to visit Lake Nakuru or Bogoria and not encounter flamingos in their thousands.

The famous view over Lake
Nakuru and its floodplain
from Baboon Cliffs (AZ)

The wilder and less busy alternative for games drives is a loop that runs south from the lake, though areas of open grassland and dense fever tree forest, towards Makalia Falls. Explore this area in the early morning, and you might drive for hours without seeing another vehicle. A landmark worth aiming for is isolated Enasoit Hill, a thickly vegetated volcanic plug whose bushed rocky slopes often hide resting lions. The thicker woodland east of Enasoit is favoured by black rhino, which are far more secretive than white rhino. On the southern boundary, the Makalia Falls plunge about 10m over a cliff surrounded by lush woodland where leopards are sometimes seen around dawn and dusk.

Nakuru town

The capital of Rift Valley province, Nakuru seems low-key and nondescript compared with Nairobi or Mombasa – dusty and cheerfully bustling, but mainly of interest for its facilities. There's a lively daily market in front of the railway station, a few moderately interesting colonial buildings (notably the members-only Rift Valley Sport Club, built in 1907), and plenty of jacarandas that come into bloom in November.

Hyrax Hill prehistoric site

Situated 4km out of town off the Nairobi Road, Hyrax Hill was inhabited some 5,000–2,000 years ago, and excavated in the 1930s by the Leakeys, who discovered some of the oldest Iron-Age artefacts known from East Africa and a Neolithic burial mound containing 19 decapitated male skeletons. Also of interest, but of unknown antiquity, are 13 *bao* games cut into the rocks behind the museum.

Menengai Crater

The northern horizon of Nakuru is dominated by the 2,278m Mount Menengai, a dormant shield volcano whose summit encloses one of the world's largest nested calderas, with an average diameter of 8km. Superb views across the crater are obtained from the rim, which is accessible by a rough 8km dirt road out of Nakuru. Menengai hasn't witnessed any significant volcanic activity in six millennia, but the steam vents and fumaroles on the crater floor are associated by locals with evil spirits: the Maa name 'Menengai' means 'Place of Demons', while its Kikuyu equivalent Kilima kya Ngoma translates as 'Devil's Mountain'.

Lakes Bogoria and Baringo

North of Nakuru, the surfaced B4 descends into a relatively arid, hot and low-lying stretch of the Rift Valley, one whose thinly inhabited and overgrazed plains display strong ecological affiliations with the parched badlands that roll northward towards Lake Turkana and the Ethiopian border. Though somewhat austere, it is a scenic part of the country, alleviated by the twin lakes of Bogoria and Baringo shimmering below the forbidding cliffs of the Rift Valley escarpment.

Practicalities

The main urban centre in the region is **Marigat**, an overgrown village that straddles the B4 about 95km north of Nakuru. The junction to Bogoria is signposted to the right shortly before you enter Marigat, while Baringo, serviced by the lakeshore village of Kampi ya Samaki (literally Camp of Fish), lies about 20km further north along the B4. In both cases, the drive from Nakuru should take around two hours, possibly longer after heavy rain. There is only one lodge at Bogoria, and it is rather mediocre, so it's best to visit this lake as a day trip from Nakuru or Baringo, or en route between them. Several good lodges dot the western shore and islands of Baringo. Banking, shopping and internet facilities are very limited in this part of Kenya, so best deal with any requirements of that sort in Nakuru town.

Accommodation

For full details of tour-operator recommended accommodation, see page 148. Here follows a few further suggestions from the author.

Upmarket
Island Camp ✆ www.island-camp.com

Moderate
Lake Baringo Club ✆ www.kenyahotelsltd.com
Lake Bogoria Spa Resort ✆ www.bogoriaspa-resort.com

Budget
Roberts' Campsite ✆ www.robertscamp.com

Partly because of their remoteness, these lakes are less frequently included on safari itineraries than Naivasha and Nakuru. Nevertheless, both attract a fair amount of tourist traffic, and the area is a favourite with birdwatchers. Bogoria peaked in popularity in the mid-1990s, when the millions of flamingos normally associated with Nakuru temporarily relocated to its shallows, and it often still hosts significant flamingo flocks today. Baringo, meanwhile, is often visited on dedicated ornithological safaris, offering the opportunity to observe several dry-country 'specials' at the southern limit of their range. Other wildlife includes the plentiful hippos and crocodiles that splash around in the shallows of Baringo, and the rare greater kudu antelope that haunts the shores of Bogoria.

The area is also of some geological interest. It was here, whilst visiting the cliffs around Baringo in 1893, that the Scots geologist John Gregory coined the name 'Rift Valley' and described the process that had led to its formation. Relicts of this tectonic activity abound today, from the steam vents that stud the caldera of the dormant volcano Korosi on the northern shore of Baringo, to the boiling geysers that erupt from the western shore of Bogoria.

Lakes Bogoria and Baringo highlights

Lake Bogoria National Reserve
☏ 051 2211987 ☉ 06.00-19.00
Situated 15km east of Marigat along a decent dirt road, this 107km^2 national reserve was created in 1973 to protect the 34km^2 Lake Bogoria, set at the base of the steep Laikipia Escarpment, and a surrounding band of acacia woodland. Too salty and alkaline to support fish, hippos or crocodiles, Bogoria is best known for the large flocks of lesser flamingo that feed on the thriving blue-green algae. The scenic highlight, at Loburu on the western shore, is the trio of primeval geysers that erupt in a steaming sulphuric haze to feed a network of multi-hued streams that drain into the lake – truly spectacular but best approached with caution, since the combination of crumbling ground and scalding water has accounted for several fatalities. As for terrestrial game viewing, there's often more livestock than wildlife to be seen in the reserve's overgrazed semi-arid acacia scrub, but the diminutive dik-dik is quite common, and it's one of the last Kenyan strongholds for the magnificent greater kudu, which is most active at dusk. Although a decent road runs along the western lakeshore, walking within the reserve is also permitted.

Lake Baringo
Typically extending over 150km^2, this beautiful freshwater lake lies at the base of the Rift Valley escarpment about 15km north of Bogoria as the

The Laburu Hot Springs fringing Lake Bogoria are a product of the same geological process that created the Rift Valley. (RT/FLPA)

White-bellied go-away bird (AZ)

crow flies. Baringo is not afforded any official protection, and its shores are inhabited by the Njemps people, who speak the same language as the Maasai, but specialise in fishing – from flimsy balsa boats – rather than cattle rearing. Despite this, it still supports a varied aquatic fauna, with outsized crocodiles, water monitors and hippos all very conspicuous. The best way to see a good variety of aquatic animals is to take a boat trip to Ol Kokwe Island, a dormant volcanic peak whose slopes are dotted with hot springs.

Baringo is one of the top birding destinations in Kenya, with more than 500 species recorded in the immediate vicinity. A varied selection of waterbirds includes the aptly named Goliath heron, the vociferous African fish eagle, and many different lapwings and other waders. The well-wooded grounds of Roberts' Campsite and Lake Baringo Club can be exceptionally rewarding too, with the likes of white-bellied go-away bird, slate-coloured boubou, northern masked weaver, white-bellied buffalo-weaver and red-and-yellow barbet all common. Better still is the eminently climbable basaltic escarpment set back some 2km west of the lakeshore – in addition to stunning views over the lake, this area is a breeding site for the splendid Verreaux's eagle, and a hotspot for 'northern specials' such as Hemprich's and Jackson's hornbill, white-crested turaco and bristle-crowned starling.

Samatian Island Lodge
🛏 www.samatianislandlodge.com

This little lodge is set in magical surroundings. Five open-plan cottages hug the shoreline of beautiful Lake Baringo - an idyllic spot to spend a few nights. The hosts are on hand to plan activities including boat rides to explore the lake and its wildlife and day trips to Lake Bogoria. For those wishing to relax and enjoy the atmosphere, the large infinity pool with its panoramic lake views and beyond to the rugged hills of the Northern Frontier District should fit the bill.

West of the Rift Valley

The far west of Kenya is dominated by the densely populated and fertile highlands that rise from the more sparsely vegetated Lake Victoria Basin. It sees few tourists, and facilities are somewhat less classy than elsewhere in Kenya, but the area is of special interest to nature lovers for hosting a range of animal species more normally associated with Uganda and West Africa. The region's top wildlife hotspots are Kakamega Forest National Reserve and Saiwa Swamp National Park, both of which allow visitors to explore on foot. Another important western landmark is Lake Victoria, the world's second-largest freshwater body, shared with Tanzania and Uganda, but as yet little developed for tourism on the Kenyan side.

Far west highlights

Kakamega Forest National Reserve

☏ 056 30603 🖥 www.kws.org
🕒 06.00–19.00

Kakamega is Kenya's largest true tropical Forest. (CG/C)

Highly recommended to anybody with a well-developed interest in wildlife, Kakamega protects the country's largest and most accessible stand of equatorial rainforest, along with a fauna whose affiliations look westward to Uganda rather than back into the rest of Kenya. It offers some of the country's best primate viewing, with seven species present, notably the spectacular black-and-white colobus monkey (see page 44), the shyer blue-and-red-tailed monkeys, and the nocturnal potto, a sloth-like relative of the bushbaby that's quite easily located by spotlight. Kakamega is one of Kenya's most alluring destinations for butterfly enthusiasts, supporting some 400 species in total, while the checklist of 360 bird species includes about three dozen forest-dwellers found nowhere else in the country, among them the spectacular great blue turaco, as well as blue-headed bee-eater, white-headed wood-hoopoe and yellow-billed barbet.

Unlike the savanna reserves further east, Kakamega is most easily explored on foot, but spotting forest wildlife can be relatively tricky, so allow yourself at least three days.

Practicalities

Very few package tours visit this part of Kenya, but most operators can make bespoke arrangements. The main urban hub is **Kisumu**, Kenya's third-largest town, set on the northeast shore of Lake Victoria about 155km by road from Nakuru. Other important towns include Eldoret, Kericho, Kakamega, Kisii and Kitale, all of which are accessible by surfaced road and offer facilities such as internet access, banks/ATMs, fuel stations, supermarkets and restaurants. Allow five to six hours to drive to most of these towns from Nairobi; less if you are coming from the Masai Mara or the Rift Valley lakes. Quality accommodation is thin on the ground, with the notable exception of the ultra-exclusive Mfangano and Rusinga Island lodges in Lake Victoria, both of which are generally reached by air from the Masai Mara or Nairobi. Elsewhere, good moderate lodgings are available in Kisumu and the Kakamega Forest, and adequate hotels can be found in other large towns.

Accommodation

For full details of tour-operator recommended accommodation, see opposite. Here follows a few further suggestions from the author.

Exclusive
Mfangano Island Lodge ⏁ www.governorscamp.com

Upmarket
Kiboko Bay Resort ⏁ www.kibokobay.com

Moderate
Imperial Hotel ⏁ www.imperialhotelkisumu.com
Kakamega Golf Hotel ⏁ www.golfhotelkakamega.com
Mago Guesthouse ⏁ www.magoguesthouse.com
Rondo Retreat ⏁ www.rondoretreat.com

Budget
Udo's Bungalows ⏁ www.kws.org

Saiwa Swamp National Park

☎ 020 29826 ⌂ www.kws.org ⏲ 06.00-19.00

Kenya's smallest national park at 3km², little-visited Saiwa forms an ideal extension to a trip to Kakamega, comprising a small forest-fringed swamp encircled by a walking trail that leads to a series of rickety wooden viewing platforms. It is possibly the best place in Africa to observe the semi-aquatic sitatunga antelope, as well as the white-bearded DeBrazza's monkey (also present in Kakamega, but seldom seen there). Bushbuck and several other primate species are present, and the birding is superb, with several western specials present, including the bright purple Ross's turaco.

Lake Victoria

Set in an elevated basin between the two main forks of the Rift Valley, Victoria is the largest lake in Africa, with a surface area of 66,800km², and it is also the source of the Nile, the world's longest river. However, the vast bulk of Victoria lies in Tanzania and Uganda, and the Kenyan portion is poorly developed for tourism probably because it lacks the scenic impact of the country's smaller Rift Valley lakes. The two main tourist draws here are Rusinga and Mfangano islands, both of which host small exclusive camps aimed mainly at game-fishing enthusiasts, though both also double as great post-safari chill-out venues. Kisumu, the main lake port, is a pleasantly unaffected town, with a languid, tropical character vaguely reminiscent of the coast, but it offers little to tourists except as a base for exploring the rest of the west.

LOWIS & LEAKEY
Privately guided safaris

Rusinga Island Lodge
⌂ www.rusinga.com

This small luxurious lodge on Lake Victoria is an idyllic spot to recharge. Seven thatched cottages, including a family room, are surrounded by lush lawns which are dotted with ancient fig trees and attract myriad bird species. Life revolves around the lake – try a wealth of watersports or fish for Nile perch or tilapia. The island is rich in fossils – the *Proconsul africanus* skull was found here by Dr Mary Leakey. Recommended for the contrast it brings to a safari.

7 Southeast Safari Circuit

The thinly populated and superficially uninteresting part of Kenya that divides Nairobi from the coast is of interest as the site of three of the country's finest national parks: Amboseli, Tsavo West and Tsavo East. Together with a host of abutting private and community sanctuaries, these parks form the most cohesive safari circuit in Kenya, in touristic terms as well as ecological. The parks of the southeast are the ones most commonly visited as an extension of a coastal beach holiday, and for those beach-lovers who simply want a quick taste of the safari experience, the private Taita Hills Wildlife Sanctuary abutting Tsavo West is particularly recommended. These national parks can also be visited individually or together out of Nairobi, with compact Amboseli being by far the most popular option thanks to its wonderful elephant viewing and stirring views of Kilimanjaro.

KEY to numbered symbols
1 Selenkay Wildlife Conservancy
2 Chyulu Hills National Park
3 Taita Hills Game Sanctuary
4 Ngulia Rhino Sanctuary

ACCOMMODATION

1 **Campi ya Kanzi** (page 160)

2 **Galdessa** (page 171)

3 **Ol Donyo Wuas** (page 160)

4 **Porini Amboseli** (page 160)

5 **Satao Camp** (page 171)

6 **Satao Elerai** (page 161)

7 **Severin Safari Camp** (page 165)

8 **Tortilis Camp** (page 161)

Amboseli National Park

☎ 0456 22251 🖰 www.kws.org ⏱ 06.00–19.00

One of Kenya's most perennially popular safari destinations, Amboseli extends over 392km² along the Tanzanian border southeast of Nairobi. Set aside as a wildlife reserve in 1899 and upgraded to become a national park in 1974, it forms the unfenced core of an 8,000km² cross-border ecosystem that includes large tracts of Maasai community land as well as a few private reserves. The park is named for Lake Amboseli, on maps a dominating blue presence, in reality a dry dustbowl that is submerged only after exceptional rains, as happened most recently in 1993. A more prominent local landmark is the jagged dome of Kilimanjaro, whose summit lies just across the border in Tanzania. Clouds permitting, Amboseli offers perhaps the most inspiring view there is of Africa's greatest mountain, a setting eulogised by the likes of Ernest Hemingway and Robert Ruark, and it is one of the few places where substantial herds of wildlife – in particular some of the region's oldest and bulkiest elephants – can be seen below the snow-capped peaks.

Amboseli highlights

The dry plains of Amboseli hold little scenic attraction in the heat of the day, when the harsh midday sun creates an appearance of dusty desiccation. All that changes towards dusk, however, when the dying sun is

Practicalities

Most people visit Amboseli on an **organised safari** out of Nairobi, some 230km away by road via the border town of Namanga, which is well equipped with filling stations, restaurants and a bank, and has a good Maasai craft market. Amboseli is a good goal for a short stand-alone safari, but it can easily be combined with Tsavo West National Park, which lies about 120km away along a poor dirt road, and is generally better for predator sightings.

Coming from Nairobi, the road as far as Namanga is surfaced and generally in good shape. However, the 60km track from there to the park entrance gate is heavily corrugated, and tolerably comfortable only when taken at speed. The **drive** takes about five hours in either direction, so those with limited time or low tolerance for jolts and dust might prefer to fly. If you want to combine Amboseli with some of the reserves north or west of Nairobi, flying is strongly recommended, as driving times can be very long (about ten hours, for instance, from the Masai Mara to Amboseli).

Amboseli is a relatively compact park, and a full day is adequate to explore its main road circuit in full. Two nights is thus the recommended minimum duration for a safari, but three nights would be better. The best game-viewing roads are those through the swamps, where you will often see herds of elephant feeding in the water. Supporting a lush groundwater forest of fever trees, Ol Tukai is the site of the park headquarters and its two oldest tourist lodges, making it a popular starting point for game drives and a good place to break up drives for a leg stretch and cold drink. Another important landmark is Observation Hill, which overlooks Lake Kioko and offers panoramic views over the rest of the park, with Kilimanjaro often visible at dusk and dawn.

Accommodation

For full details of tour-operator recommended accommodation, see page 160. Here follows a few further suggestions from the author.

Upmarket
Amboseli Serena Lodge ⌁🖰 www.serenahotels.com
Amboseli Sopa Lodge ⌁🖰 www.sopalodges.com
Ol Tukai Lodge ⌁🖰 www.oltukailodge.com

Kicked up by herds of wildebeest and other grazers, the thin volcanic ash that covers the Amboseli Plains makes for spectacular sunsets. (AZ)

refracted through a suspension of fine volcanic dust, kicked up daily by the hooves of thousands of ungulates, to colour the sky in mesmerising hues of orange and red. And it is also at dusk, or immediately after dawn, that the cloudy shroud on the park's southern horizon is most likely to dissipate, revealing Amboseli's scenic *pièce de résistance*: the spectacular, jagged snow-capped dome of Kilimanjaro towering a full 5km above the plains.

Kilimanjaro doesn't merely provide Amboseli with a splendid backdrop. The extinct volcano has been a defining influence on the ecology of the plains below. The very name 'Amboseli', derived from the Maa *empusel*, refers to the layer of grey saline volcanic ash deposited on the plains during the volcano's volatile infancy. Likewise, one must look to Kilimanjaro to resolve a conundrum first posed in 1883 by the explorer Joseph Thomson (and echoed by many subsequent visitors): 'How can such large numbers of game live in this extraordinary desert?' The answer is that molten snow and spring water from the upper slopes of Kilimanjaro drain off the mountain through a network of subterranean streams to resurface along its northern base, where they feed a ceaselessly mutating network of marshland and lakes in the otherwise arid Amboseli Plains.

Amboseli today supports an abundance of large ungulates. Wildebeest, plains zebra and Thomson's and Grant's gazelles are characteristic of the more open plains, while impala and giraffe inhabit scattered stands of *Acacia tortilis*, and muddy buffalo haunt the fringes of the swamps. However, the park's most famous and endearing residents are its elephants, which are probably the most habituated anywhere in East Africa. Whether it's a stonking elephant bull foraging shoulder deep in the marshes, or a grand matriarch and her impossibly tiny newborn walking tail-in-trunk

Amboseli Elephant Research Project

The Amboseli Elephant Research Project (AERP), supported by the African Wildlife Foundation, is the world's longest ongoing elephant study, founded in 1975 by Dr Cynthia Moss and still active today. The project monitors some 50 elephant families whose range centres on Amboseli, and it retains exhaustive records of most births, deaths and family relationships within this extended community over a 35-year period. Moss's pioneering work has been instrumental in creating a fuller understanding of elephant behaviour – it was, for instance, the first study to recognise the significance of subsonic communication – and it has gained popular recognition through wildlife documentaries such as *Echo of the Elephants*.

The presence of the AERP is the main reason why Amboseli was left largely untouched during the outbreak of commercial poaching that took such drastic toll on the elephants of Tsavo and most other parts of East Africa in the 1980s. Today, as a result, Amboseli supports an unusually high proportion of older elephants, and many individuals sport tusks to dimensions that have been consigned to memory in most other parts of the region. No less significant, though not so immediately apparent, is that the elephant herds of Amboseli were spared the traumatic social disruption that comes with large-scale poaching. Under the watchful eye of the AERP, the elephant population of greater Amboseli has more than doubled over 35 years, and it now stands at around 1,000. In addition, the elephants here have little fear of people and are very habituated to vehicles, which creates a superb opportunity to observe behaviour and social interaction at close quarters.

African jacana (AZ)

across the dusty plain, the pachydermal action at Amboseli is truly magnificent.

Predators, sad to say, are somewhat scarcer, mainly due to friction between conservation authorities and the various Maasai communities whose lands border the park. The once prolific lion population has never fully recovered from being hunted close to local extinction by Maasai evicted from the national park shortly after it was gazetted, and populations tend to fluctuate greatly from one year to the next. Cheetahs, once common, are now seldom observed, despite the apparently ideal habitat, partly because their diurnal hunting routine was so badly disrupted by safari vehicles until off-road driving was banned a few years back. Leopard, though present in small numbers, are very elusive. Far more common, but also more skittish than in many other East Africa parks, is the spotted hyena, which is often seen in 10–20-strong packs. Smaller predators such as jackals are also quite often seen.

The permanent Enkongo Narok and Olokenya swamps, near Ol Tukai village in the centre of the park, are highly alluring to birdwatchers. Over the course of a couple of days, you're likely to record some 50 water-associated species: greater jacana and long-toed lapwing mincing on the vegetated shallows, the full range of large egrets and herons working through the reeds, the gorgeous painted snipe, great white pelican and southern crowned crane. Away from the marshes, the open plains hold a variety of bustards – most commonly Hartlaub's and white-bellied – as well as the localised Pangani longclaw, a large population of secretary birds and the ubiquitous yellow-necked spurfowl. Possibly the most rewarding habitat, however, is acacia woodland, which harbours innumerable dry acacia specials: Von der Decken's hornbill, white-bellied go-away bird, red-and-yellow barbet, rosy-patched bush shrike, steel-blue whydah and black-necked weaver to name a few.

Von Der Decken's hornbill (AZ)

Kilimanjaro

Africa's highest peak and the world's tallest free-standing mountain measured from base to summit, Kilimanjaro rises some 5km above the dusty Amboseli Plains to an altitude of 5,891m. In clear weather, the snow-capped peaks form one of the most breathtaking sights on the

(AZ)

continent, but they are normally obscured in a veil of clouds that frequently disperses around dusk and dawn. And although the upper slopes of this majestic mountain actually stand within Tanzania, the best views are arguably obtained from Kenya, with Amboseli being the closest and most popular vantage point.

As its domed silhouette suggests, Kilimanjaro is a dormant volcano, one that formed about two million years ago as a by-product of the same tectonic activity responsible for creating the Rift Valley. It has two peaks, the tallest of which is Kibo, which is regarded to be dormant, not having demonstrated any notable volcanic activity in living memory. Mawenzi Peak, to the left of Kibo as viewed from the Kenyan side, is smaller, older, more pointed, and to all intents and purposes extinct. According to local Chagga legend, the two peaks are sisters, and both once had a similarly smooth head. However, Mawenzi was too lazy to collect her own firewood and kept sneaking logs from Kibo's woodpile until one day the enraged elder sister grabbed the largest log she could find and beat Mawenzi over the head, resulting the younger sister's jagged shape.

The German missionary Johan Rebmann was the first European to see Kilimanjaro, but his 1848 report of snow on the Equator was initially derided in Europe, only to be confirmed in 1861 when the first official geological survey reached the area. The first full ascent of Kilimanjaro on record was undertaken by Hans Meyer and Ludwig Purtscheller in 1889. Or maybe that was the first ascent ever, since the name Kilimanjaro, though its origin is open to debate, most likely derives from *kilema kyaro* ('impossible journey'), the initial Chagga response to European queries about trekking to the peak! Since that time, the mountain's iconic snow cap and associated glaciers have retreated by around 80%, and some experts predict that global warming will cause all permanent ice to vanish entirely by 2020.

Campi ya Kanzi
⌂ www.maasai.com

Set in the beautiful Chyulu Hills and with stunning views of Mount Kilimanjaro, this delightful camp is run in partnership with the local Maasai community. Up to 16 guests are

accommodated in six luxurious tented cottages and two suites, each with a glorious view. Fine Italian linen and locally made furniture invoke a feeling of rustic elegance, while game drives and walks led through diverse countryside provide exciting wildlife viewing. It would be easy to spend a whole week here.

Ol Donyo Wuas
⌂ www.oldonyowuas.com

In the Chyulu Hills, this lodge is a favourite for its superb hosts, remarkable architecture and the sheer variety of ways you can experience this

breathtaking wildlife area. The perfect complement to the Mara - game drives, bush walks and horse safaris are set against some of the best views of Kilimanjaro. The lodge has pioneered a predator compensation scheme that has seen local big cat populations increase. With only ten luxury suites, this traditional-style lodge is all about relaxation.

Porini Amboseli
⌂ www.porinisafaricamps.com

Simple, rustic - Porini Amboseli captures the essence of life in the bush. A traditional camp shaded by acacia trees, the nine roomy tents

are located in the unspoilt Selenkay conservation area, bordering Amboseli. Staffed almost entirely by the local community and with silver eco-rating, we highly rate this camp for the genuine interaction with the Maasai. Easily accessible from Nairobi, game viewing is still peaceful, away from the crowds, with Kilimanjaro providing a sensational backdrop.

Satao Elerai

🖱 www.sataoelerai.com

Chic eco luxury and beautiful views of Kilimanjaro make this a must on any Kenyan safari. Situated in its own private wildlife conservancy between Amboseli and Kilimanjaro, Elerai is off the beaten path yet accessible, an oasis in the wilderness. The five lodge-style suites and nine deluxe tents feature large, comfortable beds and quality linen, ensuring one of the best night's sleep in Kenya. Commitment to conservation and excellent food also come high on the list of reasons to visit.

Tortilis Camp

🖱 www.tortiliscamp.com

Close your eyes and think of Africa: Kilimanjaro rises off the plains and in the foreground a waterhole lies on the edge of a forest of the archetypal flat-topped acacia. This is Tortilis Camp, a small tented lodge of 17 en-suite tents covered with makuti thatch (including a family unit). To enhance the views, the main areas are built on a hill and there's a pool where you can escape the heat of the day. We enjoy the animal interaction, particularly with the elephants.

Tsavo West National Park

☎ 0456 22120 🖱 www.kws.org ⏰ 06.00–19.00

Extending over 9,065km², this is the smaller of two contiguous but separately administered Tsavo national parks that lie either side of the main highway connecting Nairobi to Mombasa. Kenya's second-oldest national park, Tsavo was originally gazetted in April 1948 as one practically uninhabited and tsetse-infested wilderness area extending over 21,812km², an area larger than Wales or South Africa's legendary Kruger Park. It was split into its present-day western and eastern components later the same year. Though the two parks share a common border, Tsavo West is quite different in character from its drier eastern neighbour, protecting a volcanic landscape of jagged black outcrops and solidified lava flows overshadowed by Kilimanjaro on the southwest horizon. Tsavo West is less popular with safari-goers than the Masai Mara or Amboseli, but the combination of its vast size, denser vegetation and relatively low tourist densities make for a wilder and more untrammelled safari experience. In pure game-viewing terms, it isn't quite up there with the very best Kenya has to offer, but all the Big Five are present, with black rhino being relatively easy to locate in the Ngulia Rhino Sanctuary.

Ngulia Rhino Sanctuary

Situated within the developed area of Tsavo West, the 62km² Ngulia Rhino Sanctuary, close to the lodge of the same name, was created in 1986 to protect the park's last few black rhino from commercial poachers. Enclosed by a tall electric fence, the sanctuary now harbours a population of around 60 rhinos, which receive round-the-clock protection from a dedicated anti-poaching unit. An incidental beneficiary of this high security has been a small population of elephants that were trapped within the fence when it was erected, and which had multiplied to around 160 individuals prior to the translocation of five dozen to elsewhere in the park in 2005. Open for just two hours daily (⏰ 16.00–18.00), the sanctuary has five waterholes and, with a density of around one black rhino per square kilometre, it offers one of the best chances of spotting this elusive browser in Kenya.

(WW/FLPA)

Practicalities

Tsavo West is among the most accessible of Kenya's national parks. The main Mtito Andei Gate is in the small town of the same name, about 230km from Nairobi along the Mombasa Highway. This road is surfaced in its entirety, though pot-holed in parts, and the drive from Nairobi shouldn't take longer than three hours. **Mtito Andei** itself is a thoroughly charmless small town, as might be expected of what is the main truck stop between the country's two largest cities, but it has good facilities including a few low-key hotels, many eateries and a couple of ATMs and filling stations. At the Mtito Andei Gate, a small visitors' centre consists of a museum and shop selling a limited selection of curios and interpretive material. The Tsavo Gate lies at the southern end of the developed area, about 30km past Mtito Andei.

The best way to explore the park is on an **organised road safari**, either as a two to three-night stand-alone trip out of Nairobi, or in tandem with other nearby parks such as Tsavo East or Amboseli. There are also several airstrips within the park, and **fly-in safaris** are popular, too. This is one of the easier parks to explore on a **self-drive** basis, thanks to the relative ease of access and good internal roads within the main developed area (though 4x4 may be required after heavy rain) and the presence of several self-catering cottages operated by the Kenya Wildlife Service (KWS). Game viewing is best north of the Tsavo River and we would give strong preference to lodges in this part of the park.

Accommodation

For full details of tour-operator recommended accommodation, see page 165. Here follows a few further suggestions from the author.

Exclusive
Finch Hatton's ⁒ www.finchhattons.com

Upmarket
Kilaguni Serena Lodge ⁒ www.serenahotels.com
Ziwani Voyager Lodge ⁒ www.heritage-eastafrica.com

Moderate
Ngulia Safari Lodge ⁒ www.safari-hotels.com

Tsavo West highlights

The most developed part of Tsavo West is the northern quarter, where a relatively compact circuit of game-viewing roads is bounded by the Tsavo River in the south. This area is most memorable for its bleakly surreal volcanic landscapes, which include the bizarre Chiamu Crater, situated at the top of bare conical pyramid of honeycombed black ash. More spectacular perhaps is the Shetani Lava Flow, a 200-year-old stream of solidified magma whose jagged tar-coloured rocks remain practically unvegetated, creating the impression they might have been deposited yesterday. Shetani – a Swahili word meaning 'Devil' – is avoided by locals, whose oral traditions recall that many people and animals were buried alive beneath the fast-flowing fiery lava.

Lesser kudu (AZ)

Much of Tsavo West consists of dense scrubby woodland dominated by various acacia species, and even in the most developed part of the park, the rutted roads and dense foliage ensure that a game drive never feels like a milk run. The park supports a varied selection of large mammals, but populations are less dense than in certain other reserves, and the thick vegetation can make it difficult to spot wildlife. All the Big Five are present, and elephant and buffalo sightings are all but guaranteed, as are giraffe, impala, zebra and Grant's gazelle. It is also the best place in Kenya to see the handsome but skittish lesser kudu, which often frequents riverine forests and thicketed rocky slopes. Predator sightings are rather hit and miss, but lion are reasonably common, albeit without the large manes associated with their counterparts in the Masai Mara. Birdlife is probably less exciting than in most national parks, but you can expect to see a selection of raptors, ground birds and acacia-related species. Tsavo West lies on a major bird migration route and Ngulia Lodge attracts large numbers of migrants between October and January, especially after misty nights.

One of the best birding sites in Tsavo West, Mzima Springs is also a fascinating geological phenomenon, fed by resurfaced subterranean streams that rise on the slopes of Kilimanjaro. Filtered through the porous volcanic rocks of the Chyulu Hills, this sparkling water emerges into a series of crystal-clear pools at a daily rate of more than 200 million litres, some 10% of which is diverted along an artificial pipeline to form the main source of water for Mombasa and environs. Something of an oasis in this otherwise dry part of Kenya, the lush palm and fever tree forest around

View from the underwater observation chamber at Mzima Springs (AP/A)

Mzima can be explored over 15–30 minutes on a clearly marked walking trail that leads to an underwater observation chamber built at the end of a small wooden pier in 1969. From here, you can watch shoals of fish, including a carp-like *Labeo* species, circling in an anticlockwise direction, and you may even see hippo from a fishy perspective, though these aquatic giants generally stick to the far side of the pool. The birdlife here can be excellent, ranging from the woodland-loving African paradise-flycatcher and black-headed oriole to fish eagles, kingfishers and darters and other water-related species.

Tsavo East National Park

📞 043 30049 📱 www.kws.org 🕐 06.00–19.00

Untrammelled and relatively undeveloped, Tsavo East is Kenya's largest national park, extending over 11,747km² of red earth and acacia scrub northeast of the main Nairobi–Mombasa highway. Drier and more sparsely vegetated than Tsavo West, it forms something of a transitional zone between the southern savannas and northern semi-deserts, though the general aridity is alleviated by the presence of the perennial Galana River (Kenya's second longest) and various tributaries. Flowing through it in an easterly direction for about 70km, the Galana divides Tsavo East into two unequal parts, of which the larger northern sector may be visited only with special permission. Nevertheless, even the more touristy southern sector of Tsavo East rewards visitors with its remote wilderness atmosphere, compelling sense of space, and erratic but sometimes very good game viewing – elephant are particularly common, and there's a good chance of encountering a selection of dry-country birds and mammals absent from other reserves in southern Kenya.

Dry yellow bush and sun-baked red sands are characteristic of Tsavo East's dry landscapes. (SS)

Practicalities

Tsavo East is often included as part of a longer southern safari itinerary together with Amboseli and Tsavo West, in which case the most popular entrance gates are at Voi, which lies about 310km from Nairobi along the main road to Mombasa, and at Munyani about 30km further north. Tsavo is also a popular goal for a short safari add-on to an extended beach holiday package at Malindi or Watamu. The Sala Entrance Gate is only 120km from Malindi, a two-hour drive in either direction along an adequate dirt road, and many local operators there can arrange day or (better) overnight safaris to Tsavo East at short notice. Most lodges and hotels are concentrated in and around Voi, which is undoubtedly the best area for seeing wildlife, but the pair of more remote tented camps on the Galana River offer more of a wilderness experience.

Accommodation

For full details of tour-operator recommended accommodation, see page 171. Here follows a few further suggestions from the author.

Upmarket
Voi Safari Lodge ⌁ www.safari-hotels.com
Voi Wildlife Lodge ⌁ www.voiwildlifelodge.com

Moderate
Epiya Chapeyu Camp ⌁ www.epiya-chapeyu-camp.com

Tsavo East highlights

Tsavo East has a harsh and remote character, and away from the developed area around Voi Gate it is possible to drive for hours without seeing another vehicle. The public southern third of the park protects a fairly uniform landscape of flat red plains, covered in low acacia woodland that tends to form impenetrable thickets in the northwest and becomes more thinly spread in the south. This rather monotonous landscape is broken by patches of thicker riparian woodland along the banks of the perennial Galana in the north and the seasonal Voi River further south. Most of the park's wildlife is dependent on these watercourses during the dry season, when the roads that run alongside them tend to offer excellent game viewing. After rain, wildlife disperses and game viewing is more erratic.

The Tsavo poaching war

Tsavo is famed for its prolific 'red elephants', whose unusual colouration is not a hereditary condition, but the result of rolling and bathing themselves in the red earth characteristic of the region. The elephant population is thought to have peaked in the late 1960s, when some 35,000 individuals roamed across the two parks, almost two individuals per square kilometre, an unnaturally high density attributed to the park's gradual isolation from established migration routes as a result of surrounding cultivation. This pachydermal overpopulation created environmental havoc in Tsavo, culminating with a drought in which an estimated 6,000 elephants perished of thirst or starvation in the early 1970s. The situation became so bad that selective culling was advocated by some conservationists, a controversial proposal that was heatedly contested by those who preferred to let nature run its course.

As it transpired, the culling issue was settled by an influx of Somali commercial poachers, who targeted the parks' prodigious elephants for their ivory tusks, which fetched US$300/kg on the open market. And when elephant numbers started to decline, the poachers turned their attention to the parks' black rhinos (estimated at 6,000 in 1970, the largest concentration anywhere on the continent), whose horns were prized as daggers in Yemen, and fetched up to US$30,000 apiece in the wake of the mid-70s oil price boom. By the late 1980s, Tsavos' rhinos had been poached to within a few individuals of extinction, and elephant were being lost at a rate of several thousand individuals annually – indeed, for the few safari-goers that made it to Tsavo East in these bleak times, living elephant herds were a less frequent sight than the piles of tuskless cadavers left behind by poachers. Many people justifiably feared that Kenya's rhino and elephant would disappear entirely by the turn of the century.

Fortunately, the trend was reversed in the early 1990s, by which time the elephant population of the Tsavo region had plummeted to an estimated 6,000, less than 20% of its 1960s peak. Key factors in eradicating the poaching were an international CITES ban on the sale of ivory, and the unification of the country's disparate conservation bodies into the Kenya Wildlife Service (KWS) under Richard Leakey. In 1992, President Moi backed up the symbolic public burning of Kenya's entire government ivory stock by implementing a 'shoot-on-sight' policy to poachers. As a result, poaching is practically a thing of the past in Tsavo, the elephant population now stands at around 12,000, and the black rhino population has increased from a mere three confirmed individuals in 1986 to around 150 today.

The most reliable game-viewing circuit follows the Voi River east from the eponymous entrance gate as far as Aruba Dam. The clifftop Voi Safari Lodge, near the entrance gate, is emphatically worth a look: it offers commanding views across the surrounding plains, a muddy waterhole that frequently attracts large herds of elephant and buffalo, and the opportunity to see several smaller rock-dwelling creatures including red-winged starling, red-headed agama lizard and rock hyrax. The open country around the entrance gate is a good place to look for cheetah, impala, Coke's hartebeest, zebra and gazelle, while lions are frequently seen below the shady trees surrounding Aruba Dam, constructed on the Voi River in 1951 as the only permanent water source in this otherwise arid part of the park. Roads running north from the Voi River towards the Galana River pass through scrubby plains that support relatively low concentrations of wildlife. However, this habitat is favoured by several localised dry-country species, notably gerenuk, fringe-eared oryx and hirola, the last an endangered northeast Kenyan endemic that was introduced to this part of Tsavo East in the 1960s. The burnt sepia landscape is also brightened up by the presence of several colourful dry-country birds, including golden pipit, vulturine guineafowl, golden-breasted starling and various barbets, bee-eaters and hornbills. Furthermore, it is the southernmost haunt of the localised Somali ostrich.

A somewhat surreal sight in this otherwise austere landscape, the palm-fringed Galana River, also known as the Sabaki, drains a 70,000km^2 catchment area embracing Kilimanjaro and Nairobi National Park. Its most significant landmark is Lugard Falls, a sequence of rapids that flow rapidly across a bed of black dolomite striated with white quartzite rocks. Downriver of the falls, there's a good hippo pool where crocs are also usually present. Riparian forest associated with the Galana is inhabited by large numbers of elephant and buffalo, as well as black rhino and lesser kudu, and game-viewing roads follow the river all the way east to Sala Gate.

A major landmark in the west of the park, situated about halfway along the 30km road between the Munyani and Voi

The red-winged starling is often associated with cliffs. (NB/FLPA)

Lugard Falls on the Galana River (NP/C)

entrance gates, Mudanda Rock is regularly and somewhat fancifully compared to Ayer's Rock in Australia. This 1.5km long inselberg is too small to stand the comparison, but approached with realistic expectations, it is an impressive sight, run through by a series of quartzite striations alluded to in its name, which means 'strips of drying meat'. The crest of the rock offers stirring views across to the flat plains to the distant Galana River, and it also overlooks a waterhole where elephant and buffalo gather to drink and wallow, and leopard sometimes emerge towards dusk.

Galdessa

🖰 www.galdessa.com

Galdessa has a coastal/bush relaxed feel – we love the earthy colours and natural woods. The camp is located along the Galana River under fringed doum palms with 12 spacious thatched and semi-tented bungalows on wooden platforms. Private Galdessa can be booked on an exclusive basis for extra luxury including dedicated staff and a separate dining room and lounge. The camp's commitment to conservation includes working with the KWS on a black rhino re-introduction project.

Satao Camp

🖰 www.sataocamp.com

20 tents are positioned in a semi-circle shape around the camp's own waterhole, which is floodlit at night allowing you to view passing wildlife 24 hours a day from the comfort of your own veranda. In the heart of the national park, it is *the* place to stay for guests looking for a short safari to combine with a longer beach holiday. At just four hours' drive from Mombasa's south coast you'll be in the camp ready to board Satao's own 4x4 purpose-built safari vehicle in no time.

Voi, Taveta and surrounds

With a population approaching 25,000, Voi is substantially the largest town along the main highway that runs through the wild bush country separating Nairobi from Mombasa. Named after a powerful 17th-century Akamba leader and situated alongside the eponymous river, Voi emerged as an important commercial, agricultural and administrative centre following the arrival of the Uganda Highway from Mombasa in 1898. Today, it stands only 7km from the main entrance gate to Tsavo East, and is the junction town for the C104, a 120km road that runs west to the small town of Taveta on the Tanzanian border. Although Voi and Taveta are of limited interest to tourists, the road that connects them is flanked by private wildlife sanctuaries, most famously Taita Hills, and Taveta lies within easy striking distance of the lovely lakes Jipe and Chala.

Voi and Taveta highlights

Taita Hills

Rising to 2,208m about 50km west of Voi by road, this isolated range is the most northerly of the Eastern Arc Mountains, a geologically affiliated series of 13 massifs whose ancient forests are known for their high level of endemism. Taita is the only one of these montane islands to fall outside Tanzania, and though the extent and biodiversity of its forest is relatively small, it is renowned among birdwatchers as the only place to see the Taita thrush. This colourful montane forest endemic has an estimated global population of 1,350 individuals confined to three forest patches in Taita, of which the most accessible is Ngangao (13km from the town of Wundanyi). Other endemics include the Taita apalis, the Taita white-eye and a species of African violet, and it is a good site for the rare Taita falcon. The cultivated breezy hills, inhabited by the industrious Taita people, make for a refreshing climatic contrast to the hot dry plains below, covered in lush tropical cultivation and montane forest. Cultural sites include the Cave of Skulls at Ngomenyi, 2km from Wundanyi, and a pretty church founded in 1906 at Mbale.

Taita Hills Wildlife Sanctuary

☎ 043 30270 🖰 www.sarovahotels.com
Situated some 38km west of Voi along the road to Taveta, this misleadingly named private sanctuary doesn't lie on the Taita Hills but below them, where it shares an unfenced border with Tsavo West National Park, and protects a similar habitat of thorny scrubland. The 110km² sanctuary was established in 1972 and is home to at least 50 mammal and

Practicalities

Most tour operators in Mombasa, Nairobi or elsewhere offer stand-alone **road and fly-in safaris** to the two game lodges in Taita Hills Wildlife Sanctuary, which can also be included in broader safari itineraries around southern Kenya, as can the lodge in Lumo. The drive from Mombasa will take around three hours and the drive from Nairobi four hours, and road conditions are usually good the whole way. Most safaris to Taita Hills are for one night only, but we would recommend two nights to make the most of the wonderful elephant sightings at Salt Lick Lodge, whilst also getting in a couple of game drives.

Although **Voi** is the largest and best-equipped town in this part of Kenya, tourist traffic is almost entirely transient, comprising safari vehicles *en route* to Tsavo East National Park, whose main gate lies just 7km out of town. There are a few good lodges around the park entrance gate (see listings for Tsavo East on pages 167 and 171), and the energetic town centre is well equipped with filling stations, shops, restaurants, internet cafés, banks and ATMs. It is the best base for exploring the forests of the Taita Hills, which lie about an hour's drive away, and are sometimes included on dedicated ornithological tours of Kenya.

Taveta is a smaller town with fewer facilities, but it is the site of a major border crossing into Tanzania and it springs to life on market days (Wednesday and Saturday). It is a good base for self-drive excursions to Lakes Chala and Jipe, and has a few basic lodges. However, the Taveta area lacks any decent tourist accommodation following the closure of an eponymous lodge on the rim of Lake Chala a few years back.

Accommodation

Upmarket
Sarova Salt Lick Game Lodge ⌂ www.sarovahotels.com
Sarova Taita Hills Game Lodge ⌂ www.sarovahotels.com

Moderate
Lions Bluff Lodge ⌂ www.lionsblufflodge.com

300 bird species, though there is some seasonal fluctuation in numbers, with elephant and buffalo populations being especially dense at the end of the dry season (September into November). Giraffe and Coke's hartebeest

are among the more common ungulates, three lion prides are resident, as is a small population of cheetah, and night drives offer a good chance of spotting secretive nocturnal species such as leopard, hyena, white-tailed mongoose, honey badger and genet. The sanctuary is most often visited on a stand-alone overnight safari package from the coast, which can be arranged through any operator, inclusive of meals and activities. Two lodges

Coke's hartebeest (AZ)

are set within the reserve, both under the same management, and while Taita Hills Lodge is marginally the more comfortable, Salt Lick Lodge – a bizarre stilted construction whose bunker-like architecture reflects the several World War I battles fought in the vicinity – is wonderfully positioned for in-house nocturnal wildlife viewing, with elephants often gathering here in their hundreds.

Lumo Community Wildlife Sanctuary

℆ 072 3266606 ⬨ www.lionsblufflodge.com 🕓 06.00-18.00

Situated 50km west of Voi along an ancient wildlife corridor between Tsavo West and East, this 600km² sanctuary started life in 1993 when the local Lualenyi, Mramba and Oza people decided to amalgamate part of their traditional tribal lands for the development of a community ecotourism project in conjunction with the African Wildlife Foundation. The sanctuary borders Tsavo West and protects a similar range of large

Breathtaking vistas at the Lumo Community Wildlife Sanctuary (LBL)

mammals to its larger neighbour, with all but one of the so-called Big Five being present, the exception being black rhino. Day visitors with private transport are permitted to explore the limited road system under their own steam, but the reserve caters mainly to overnight visitors following the 2004 opening of a spectacularly sited and eco-friendly 12-unit tented camp called Lions Bluff Lodge. Tourist volumes are low, and because the reserve lies outside the national park system, it offers a wider range of guided walks and night drives in addition to the usual game drives.

Lake Chala

Situated 8km from Taveta along the Oloitokitok road, this beautiful crater lake, which lies on the southern footslopes of Kilimanjaro bordering Tanzania, is almost 3km in diameter, yet it remains practically invisible until you topple over the caldera rim in which it nestles. The scenery alone justifies a visit, especially when Kilimanjaro emerges from the clouds on the northern horizon. But if you want to reach the rocky shore, which is hemmed in by sheer cliffs draped in tropical greenery, a steep footpath leads down there from the eastern rim. The translucent turquoise water plunges almost vertically to a depth that remains undetermined, and locals claim that a menagerie of mysterious and malignant Nessie-like beasties lurk below. Terrestrial wildlife is in short supply, but crocodiles are certainly present, as is the endemic cichlid *Oreochromis hunteri* and an abundance of waterbirds. Swimming cannot be recommended following a fatal crocodile attack in 2002.

Lake Jipe

In direct contrast to nearby Chala, Lake Jipe, set on the Tanzanian border some 25km south of Taveta, is a large, shallow sump fringed by dense bed of papyrus in parts. It lies on the little-visited southern border of Tsavo West, below Tanzania's spectacular North Pare Mountains, and on a clear day you will also see Chala crater outlined on the flat plain to the east, and Kilimanjaro on the northern skyline. Elephants are frequent visitors to the shore, especially in the dry season, and hippo and crocodiles are everywhere, necessitating a certain amount of caution when walking close to the lakeshore. The birdlife can be terrific, with specialities such as lesser jacana, African water rail, pygmy goose, black egret and black coucal most easily seen if you head out to the open water in a local boat. Between Taveta and Lake Jipe, it's worth stopping at Grogan's Castle, an idiosyncratic 1930s construction built on a tall volcanic plug as the home of Ewart Grogan, an eccentric Scot settler best remembered for his pioneering foot journey from the Cape to Cairo, undertaken between 1898 and 1900.

8 The Coast

The Swahili coast of Kenya conforms effortlessly to every travel brochure archetype of a tropical beach nirvana: a seemingly endless succession of white sandy beaches lapped by the warm blue waters of the Indian Ocean, ventilated by a butterfly-light sea breeze, and overhung by swaying coconut palms. In fact, for a country widely regarded to be the quintessential land of the safari, Kenya could make a more than passable stab at marketing itself as one of the world's great beach destinations. And certainly, if your idea of a perfect holiday amounts to lounging about in a shaded deckchair, trashy novel in hand, with no ambition more burning than the acquisition of an enviable tan – well, beaches truly don't get much better than Kenya's finest.

Choosing an itinerary

Dodori NR

Kiunga MNR

Kiwayu

Bodhei

Pate

Manda Tato

50km

25 miles

Makowe

Manda

LAMU

Lamu

R Tana

Tana River Primate Reserve, Garissa

C112

Witu

Indian Ocean

Garsen

Tana Delta

TRIED & TESTED

ACCOMMODATION

1 **Afrochic** (page 189)

B8

Mambrui

Marafa Depression

MALINDI

Malindi MNP

Gedi ruins

R Sabaki

Watamu

Watamu MNP

C103

Arabuko-Sokoke NP

Tsavo East NP

KILIFI

C107

Kaloleni

Jumbo la Mtwana

Mtwapa

Mombasa MNP

Mariakani

Rabai

North beaches

Nyali Bridge

Maseras

Mombasa Island

Likoni

MOMBASA

Mwaluganje Elephant Sanctuary

Kwale

DIANI

Diani Chale MNP

Shimba Hills NR

C106

Chale

The Coast

R Ramisi

A14

Funzi

Ramisi Delta

Shimoni

Lunga Lunga

Kisite

Tanzania

Mpunguti MNP

Wasini

There is much more to the Kenyan coast than a stock seaside holiday in tropical surroundings. Offshore, a string of reefs teems with a kaleidoscope of colourful fish, offering some of the best snorkelling and game fishing in the world. Back on terra firma, there's great game viewing to be had at the likes of Shimba Hills National Reserve, while the pedestrian-friendly Arabuko-Sokoke National Park protects a tract of coastal forest rich in endemic birds and mammals. The coast also has a strong sense of place and history, notable for the cultural cohesion of the Swahili people, the antiquity of ports such as Lamu and Mombasa, and mysterious jungle-bound ruins that pay testament to an ancient trade that has flourished intermittently since medieval times.

Tourists with limited time will generally visit only one of the towns or beach resorts described in this chapter, possibly using it as a base for further exploration. Which one you should choose will depend greatly on your personal needs and interests. If these are sedentary and strongly beach-oriented, the resort-like beaches flanking Mombasa – Diani, Nyali and Shanzu – should be ideal. For more active travellers with an interest in marine and terrestrial wildlife, Watamu or nearby Malindi would be my suggestion. And for those whose interests are mainly cultural and historical – or who enjoy a more urban setting – the pick would have to be Lamu.

Mombasa and the south coast

Kenya's largest port and second-most populous city is not the tourist magnet one might expect. It's more accurate perhaps to refer to it as a tourist funnel. As the terminus of the main highway and railway connecting Nairobi to the coast, and site of the country's second-busiest international airport, this is the first port of call for most coast-bound travellers, but few actually spend any time in the city, preferring instead to head directly to one of the nearby beach resorts. There's some sense in this, as the bustling city centre might prove a daunting prospect for fresh arrivals to the coast. But once you are settled into your hotel, Mombasa is well worth exploring: the Old Town in particular possesses a tropical languor, organic layout and sense of historical continuity that places it a world away from the breezy modernity and Westernisation of Nairobi.

History

Mombasa is a city of considerable antiquity. Local oral tradition links its foundation with one Shehe Mvita, an educated medieval leader of Arabian descent. Mombasa is first mentioned by name in the writings of the 12th-century Arab geographer Al Idrisi, at which time it was a prosperous town trading in spices, gold and ivory with ships from Arabia and Asia. In 1331, the Moroccan adventurer Ibn Buttata spent a night

View towards Mombasa (PCL/A)

there, noting that its Islamic residents were 'a religious people, trustworthy and righteous' and that their mosques were 'expertly built'. By the 15th century, Mombasa had probably superseded Kilwa (in present-day Tanzania) as the pre-eminent trade centre along the East African coast.

In 1498, the Portuguese navigator Vasco da Gama landed at Mombasa *en route* to India and met with a hostile reception. The Portuguese returned in 1505 to launch an uneven naval bombardment on Mombasa, razing most of the buildings and forcing those inhabitants who survived to flee inland. Initially, Portugal showed no interest in settling at Mombasa and preferred Malindi as its regional base. Nevertheless, it launched further attacks on Mombasa in 1528 and 1589, and finally relocated its base to the city in 1593, when Fort Jesus was built. Mombasa was formally made a Portuguese colony, subordinate to Goa, in 1638.

Following a 33-month naval siege, Fort Jesus was captured by Omani Arabs in 1698, and though the Portuguese reoccupied it briefly in 1728, Mombasa essentially remained under Omani/Zanzibari rule until the 1880s, when it was leased to British East Africa (later Kenya) by the Sultan of Zanzibar. Mombasa served as capital of British East Africa until that role was usurped by Nairobi, and it saw a great deal of development under British rule, as the main sea harbour serving East Africa and the coastal terminal of the Uganda Railway. Its fortunes have declined somewhat in recent decades, partly as a result of the diminished importance of maritime transport and the rise of Dar es Salaam in Tanzania, but it remains a busy commercial city with a predominantly Islamic population estimated at around one million.

Mombasa was the main gateway to the Kenyan interior before the days of scheduled flights. (SI/C)

Mombasa highlights

Mombasa Old Town

Running adjacent to the old harbour immediately north of Fort Jesus, Mombasa's fascinating Old Town comprises a compact maze of narrow alleys that can be covered in an hour's stroll, longer if you fancy the occasional stop at a roadside coffee stall or juice shop. This is the oldest

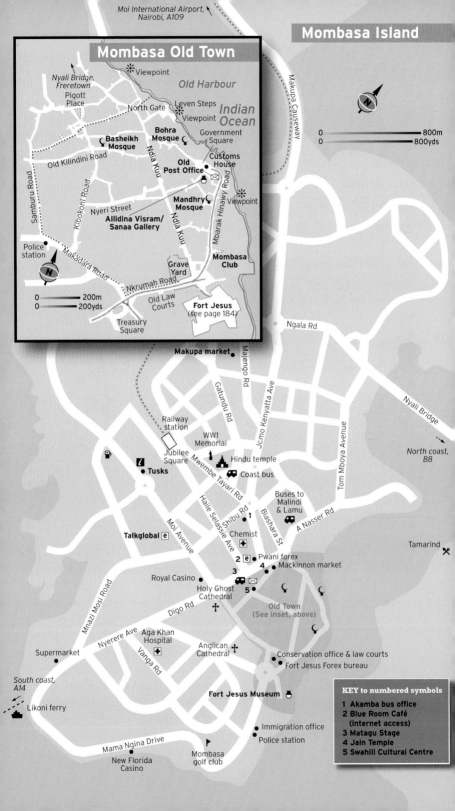

Mombasa Island

Mombasa Old Town

- Nyali Bridge, Freetown
- Pigott Place
- North Gate
- Viewpoint
- Leven Steps
- Viewpoint
- *Indian Ocean*
- Old Harbour
- Basheikh Mosque
- Bohra Mosque
- Government Square
- Old Kilindini Road
- Old Post Office
- Customs House
- Ndia Kuu
- Kibokoni Road
- Nyeri Street
- Mandhry Mosque
- Allidina Visram/ Sanaa Gallery
- Ndia Kuu
- Viewpoint
- Samburu Road
- Police station
- Makadara Road
- Grave Yard
- Mombasa Club
- Mbarak Hinawy Road
- Nkrumah Road
- Old Law Courts
- Fort Jesus (see page 184)
- Treasury Square

0 — 200m
0 — 200yds

Moi International Airport, Nairobi, A109

0 — 800m
0 — 800yds

- Makupa Causeway
- Ngala Rd
- Makupa market
- Majengo Rd
- Gatundu Rd
- Nyali Bridge
- Railway station
- WW1 Memorial
- Jubilee Square
- Hindu temple
- Coast bus
- Tusks
- Jomo Kenyatta Ave
- Mwembe Tayari Rd
- North coast, B8
- Tom Mboya Avenue
- Buses to Malindi & Lamu
- Shibu Rd
- **1**
- Chemist
- Biashara St
- A Nasser Rd
- Talkglobal
- Halie Selassie Ave
- Moi Avenue
- **2** e Pwani forex
- **4** Mackinnon market
- **3**
- Royal Casino
- **5**
- Holy Ghost Cathedral
- Old Town (See inset, above)
- Tamarind
- Mnazi Mosi Road
- Digo Rd
- Nyerere Ave
- Aga Khan Hospital
- Vanga Rd
- Anglican Cathedral
- Conservation office & law courts
- Fort Jesus Forex bureau
- Supermarket
- South coast, A14
- Likoni ferry
- Fort Jesus Museum
- Immigration office
- Police station
- Mama Ngina Drive
- New Florida Casino
- Mombasa golf club

KEY to numbered symbols
1 Akamba bus office
2 Blue Room Café (Internet access)
3 Matagu Stage
4 Jain Temple
5 Swahili Cultural Centre

Practicalities

Central Mombasa squats on a small offshore island linked to the mainland by Makupa Causeway in the west, Nyali Bridge in the north and Kilindini Ferry in the south. Most people arrive at **Moi International Airport**, 10km from the city centre via Makupa Causeway, and pre-arrange a shuttle or transfer to their beach hotel, though taxis are also available and charge fixed fares. The main **bus station** and **railway station** are both in the city centre and are also serviced by

Accommodation

For full details of tour-operator recommended accommodation, see page 189. Here follows a few further suggestions from the author.

Upmarket
Diani Beach Reef Resort & Spa ⌖ www.dianireef.com
Indian Ocean Beach Resort ⌖ www.jacarandahotels.com
Mombasa Serena Beach Hotel & Spa ⌖ www.serenahotels.com
Pemba Channel Lodge ⌖ www.pembachannellodge.com
Sarova Whitesands Spa & Resort ⌖ www.sarovahotels.com
The Sands At Nomad ⌖ www.thesandsatnomad.com

Moderate
Bamburi Beach Hotel ⌖ www.bamburibeachkenya.com
Mwaluganje Elephant Camp ⌖ www.travellersbeach.com
Nyali Beach Hotel ⌖ www.nyalibeach.co.ke
Papillon Lagoon Reef ⌖ www.rexresorts.com
Reef Hotel ⌖ www.reefhotelkenya.com

continuously settled part of Mombasa, and several of its mosques have been on the same site for centuries, most notably Basheikh Mosque, reputedly founded about 800 years ago, though the building itself is relatively new. The two main roads through the old town, Ndia Kuu and Sir Mbarak Hinawy, are lined with two- and three-storey buildings dating to 1870–1930 and combine British colonial influences with more ornate oriental and Arabic flourishes such as fine fretwork balconies, elaborately carved window frames, and studded Zanzibari-style doors. Government Square, halfway along Sir Mbarak Hinawy Road, is surrounded by period buildings, including the fish market, the Old Customs House, the original taxis. Hotels on the northern beaches can be reached from the city centre or airport in less than 30 minutes, but you should allow at least two hours to get to Diani or any other hotel south of the city, where travel times depends on the many vagaries associated with the Kilindini Ferry. In the city centre, there is no shortage of internet cafés, banks, ATMs, restaurants and other amenities, especially on the main commercial thoroughfares of Nyerere Road, Nkrumah Road and Moi Avenue, but tourist accommodation is thin on the ground as most hotels are on the beaches north or south of town.

Shimba Lodge www.aberdaresafarihotels.com
Voyager Beach Resort www.heritage-eastafrica.com

Budget
Castle Royal Hotel www.sentrim-hotels.com
Diani Sea Lodge www.kenya-hotels.de
Lotus Hotel www.lotushotelkenya.com
Shimoni Reef Lodge www.shimonireeflodge.com

Eating out

Ali Barbour's (seafood) Diani Beach ☎ 041 3202033
Castle Terrace (Continental & seafood) Castle Royal Hotel, Moi Av ☎ 041 315680
Charlie Claws (seafood buffet) Wasini Island ☎ 040 3202331
Galaxy (Chinese) Archbishop Makarios St ☎ 041 2311256
Il Covo (Italian) Bamburi Beach ☎ 041 5487481
Sher-E-Punjab (Indian) Diani Beach ☎ 041 3202116
Tamarind (fresh seafood & Swahili) Silo Rd ☎ 041 474600

post office, and the former abode of the merchant Allidina Visram. Nearby, the whitewashed Mandhry Mosque was built in the 1570s alongside a well whose potable water is protected by an ornate front built in 1901. Although it had become very run-down by the turn of the millennium, the Old Town has since been infused with a mood of

Balcony in Mombasa's Old Town (AZ)

rejuvenation following the renovation of many once dilapidated buildings as boutiques, galleries or craftshops. At the same time, it has a striking sense of community, with most businesses remaining small family-run affairs, and everybody seems to know everybody else – in many respects, it feels more like a self-contained village than the heart of a large city.

Fort Jesus National Museum

📞 041 312839 🖥 www.museums.or.ke ⏰ 08.00-18.00

Mombasa's best-known landmark, Fort Jesus lies at the seafront end of Nkrumah Road, opposite the Old Town. Built for the Portuguese in 1593, it was the most strategically important building on the Swahili coast for the first three centuries of its existence, and it changed hands more than a dozen times over that period. The longest battle in its history was a 33-month Omani naval siege that claimed the lives of more than 1,000 Portuguese soldiers and 5,000 Swahili residents, and culminated in its annexation to Oman in 1898 after the Portuguese captain was shot and beheaded. Fort Jesus diminished in significance during the colonial era, when it served as military barracks and then a prison, but the original plan is largely intact, despite several renovations and additions over the years, and it still cuts an imposing figure above Mombasa Harbour, where the 2.5m-thick seaward walls rise a full 16m from the coral base to the fortified turrets. Now a museum, it houses an impressive collection of artefacts

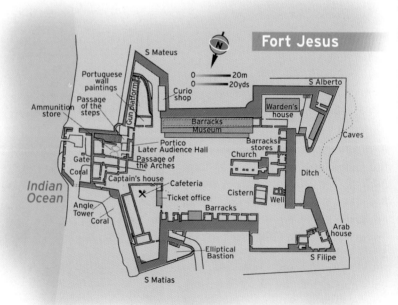

The imposing seaward walls of Fort Jesus dominate Mombasa's old harbour. (SS)

unearthed during excavations, including Chinese porcelain and Arabic earthenware, while a striking panel of wall paintings executed by an unknown Portuguese sailor before 1639 can be seen in *situ*.

North beaches

The only road conduit between Mombasa Island and the coast further north is the 400m Nyali Bridge, built in the early 1980s to replace what was the world's longest pontoon bridge, the remains of which are still clearly visible. Immediately north of the bridge, Kongowea Junction is the site of Freretown (named after Sir Bartle Frere), where the Anglican Church settled thousands of free slaves between 1874 and 1888 to form a thriving self-sufficient Christian community, relics of which include the Freretown Bell, erected to warn the community of impending danger, and the attractive Emmanuel Church built in 1889. Kenyatta municipal beach, 7km north of Kongowea, is the main public beach servicing Mombasa; swimming is pleasant at high tide, and it's a good place to arrange glass-bottomed boat excursions into the Mombasa Marine National Reserve, but it can get busy on weekends and holidays. By contrast, the more southerly Nyali and more northerly Bamburi and Shanzu beaches are more quiet and exclusive, used primarily by the upmarket resorts that line them.

Seaside activities aside, a number of popular attractions lie a short distance inland of the north beaches. About 1km past Kongowea, the **Bombolulu Workshops and Cultural Centre** (✆ 041 471704 ✆ www.apdkbombolulu.org ◷ 08.00–17.00) is a highly regarded craft centre selling leatherwork, basketry, woodcarvings and jewellery made on site at five workshops that create employment for more than 150 disabled people. Opposite Kenyatta Beach, the admirable Haller Park (📞 041 548 5901 🖰 www.lafargeecosystems.com 🕐 09.00–17.00) is a reclaimed limestone quarry run through by a 90-minute nature trail that passes enclosures inhabited by giraffe, hippo, buffalo, antelope and other introduced wildlife. Another reclaimed limestone quarry, this time at Shanzu, is the site of **Ngomongo Village** (📞 072 1746093 🖰 www.ngomongo.com 🕐 09.00–17.00), which offers a highly informative and worthwhile two-hour guided tour through ten reconstructed traditional villages representing tribes such as the Maasai, Mijikenda, Akamba, Pokot and Luo. Any hotel or resort can arrange a visit to these sites, as well as diving and snorkelling excursions in the offshore reefs protected by the Mombasa Marine National Reserve.

Jumba la Mtwana

Situated at the end of a 4km dirt road running east from Mtwapa, Jumba la Mtwana is arguably the most mysterious and compelling of several ruined Swahili trading ports on the Kenyan coast south of Gedi. Chinese porcelain unearthed during excavations in 1972 suggest the town was founded before AD1350 and abandoned a century later, but no written records of a town here exist, and – as with Gedi – its original name is long forgotten. It must once have been a very substantial settlement, blessed with a breezy beachfront setting near the mouth of Mtwapa Creek and an ample supply of fresh water. Today, gigantic fig and baobab trees erupt from the old coral rag walls, but several buildings remain recognisable, including four houses and three mosques, the best preserved of which has arched doorways and an intact mihrab.

Diani Beach

When tourist brochures refer to Mombasa as a seaside holiday destination, they're generally talking about Diani Beach, a long, idyllic expanse of palm-fringed white sand set some 30km south of the city itself. Lined with dozens of resort hotels, Diani is the focal point of Kenya's all-inclusive beach package scene; it can feel quite touristy for East Africa, but the beaches remain blissfully uncrowded by Mediterranean standards, marred only by the presence of somewhat persistent 'beach boys' selling everything from illegally gathered shells to snorkelling trips. The surfaced road connecting the Diani resorts offers a good range of tourist amenities, including ATMs, internet cafés, car rental agencies, supermarkets, laundrettes, DVD rental stores, restaurants and craft markets. The hotels and tour operators here offer a wide selection of excursions, from short safaris to Shimba Hills, Tsavo East or Taita Hills, to marine activities such as diving, snorkelling, windsurfing and game fishing.

Traditional dhows launching from Diani Beach. (NP/C)

On the landward side of the road, relict patches of coastal forest support quite a bit of wildlife. You're unlikely to encounter the elephants that still found their way onto the beach until the 1930s, but Sykes, vervet and Angola colobus monkeys remain common, along with forest birds such as trumpeter hornbill and Schalow's turaco. Raise your eyes skyward, and you'll see one of 26 wire-and-plastic cased 'colo-bridges', erected by an NGO called the Colobus Trust to allow monkeys to cross the road aerially rather than be exposed to speeding traffic. At the Tiwi River mouth on the north end of the beach, the 16th-century Kongo Mosque is tucked away in a stand of baobabs.

Shimba Hills National Reserve

📞 040 4159 🖥 www.kws.org ⏱ 06.00-19.00; guided walks to Sheldrick Falls 10.00 and 15.00

This underrated reserve, established in 1968, seldom features on safari itineraries, but it makes for an excellent short excursion from Diani Beach, offering breezy respite from the coastal humidity in a scenic 250km² expanse of rolling grassland and forested slopes. Shimba is best known as the last Kenyan stronghold of the handsome sable antelope, which is easily seen on game drives, and it also hosts healthy populations of giraffe, zebra, warthog, elephant, buffalo and (more elusively) leopard. Set partly within the reserve, Kenya's second-largest coastal forest supports rare cycads, orchids and the

Shimba Hills is the sole Kenyan refuge for the sable antelope. (AZ)

endemic *Diospyros shimbaensis*, along with Angola colobus, blue duiker and suni, and a host of forest-dwelling birds (notably green-headed oriole). On the eastern escarpment, Elephant Lookout offers fabulous views back to Diani, and it's the starting point for a two-hour guided walk to the 21m-high Sheldrick Falls. Visits to Shimba can be arranged at short notice through any beach resort or tour operator at Diani, less than an hour's drive away, or you can visit under your own steam in a 4x4. Do stop for lunch, or better still stay overnight, at Shimba Lodge, a coastal variant of Treetops whose jungle-like setting attracts plentiful wildlife, notably the diurnal red-bellied coast squirrels and nocturnal greater bushbabies that clamber around the balcony.

Mwaluganje Elephant Sanctuary

☏ 040 2104221 ☉ 06.00-18.00

An unfenced northern extension of Shimba Hills, this community sanctuary comprises 36km² of rolling cycad- and baobab-studded hills donated by the 200 Mijikenda families who all get a share of proceeds raised by tourism. Buffalo, leopard, zebra, waterbuck, warthog and sable antelope are all present, but as the name suggests, elephants are the prime attraction, and they are much more likely to be seen here than at Shimba. There's a decent road network, but the most reliable game-viewing site, 9km from the entrance gate, is the Mwaluganje Elephant Camp, a lovely little bush lodge that overlooks a small waterhole favoured by thirsty elephants – day visitors are welcome to visit the camp for drink or meal. A traditional *kaya* ('sacred forest') can be visited on foot by prior arrangement.

Shimoni and Wasini

Only 10km from the Tanzanian border, Shimoni – 'Place of the Hole' – is a low-key fishing village that flourished briefly in the late 19th century, when it served as the first headquarters of the British East Africa Company, but has been pretty quiet ever since. A few relics from Shimoni's heyday survive, notably a derelict district commissioner's residence and a small military

The Coral Garden at Wasini (AZ)

cemetery, but the main attraction is the caves alluded to in its name. Held sacred by the local Digo people, this gloomy labyrinth once served as a holding pen to incarcerate slaves captured in the interior before they were shipped to Zanzibar. Chains and hooks dating to the slaving era are embedded in the walls, and there's a slightly saline well from where the slaves were forced to drink.

Another worthwhile local attraction, divided from Shimoni by a narrow channel, the 5km^2 Wasani Island is named for the Chinese ('Wa-Cini' in Swahili) whose ancient trade link with this part of Kenya is reinforced by the presence of a pillar tomb inset with Ming porcelain. The highlight of Wasini is its so-called 'Coral Garden', a bleakly attractive landscape of partly exposed coral outcrops, sand flats and mangroves that can be explored from a boardwalk managed as a community project by a local women's group. You'll see plenty of hermit crabs and mudskippers here, as well as the odd seabird, and a dusk visit might be rewarded with a sighting of the spectacular coconut crab, the world's largest terrestrial crustacean. Several operators run day trips from Diani to Shimoni, taking a spectacular seafood lunch at Wasini's legendary Charlie Claws Restaurant, so it can get busy between 09.00 and 16.00, but few people stay overnight.

THE ZAMBEZI SAFARI
& TRAVEL CO. LTD

Afrochic
www.elewana.com/afrochic

Small really is beautiful at Afrochic, a ten-bedroom boutique hotel right on the white sands of Diani Beach. Guests are made to feel truly spoilt at this villa-style residence, with meals prepared beachside, in the privacy of your room or in the elegant dining room. The five-star quality and elegant décor will appeal to those ready for some post-safari pampering, whilst a soothing massage will revitalise the most weary of travellers.

Malindi and Watamu

Separated by 15km of beautiful Indian Ocean frontage, Watamu and Malindi rank among the most popular and worthwhile coastal destinations in Kenya, both in themselves and for the wide range of marine and terrestrial excursions on offer. However, the two towns could scarcely be more different in character. Malindi, with a population of 120,000, is a large historic seaside town studded with architectural relicts dating back to before the Portuguese era, plenty of upper mid-range accommodation, a lively

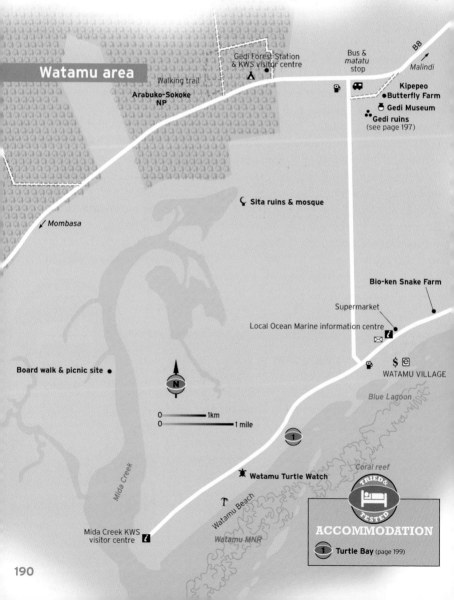

Watamu area

Gedi Forest Station & KWS visitor centre

Walking trail

Arabuko-Sokoke NP

Bus & matatu stop

B8

Malindi

Kipepeo ● Butterfly Farm

☃ Gedi Museum

Gedi ruins (see page 197)

ʕ Sita ruins & mosque

↙ Mombasa

Bio-ken Snake Farm

Supermarket

Local Ocean Marine information centre

Board walk & picnic site ●

N

0 ———— 1km
0 ———— 1 mile

$ ⊟
WATAMU VILLAGE

Blue Lagoon

1

Watamu Turtle Watch

Coral reef

Mida Creek

Mida Creek KWS visitor centre

Watamu Beach

Watamu MNR

TRIED & TESTED

ACCOMMODATION

1 Turtle Bay (page 199)

beachfront restaurant scene, and plenty of other urban distractions. Watamu, by contrast, comes across as a jumped-up fishing village, flanked by a string of exclusive upmarket hotels overlooking Turtle Bay – unquestionably the most scenically memorable beach in Kenya, an idyllic stretch of fine white sand subverted by an offshore archipelago of ragged coral formations that burst from the sea like giant mushrooms. Malindi will appeal more to those who enjoy city settings, while Watamu offers more to nature-lovers, but either resort forms a useful base from which to explore such diverse attractions as the Malindi Marine National Reserve, Gedi Ruins and Arabuko-Sokoke National Park and Sokoke Forest.

History

Little concrete is known about this part of the Kenyan coast prior to the 12th century, when the existence of Malindi was first documented by the Arab geographer Al Idrisi. Malindi has been inhabited more or less continuously ever since Al Idrisi's time, and the area was an important centre of maritime trade throughout the pre-Portuguese era. Indeed, the renowned Chinese explorer Zheng He, sponsored by the Ming government, visited Malindi in 1414, receiving a gracious welcome from the local sultan, who sent a personal envoy back with the fleet to China, along with a live giraffe, a gift that delighted its recipients. By comparison, Watamu is a settlement of little historical significance, but it lies only a few kilometres from the ruined city of Gedi, which flourished in medieval times.

For much of its history, Malindi has been the main trade and military rival of more powerful Mombasa, to which it still plays second fiddle today. It was largely as a result of this rivalry that the Sultan of Malindi offered the warmest of receptions to the Portuguese fleet of Vasco da Gama when it arrived there in 1498, just days after it had been evicted from Mombasa. Soon after, the sultan entered into an enduring alliance of convenience with Portugal, and Malindi formed the main base of Portuguese coastal operations until 1593, when both allies relocated to Mombasa. Malindi was revived as a low-key trade centre with the return of its traditional rulers in the late 17th century, following the Omani capture of Mombasa and effective evacuation of the Portuguese from the coast north of present-day Mozambique.

Malindi and Watamu highlights

Malindi Old Town

Malindi is Kenya's second-largest coastal port, and one of its oldest. However, a succession of destructive fires prior to the 19th century destroyed many of its older buildings, as a consequence of which there are fewer historical landmarks than might be expected. The most significant

Practicalities

Watamu and Malindi lie 105km and 120km north of Mombasa respectively, a drive of roughly 90 minutes on the surfaced B8. There are **flights** to Malindi from Mombasa, Lamu and Nairobi; the airport lies about 3km from the town centre and taxis can transfer you to any beach hotel there or on Watamu. Malindi has the better facilities of the two towns, including several banks with

Accommodation

For full details of tour-operator recommended accommodation, see page 199. Here follows a few further suggestions from the author.

Exclusive
Tana Delta Dunes ⌂ www.tanadelta.org

Upmarket
Blue Bay Club ⌂ www.igrandiviaggi.it
Dream of Africa ⌂ www.planhotel.com
Hemingway's ⌂ www.hemingways.co.ke
Tana River Camp ⌂ www.tanadelta.org

Moderate
Eden Roc Hotel ⌂ www.edenrockenya.com

Islamic monument is a pair of 15th-century pillar tombs standing in front of the seafront Friday Mosque. Relicts of the Portuguese era include a small thatched chapel built in the early 16th century, and the limestone cross erected by the Portuguese navigator Vasco da Gama in 1499 which stands on a windswept coral peninsula about ten-minutes' walk further out of town (see page 7). The British colonial era is represented by the fantastically run-down double-storey district commissioner's residence, erected in 1890 opposite what is now Uhuru Park. The three-storey waterfront 'House of Columns', an Indian trading store built c1890, is now the **National Museum of Malindi** (⌂ www.museums.or.ke ☼ 08.00–18.00); displays include a stuffed coelacanth weighing 77kg and a rare collection of carved Gohu burial totems, while the top-floor Webb Memorial Library includes several rare out-of-print volumes dedicated to coastal history and culture.

ATMs, a few internet cafés, several tour operators and car-rental agencies, an excellent selection of restaurants, and some good shops. Watamu, though smaller, is also very tourist friendly, but there's no ATM, internet facilities are limited to the smarter hotels, and shopping opportunities are few. Any hotel or operator can set up diving and snorkelling excursions, day trips to the likes of Gedi, Arabuko-Sokoke or the Marafa Depression, or overnight safaris into Tsavo East, whose Sala Gate lies 90 minutes' drive west of Malindi.

Malindi Beach Resort ⌁ www.planhotel.com
Tropical Beach Hotel ⌁ www.planhotel.com

Budget
Malindi Cottages ⌁ www.kenyabeach.com/kenya-travel

Eating out

Baby Marrow (homemade pasta & seafood) Vasco da Gama Rd, Malindi ☎ 073 3801238
Da Gama Restaurant (Indian, Italian & seafood dishes) Vasco da Gama Rd, Malindi ☎ 042 31942
I Love Pizza (pizza) Vasco da Gama Rd, Malindi ☎ 042 20672
Tangeri (Italian, seafood & vegetarian) Vasco da Gama Rd, Malindi ☎ 042 20414

Malindi Marine National Reserve

Offering some of the most stellar diving and snorkelling opportunities in East Africa, this is Africa's oldest marine reserve, gazetted in 1979 to protect some 213km² of beaches, offshore reefs and open water, starting at Malindi in the north and running south via Watamu and Turtle Bay to Mida Creek to Malindi via Watamu. The reserve incorporates the Malindi and Watamu marine national parks, and more than 300 species of reef fish have been recorded. For snorkelling, the maze-like coral gardens protected within Turtle Bay are difficult to beat, offering

A turtle in Malindi Marine Reserve (A/D)

the combination of easy access, calm water, good visibility and a kaleidoscopic array of reef fishes. Diving is usually undertaken further out to sea, on the main reefs, where you might also encounter whale sharks and any of four recorded species of marine turtle. Most hotels offer daily snorkelling excursions, with the exact timing depending on tides, and several also have dive schools. Snorkelling trips in private glass-bottomed boats can also be arranged directly with captains in both Malindi and Watamu. Fishing is prohibited in the national park, but the larger hotels can arrange game-fishing trips further out to sea.

Mida Creek

☎ 073 3626573 or 072 3422610 ⏰ sunrise to sunset

Separated from the open sea by the Watamu Peninsula, this large wide creek, renowned for its marine birdlife, was recently developed for tourism by a local community group that erected a 260m stilted boardwalk through the surrounding mangroves to a small hide above the sand flats. Clearly signposted from the main Mombasa road, the creek is an important wintering site for Palaearctic migrants such as the localised crab plover and grey plover, and the checklist of 70 aquatic species also includes dimorphic egret, mangrove kingfisher and greater flamingo, while

Pillar tombs

Though most medieval Swahili architecture is clearly influenced by styles associated with the Islamic places of origin of the Arabs who settled there, there are also several local innovations. The most important of these is the pillar tomb, a narrow grave marker that might stand several metres tall, and which has no counterpart in any other Islamic culture – indeed, some experts think it is an adaptation of the more overtly phallic stelae fields that scatter southern Ethiopia. Pillar tombs have been around since medieval times, and many are inscribed with Islamic dates, including one of the two superb examples to be seen in central Malindi.

(AZ)

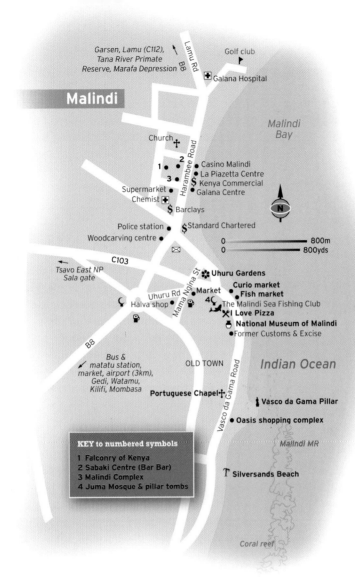

the surrounding coastal scrub hosts the spectacular carmine bee-water and less striking but very rare Sokoke pipit. The quality of birding from the boardwalk depends on tidal factors, so call in advance and talk to one of the knowledgeable guides for advice about timings.

Arabuko-Sokoke National Park

📞 042 3246 🖥 www.kws.org 🕐 06.00–19.00

East Africa's most extensive tract of coastal forest is protected within this 420km² national park, whose eastern boundary follows the main coastal road from Kilifi Creek north to Watamu. The forest might come across as rather low-key by comparison with the celebrated safari destinations that lie further inland, and it receives relatively few visitors, but it is readily accessible from the main road, and unusually pedestrian-friendly. It is also one of Kenya's most important protected areas in terms of global biodiversity, providing a stronghold to six globally threatened bird species (among a checklist of 230), four endemic butterfly species, and globally threatened and near-endemic mammals such as Ader's duiker, Sokoke dog mongoose and the delightful yellow-rumped elephant-shrew. A resident population of 120 elephants is furtive and seldom seen, but you are sure to see their distinctive large pats splattered along the road.

Sokoke scops owl is near-endemic to this part of Kenya. (NB/FLPA)

A network of roads and walking trails runs inland from the various gates to Arabuko-Sokoke. In a vehicle, the 14km motorable track running from Mida Gate to Nyati Viewpoint offers the best compact introduction to the forest's main habitats, passing first through mixed evergreen forest studded with the prehistoric-looking cycad *Encephalartos hildebrandtii*. After 4km (2.5 miles), mixed forest gives way to *Brachystegia* woodland, home to highly sought species such as Sokoke pipit, chestnut-fronted helmet-shrike, little yellow flycatcher and Amani sunbird. Past lily-covered Whistling Duck Pond, which often hosts waterfowl, the track ascends through dense *Cynometra* woodland to Nyati Viewpoint, which offers sweeping views across the canopy to the coastline. Other sites of interest include the Arabuko Swamp, on the park's northern boundary, and – best visited at dusk – the Komani Track, where local guides are usually able to track down the near-endemic Sokoke scops owl, an endangered small owl first described as recently as 1965. Dakacha, a short distance outside the park's northern boundary, is the most reliable site for the endemic Clarke's weaver, arguably the most alluring of the forest's many rare birds.

Gedi ruins

☎ 020 2335801 🖰 www.museums.or.ke 🕐 07.00–18.00

Probably the most popular goal for day trips out of Watamu or Malindi, the ruined city of Gedi, enclosed by the tangled undergrowth and towering canopies of Arabuko-Sokoke, is also the largest and most haunting medieval ruin on the Kenyan coast. It was founded between the 11th and 13th centuries, on what was then an arm of the Sabaki River, possibly in

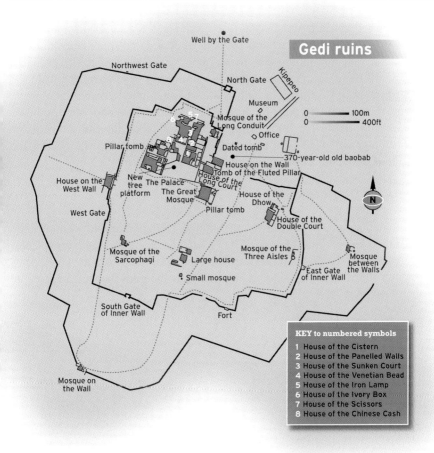

Well by the Gate

Gedi ruins

Northwest Gate

North Gate

Kipepeo

Museum

Mosque of the
Long Conduit

Office

0 ___ 100m
0 ___ 400ft

Pillar tomb

Dated tomb

370-year-old old baobab

House on the Wall

Tomb of the Fluted Pillar

House on the
West Wall

New
tree
platform

The Palace

House of the
Long Court

The Great
Mosque

House of the
Dhow

West Gate

Pillar tomb

House of the
Double Court

N

Mosque of the
Sarcophagi

Large house

Mosque of the
Three Aisles

Mosque
between
the Walls

East Gate
of Inner Wall

Small mosque

South Gate
of Inner Wall

Fort

Mosque on
the Wall

KEY to numbered symbols
1 House of the Cistern
2 House of the Panelled Walls
3 House of the Sunken Court
4 House of the Venetian Bead
5 House of the Iron Lamp
6 House of the Ivory Box
7 House of the Scissors
8 House of the Chinese Cash

the wake of a secession dispute at Malindi 16km to the north. The city grew prosperous on a flourishing maritime trade, extending over 20ha in its medieval peak, and it must have supported at least 2,000 people prior to being abandoned in the 1530s in the aftermath of the Portuguese destruction of Mombasa. And yet its original name, indeed its very existence, goes undocumented in any surviving source – Gedi, or more accurately Gede – dates to a 17th-century reoccupation by Oromo nomads and translates as 'Precious' in allusion to the abundant water held by its network of deep stone wells.

Set aside at least two hours to explore the site properly, starting at the Gedi Museum, where artefacts from as far afield as India, Egypt, Arabia and Spain pay testament to the city's place in the medieval trade network. A clear footpath runs from the museum through the original town centre, which is still dominated by a 900m² Sultan's Palace that was built in the 15th century and housed at least three generations of ruler, all of whom are buried beneath an adjacent pillar tomb (see page 194). There are also eight mosques dotted around the site, while a dated tomb erected in the Islamic year 802 (equivalent to AD1399) helped determine the probable time frame of Gedi's occupation. For a monkey's-eye overview, scale the birdwatching platform placed high in a baobab tree between the mosque and the palace (see page 6). And wildlife enthusiasts shouldn't omit the longer footpath that leads through the shady forest interior to the inner and outer city walls – monkeys are often seen here, and it's a good place to look for forest birds and the yellow-rumped elephant-shrew.

Marafa Depression

🕐 06.00–18.00

Situated about 35km northwest of Malindi, this miniaturised version of the Grand Canyon, also known as Hell's Kitchen, is studded with spectacular demoiselles (eroded sandstone pillars) that stand up to 30m tall. Locals claim that the depression was created when the gods invoked a torrential

The Marafa Depression is also known as Hell's Kitchen. (TM/A)

storm to punish a Giriama tribe so wealthy that its people washed their bodies with milk rather than water. Managed as a low-key community project, the valley is most impressive in the soft early morning light, when the layered columns glow sugary pink, and it can be explored along a 3km footpath from the fenced car park.

Tana River Primate Reserve

📞 046 2035 🖱 www.kws.org ⏱ 06.00-19.00

Remote and underpublicised, this 28km² reserve protects an isolated and ecologically unique stretch of riparian forest flanking the Tana River north of Garsen. It exists primarily to protect the only remaining habitat of two endemic monkey species, the Tana River red colobus and Tana mangabey, whose affinities suggest an ancient link with the forests of the Congo Basin. Both monkeys are listed as critically endangered by the IUCN, with populations of fewer than 1,000 individuals, but they are quite easily seen within the reserve. Other wildlife includes typical northern species such as Grevy's zebra and reticulated giraffe, a small population of the endangered hirola, and more than 250 bird species including Pel's fishing owl, Fischer's turaco, east coast akalat, brown-breasted barbet and the endemic and possibly extinct Tana River cisticola. The reserve is seldom visited, but several operators in Malindi offer organised overnight tours based at the upmarket Tana River Camp.

TRIED & TESTED

rainbow tours

Turtle Bay
🖱 www.turtlebay.co.ke

Incredible value, this all-inclusive resort is only 2½ hours north of Mombasa, on Watumu Beach. Turtle Bay is the only silver eco-rated hotel on the coast. There's a vast choice of activities, from watersports and beach games, to arts and crafts. Tarzan's Tree House and Kids' Fort keep younger children occupied and, for adults seeking some peace, there's a child-free section with pool. An astonishing number of repeat bookings illustrate why this hotel tops our list for families as well as couples.

The Lamu Archipelago

Separated from Malindi by 200km of dusty road, the sleepy Lamu Archipelago – comprising Pate, Manda and Lamu islands, as well as several smaller islets – is the most remote tourist focus on the Kenyan coast, with few of the attributes one would associate with a conventional seaside resort. True, the archipelago is liberally endowed with idyllic beaches, and the offshore reefs offer sublime snorkelling, but for most visitors the islands' main attraction is Lamu town, a UNESCO World Heritage Site whose architectural cohesion, historical continuity and cultural integrity are unmatched by any other Swahili settlement of comparable vintage.

Lamu town is at once an impenetrable anachronism and oddly cosmopolitan in mood, a paradox it has managed to sustain since the late 1960s, when the nearby beaches were transformed into makeshift campsites along the hippy overland trail. Indeed, something of an alternative ethos still permeates this otherwise devoutly Islamic town, from the fruit juice- and pancake-based menus beloved of its many restaurants to the imported cassettes that blare through the whitewashed alleys between mosque calls. And yet Lamu is the only East African town of comparable size where the alleys are still ruled by donkeys, whose plodding supremacy somehow epitomises the soporific, time-warped atmosphere, and is challenged, at last count, by a grand total of three motorised vehicles.

Winding alleyways are part of Lamu's charm. (AZ)

Contrary to any images of cultural austerity conjured up by the phrase 'traditional Islamic settlement', there is something irresistibly easy-going about Lamu, a delicious tropical languor that frequently induces visitors with flexible itineraries to stay on and on, filling the days by arbitrarily wandering the alleys, stopping for the occasional fruit juice or beer, chatting to locals and other travellers, or just lounging on the rooftop of your hotel. But the archipelago offers plenty of opportunities for further exploration, whether that means taking a gentle stroll to the nearest beach, donkey trips to the other side of the island, snorkelling excursions on a local dhow, visiting old Swahili ruins, or the more adventurous crossing to Pate Island.

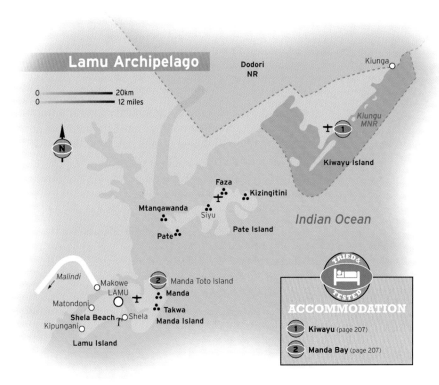

History

The Lamu Archipelago is the site of the oldest-known Islamic structures on the Swahili coast, namely the architecturally undistinguished Shanga Ruins on Pate Island, which date to the 8th century AD and were abandoned a century later. Most of the archipelago's more substantial towns – Pate, Siyu, Faza, the abandoned port of Takwa, and of course Lamu itself – are of considerable antiquity. Pate is probably the oldest extant settlement in Kenya, founded by Omani refugees in the 9th century, and while little is known about the foundation of Lamu town, it certainly functioned as an important trade centre by the 14th century. The ports of Lamu Archipelago have experienced their fair share of economic slumps and revivals over the centuries, but while periods of intense local military rivalry are on record (persistent attacks from Pate, for instance, are thought to have contributed to the demise of Takwa), the islands generally somewhat aloof from the political and military machinations associated with the rivalry between Mombasa and Malindi prior to the Omani occupation of the mid-19th century. Lamu town was an important administrative outpost in the colonial era, but today the entire archipelago feels remote from the Kenyan mainstream.

Practicalities

Lamu - or more accurately Mokowe, on the mainland 30 minutes' ferry ride distant - can technically be reached by road from Malindi, but it's an uncomfortable trip, and occasional outbreaks of banditry provide further dissuasion. There are usually a few **flights** daily from Nairobi, Mombasa and/or Malindi, landing on the airstrip at Manda Island, a short boat transfer away from Lamu town and its many hotels. Once settled in, Lamu town is most easily explored on foot, while regular dhows ply back and forth between the main jetty and nearby Shela Beach (also within walking distance of town). Any hotel, tour operator or tout can arrange dhow trips to neighbouring islands, and there is also an unpredictable daily ferry to Pate. Facilities in Lamu town include many hotels and restaurants, a waterfront KCB bank with an ATM, a few cafés offering (rather slow) internet access, and some good shops. Facilities elsewhere on the archipelago are practically non-existent. Bear in mind that for all its tourist-friendly veneer, Lamu is deeply Islamic and it is advisable to dress modestly away from recognised tourist beaches.

Accommodation

For full details of tour-operator recommended accommodation, see page 207. Here follows a few further suggestions from the author.

Exclusive
Kipungani Explorer ⌖ www.heritage-eastafrica.com

Upmarket
Peponi Hotel ⌖ www.peponi-lamu.com

Moderate
Lamu House ⌖ www.lamuhouse.com

Budget
Yumbe House ⌖ www.yumbehouse.com

Lamu highlights

Lamu town (ss)

Lamu town

Founded in medieval times, Lamu lends itself to casual exploration on foot, and while it is easy to become temporarily disorientated within the labyrinthine alleys, the predictable terrain – sloping gently towards a 2km waterfront – means you're unlikely to remain so for very long. Lamu has changed little in shape in recent centuries, and it undoubtedly ranks as the best-preserved harbour town anywhere on the Swahili coast. Strikingly, where most of its peers are either ruinous, or form quaint traditional quarters within large modern cities, Lamu is flanked neither by industrial works nor by modern suburbia. Instead, it rises in isolation from the coastal scrub, a compact labyrinth of shady, cobbled alleyways and whitewashed buildings that amounts to something far more satisfying than the sum of its individual architectural landmarks.

As might be expected of such a lived-in settlement, Lamu recognises few divisions between residential and business districts. Private homes, hotels, restaurants, mosques and shops jostle alongside each other on the main roads and back alleys, and the strong tourist presence passes unnoticed by the playing children, the old men who sit chatting on the pavement, or the bui-bui draped women that slink silently between residential doorways. Most houses are two or three storeys high, and built to a traditional design, with shady inner courtyards and verandas, elaborately carved wooden doors, and high plastered ceilings supported by poles of mangrove timber. Rooftop verandas are a memorable feature of Lamu, offering an opportunity to catch a sea breeze by day, and often hauntingly beautiful after dark, with palm trees swaying beneath a pristine night sky, and a flow of gossip from the streets below punctuated by the insane braying of donkeys.

Situated along the narrow channel separating Lamu Island from Manda islands, the archipelago's main town could easily be mistaken for a river port, despite the unmistakable saline smell that permeates the waterfront, which was extended seaward by one block as a result of land infill in the mid-19th century. The most important waterfront landmark, the **Lamu Museum** (⌂ www.museums.or.ke ☉ 09.00–18.00), built as a colonial governor's residence in 1891, houses a selection of traditional Swahili musical instruments, including a pair of ancient Siwa horns, alongside displays about the urban evolution of Lamu town and various coastal

Lamu town

Swahili House Museum

Kenyatta Road

Matondoni

Donkey Sanctuary

Harambee Avenue

Silversmiths

Lamu Museum

Catholic church ✝

Ferries to Pate Island

Kenya Commercial $

Lamu Channel

Waterfront

Supermarket

Pwani Mosque ℭ

Immigration office

Main Square

Lamu Fort (Environmental Museum)

Manda Jetty (boats to Manda Island & dhows to Shela Beach)

✉

Market ●

German post office museum

Harambee Avenue

18th-century mosque

Riyadha Mosque, police station

Kenyatta Road

Health centre ✚

N

Lamu bookshop ●

0   100m
0   100yds

Shela Beach

Bus office

cultures. Note that the hefty entrance charge to this museum includes entry to the Swahili House Museum, Lamu Fort and German Post Office Museum, so best to visit all these sites on the same day.

A block inland, Harambee Avenue, once the main waterfront, is now the town's busiest thoroughfare, lined with small shops, boutiques, cafés and restaurants. Also here, stranded from its original waterfront location, Lamu Fort is a double-storey stone structure, built by the Sultan of Oman in the early 19th century, and now used as an environmental museum and community centre. Other important landmarks include the Swahili House Museum, a restored 18th-century house complete with inner courtyard, and the German Post Office established in 1888 to service the nearby German Protectorate at Witu and now a museum. Riyadha Mosque is the most prestigious place of worship in Lamu, built in 1900 by a Yemenite settler called Sharif Habib Salih, and an important pilgrimage site during the Maulidi Festival. Of greater antiquity is the 14th-century pillar tomb that stands behind this mosque, and Pwani Mosque, opposite the fort, which dates to 1370, though nothing of the original building remains.

Shela

The most popular beach on the archipelago, situated about 3km southeast of Lamu town (about 40 minutes' walk, quicker by passenger dhow), this fabulous swathe of soft white sand follows the coast for more than 10km. It's one of the few Kenyan beaches to lack a protective reef, so the sea is relatively cool and

Shela Beach (AZ)

there's even the odd wave – swimming is generally safe, but you might want to check locally if conditions look rough. It's also inadvisable to wander too far out of eyeshot, as occasional muggings are reported, and the lack of shade makes sunblock all but essential. If you can tear yourself away from the beach, the tiny adjoining village of Shela, founded about 400 years ago by refugees from Takwa (see below), boasts a striking Friday Mosque, whose conical whitewashed minaret, built in AD1829, stands 18m tall and has an internal spiral stairwell of 58 steps.

Matondoni

The picturesque fishing village of brick-and-thatch huts lies on the opposite side of Lamu Island to the eponymous town. It comes across as a particularly industrious spot, with people weaving mats and baskets or crushing maize wherever you go, though its main claim to fame is as a dhow-building centre. The best way to visit – easily organised through any hotel – is on the back of a donkey, a trip that takes up to two hours in either direction, depending on how stubborn he or she is. The trip also offers the opportunity to explore the island's interior, which can be mercilessly hot and dry – bring a hat! – and supports a cover of thorny acacias and shadier mango trees. The acacia scrub rattles with birdlife; look out for the dazzling carmine bee-eater.

Manda Island

A popular target for dhow trips out of Lamu town, Manda, the smallest of the archipelago's three main islands, is separated from Lamu by a narrow channel, but the absence of potable water means it is practically uninhabited today. The Swahili trading centre of Takwa formerly stood on the opposite side of the island to Lamu (about 5km from the modern airstrip), only to be abandoned in the early 17th century following a long war with Pate and an increase in the salinity of the water supply.

The **Takwa ruins** (🖰 www.museums.or.ke ☉ 09.00–18.00) can be visited today, and include a striking Friday Mosque with a large pillar tomb rising from its wall – site of a biannual pilgrimage from Shela, which was founded by refugees from Takwa. Dhow trips from Lamu usually combine a visit to Takwa with snorkelling at nearby Manda Toto (literally 'Child of Manda'). This uninhabited coral islet, an important breeding site for marine birds, is also a magnet for masses of colourful reef fish, and is sometimes visited by whale sharks, dolphins and marine turtles.

Manda Island – postcard perfect (MB)

Pate Island

The largest island in the archipelago, Pate is the site of three absorbingly time-warped small towns that make Lamu seem positively urbane by comparison. Getting to the island is easy enough, whether you charter a dhow, or surrender to the combination of tides, winds and whimsy that dictate the schedule of daily water-taxis from Lamu Town, but tourists remain such a rarity that no formal accommodation exists. Faza, the largest of Pate's ancient towns, boasts relatively few antiquities, having been razed in the 16th century by the Portuguese, who settled there briefly. It's best-known building now is the ruined Shala Fatani Mosque, which was built during Faza's 18th-century revival as a Swahili trade centre.

An altogether more bizarre prospect is the town of Pate, which was founded in the 9th century by Omani refugees, peaked under the Nabahani dynasty during the 12th–15th centuries, and enjoyed a second heyday as a prosperous centre of Swahili craftsmanship in the 18th century. The present-day town, with its narrow alleys and towering three-storey stone homesteads, feels like the labyrinthine heart of an old city, when in fact it comprises a mere 100-odd houses surrounded by mangroves, palms and the substantial ruins of its medieval incarnation. Also of great interest is Siyu, which was a renowned centre of Islamic scholarship supporting a population of 20,000 prior to the Omani occupation of 1847, and is still the site of the immaculately preserved Fort Siyu, built in the mid-19th century.

Kiwayu Island

This pencil-shaped island lies beyond Pate and is notable for its idyllic beaches, excellent snorkelling and game fishing, and total sense of isolation. It falls within the Kiunga Marine Reserve, which protects some 60km of coastline and dozens of calcareous reefs and islands north of Lamu. Marine life includes the rare dugong and several species of marine turtle. The facing mainland, protected in the Dodori and Boni national reserves, is home to substantial numbers of elephant.

Aardvark SAFARIS LTD

Kiwayu
www.kiwayu.com

18 thatched bandas sit snugly among the dunes on this glorious sandy shoreline. Rarely visited by anyone other than local fisherman, this is a wonderful place to recharge – each spacious and comfortably furnished cottage has a private veranda, with hammock or day bed, and panoramic views across the lagoon. Menus include fabulous fresh seafood and simple Italian dishes. The bay is perfect for watersports - snorkelling and fishing are great seasonal activities. Mangrove trips in motorised canoes are a fun way to explore.

Aardvark SAFARIS LTD

Manda Bay
www.mandabay.com

This 16-cottage luxurious beach-front lodge is an idyllic spot to relax pre- or post-safari. Pretty thatched rooms are strung along a sandy shore, each with handcrafted furniture and a private veranda. The chef serves some of the best food we've come across on the Lamu Archipelago with fresh fish a real speciality. Activities include fishing, waterskiing, diving and trips on *Utamaduni* – the lodge's beautifully restored traditional dhow. A little more expensive than some in the area, but among the best Kenyan beach properties we know.

9 Central and Northern Safari Circuits

From snow-capped Mount Kenya to the parched Chalbi Desert, the vast swathe of Kenya that runs north from Nairobi towards the Ethiopian border is characterised by climatic extremes. Broadly, the area consists of three main ecological regions: the cool and well-watered central highlands immediately north of Nairobi, the lower-lying and drier badlands that run further north from Samburu and Buffalo Springs national reserves to remote Lake Turkana, and a transitional zone comprising the likes of Meru National Park and the Laikipia Plateau. Some of Kenya's finest game viewing is to be had here. Reserves such as Meru, Laikipia and Samburu-Buffalo Springs possess an altogether more remote and rugged character than their southern counterparts, and host a fascinating array of dry-country wildlife. By contrast, the central highlands are studded with tree hotels designed for observing animal behaviour, and Mount Kenya itself is the country's top hiking destination.

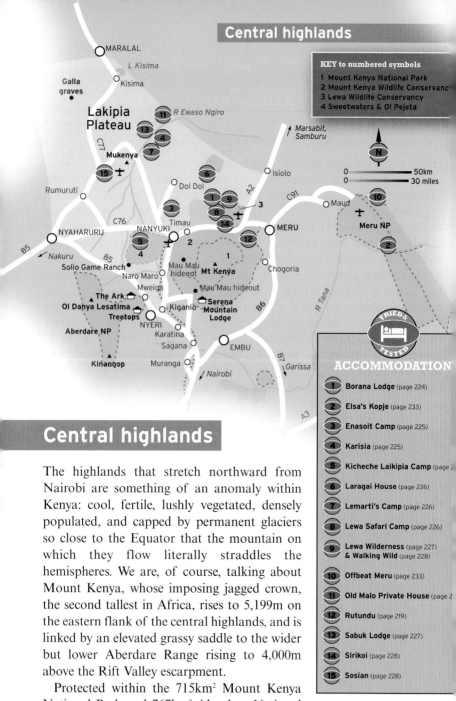

KEY to numbered symbols

1 Mount Kenya National Park
2 Mount Kenya Wildlife Conservancy
3 Lewa Wildlife Conservancy
4 Sweetwaters & Ol Pejeta

ACCOMMODATION

1 Borana Lodge (page 224)
2 Elsa's Kopje (page 233)
3 Enasoit Camp (page 225)
4 Karisia (page 225)
5 Kicheche Laikipia Camp (page)
6 Laragai House (page 226)
7 Lemarti's Camp (page 226)
8 Lewa Safari Camp (page 226)
9 Lewa Wilderness (page 227) & Walking Wild (page 228)
10 Offbeat Meru (page 233)
11 Old Malo Private House (page 2)
12 Rutundu (page 219)
13 Sabuk Lodge (page 227)
14 Sirikoi (page 228)
15 Sosian (page 228)

Central highlands

The highlands that stretch northward from Nairobi are something of an anomaly within Kenya: cool, fertile, lushly vegetated, densely populated, and capped by permanent glaciers so close to the Equator that the mountain on which they flow literally straddles the hemispheres. We are, of course, talking about Mount Kenya, whose imposing jagged crown, the second tallest in Africa, rises to 5,199m on the eastern flank of the central highlands, and is linked by an elevated grassy saddle to the wider but lower Aberdare Range rising to 4,000m above the Rift Valley escarpment.

Protected within the 715km² Mount Kenya National Park and 767km² Aberdare National Park, the two great massifs of the central highlands share many ecological affinities, supporting most of Kenya's extant Afro-montane forest and Afro-alpine moorland. And yet they also represent extremes of geological antiquity. Mount Kenya, an extinct volcano, erupted into existence some three million years ago, long after our earliest bipedal ancestors strode across the Rift Valley floor. The contorted folds of the Aberdares, by contrast, are among the most ancient in East Africa, dating to before the Age of Dinosaurs.

The montane forests of the central highlands harbour an outstandingly varied fauna, including forest specialists such as Sykes monkey, black and white colobus, Harvey's red duiker, bushbuck, and isolated easterly populations of the scarce bongo antelope and giant forest hog. More surprising, perhaps, is that all of the Big Five still survive here in significant numbers, with elephant and buffalo being especially numerous. Set at a higher altitude than the forest, generally above the 3,000m contour, the Afro-alpine zone is an otherworldly landscape of open moorland studded with bizarre giant forms of heather, lobelia and groundsel, accessible only to dedicated hikers.

During the colonial era, the combination of an agreeable climate, arable soils and proximity to Nairobi ensured that the central highlands were heavily settled by European farmers. In the 1930s, it lay at the heart of the notorious 'Happy Valley' scene, and two decades later its vast forests provided refuge to the Mau-Mau in their fight for independence. Today, the region remains the breadbasket of Kenya, though the sprawling agricultural estates of colonial times have mostly been carved up into *shambas* (subsistence smallholdings) where Kikuyu and other Bantu-speaking agriculturists tend their papayas, bananas, coffee and other tropical crops.

Endemic giant groundsel and lobelias on the Mackinder route, Mt Kenya National Park (IB/FLPA)

Practicalities

All **road safaris** to northern reserves such as Samburu-Buffalo Springs or Meru National Park will pass through the central highlands, whether that's *en route* from Nairobi (two to three hours' drive from most landmarks in the region) or the Rift Valley town of Nakuru (less than an hour's drive from Nyahururu). The main road through the region, encircling Mount Kenya, comprises the A2 through Naro Moru and Nanyuki on the west side of the mountain, and the eastern B6 via Meru, Chogoria and Embu. Branching northwest from the southern base of the ring road, flanked by the Aberdares to the west, is the B5 through Nyeri and Nyahururu. All these roads are surfaced and in good condition, but winding stretches should be taken carefully, if only to allow for dangerously fast local traffic.

The central highlands is a popular goal for dedicated hikers who want to climb Mount Kenya, a three to seven-day trip discussed further in the box on page 214. For more sedentary visitors, the main attraction is the trio of

Accommodation

For full details of tour-operator recommended accommodation, see page 219. Here follows a few further suggestions from the author.

Exclusive
Mount Kenya Safari Club ⌐Ů www.fairmont.com

Upmarket
Serena Mountain Lodge ⌐Ů www.serenahotels.com

Central highlands highlights

Aberdare, Treetops and The Ark

Although Aberdare National Park can be explored independently in a sturdy 4x4, very few tours actually do this, preferring instead to stay at one of the two legendary tree hotels on its forested slopes, namely Treetops and The Ark. These are effectively game lodges that double as hides: stilted timber-based monoliths that span several stories and are oriented to maximise the viewing possibilities over a waterhole, allowing tourists weary of bumping around the dusty savanna reserves to put up their legs and wait for the animals to come to them. In both cases, the tree hotels are run out of base hotels outside the park, and all overnight visitors are tree hotels on the forested slopes of the Aberdares or Mount Kenya, which offer great nocturnal game viewing. Overall, however, few safaris linger long in the highlands, either shooting through in a day *en route* to a more northerly destination, or including a one-night stop at one of the tree hotels. Worthwhile stops for those in transit include Thomson's Falls on the outskirts of Nyahururu, the Outspan Hotel in Nyeri, the Mount Kenya Wildlife Conservancy near Nanyuki, the wildlife-packed Solio Game Ranch and any of several places where the road crosses the Equator.

The region is scattered with medium to large towns such as Nyeri, Nanyuki, Nyahururu, Meru and Embu. All feel a touch anonymous, but they are also pleasant and easy-going places, and well equipped in terms of tourist facilities, including internet cafés, banks with ATMs, supermarkets, filling stations and adequate restaurants and hotels. Few tourists stay overnight in any of these towns, but many will stop there to do last-minute shopping, change money or check email before heading out to one of the more remote game reserves covered later in the chapter.

The Ark ⌁ www.fairmont.com
The Outspan ⌁ www.aberdaresafarihotels.com
Treetops ⌁ www.aberdaresafarihotels.com

Moderate
Naro Moru River Lodge ⌁ www.alliancehotels.com
Thomson's Falls Lodge ⌁ www.laikipia.org

Budget
Mount Kenya Youth Hostel ⌁ www.flechser.de/contact/mtkenyahostel.htm

bussed there as one group in the late afternoon, returning to the base hotel first thing in the morning.

One of East Africa's most celebrated hotels, **Treetops** (for contacts, see above) started life in 1934, as a basic tree-house construction overlooking a waterhole enclosed by forest. It shot to instant fame when it hosted the young Princess Elizabeth on the fateful night of 5 February 1952, during which King George VI died, and the princess, unbeknown to herself or to her game-viewing companions, became the uncrowned Queen of England. The hotel has expanded greatly since then, but it retains an Edwardian smoking-room ambience with its wood-panelled walls covered in memorabilia of various royal and presidential visits. Sadly, however, the

The Ark tree hotel (AZ)

forest that once surrounded the lodge has not fared so well, and while the likes of elephant and black rhino still visit Treetops most nights, the setting is now far too open to attract forest specialists such as giant forest hog, Sykes monkey and black-and-white colobus.

A more modern construction built higher on the slopes of the Aberdares, **The Ark** (for contacts, see page 213) may lack the musty period ambience and prestigious royal associations that make Treetops a real 'one of a kind', but this is amply compensated for by the superior game viewing. Most of the so-called Big Five will be seen on any given night,

Climbing Mount Kenya

As Africa's second-highest mountain, Mount Kenya will never attract a level of tourist interest comparable to the continental summit of Kilimanjaro. Furthermore, its tallest peak, Batian, is only accessible to experienced climbers with specialist equipment, leaving the 4,985m-high Lenana as the highest summit accessible to ordinary hikers. However, if conquering peaks is not your primary concern, then hiking on Mount Kenya offers similar exposure to the full spectrum of Afro-montane vegetation and wildlife, but with the advantages of being less crowded than the more popular routes up Kilimanjaro, significantly less expensive, less likely to induce severe altitude-related illness, and less often treated as a single-minded exercise centred upon reaching the summit.

The climb to Lenana is an extended uphill slog that requires no climbing experience, but it should not be undertaken lightly. A reasonable degree of fitness and stamina is a prerequisite, as is an experienced local guide and adequate gear to protect against the wet weather and sub-zero temperatures that might induce hypothermia, occasional blinding blizzards, and the potentially lethal effects of a rapid ascent to high altitude. For this reason, its strongly advised to arrange hikes with a reputable operator that has specialist knowledge of the mountain and employs experienced guides and porters, and to spend at least three nights on the mountain before ascending Lenana. If time permits, a week will allow you a full day to explore each of the forest and moorland zones from a base, and it will minimise the effects of altitude.

and occasionally it attracts the full house. Other secretive nocturnal creatures such as genet and white-tailed mongoose are regular, as are various forest monkeys and the likes of giant forest hog and Harvey's red duiker, but it no longer attracts the endangered mountain bongo with any regularity. The elevated wooden platform that links the lodge to the parking area provides a good vantage point for seeing forest and highland birds such as rufous-chested sparrowhawk, scaly francolin, Hartlaub's turaco, Doherty's bush-shrike, Hunter's cisticola, thick-billed seedeater, yellow mountain warbler, golden-winged sunbird and mountain greenbul.

Trekkers in fen landscape, Mt Kenya National Park (IB/FLPA)

Several ascent routes can be taken. The easiest and most popular, as pioneered by John Gregory and Sir Halford Mackinder in the 1890s, is the Naro Moru Route up the west side of the mountain. This follows the Naro Moru River uphill from the eponymous town to its glacial source, and can be completed as a three-day round trip using the Meteorological Station (3,050m) as a starting point, but an extra day reduces the risk of altitude-related illness. Almost as popular and the most beautiful is the Chogoria Route, which starts at the town of the same name on the eastern side of the mountain, and requires a minimum of four to five days. Longer still, the little-used Sirimon Route, a beautiful and relatively gradual ascent from the northwest, is recommended for those with a strong interest in Afro-alpine flora and wildlife. It is worth talking through these options with an experienced operator before making any decision.

Serena Mountain Lodge

The only hotel set in the forest zone of Mount Kenya, immediately outside the national park boundary, Mountain Lodge is a similar set-up to the

Game viewing from the balcony of Serena Mountain Lodge (AZ)

tree hotels of the Aberdares, overlooking a swampy pool encircled by lush gallery forest and capped by the ragged glacial peaks of Africa's second-highest mountain. Though less well known than its Aberdare counterparts, it is vastly superior when it comes to game viewing; indeed, it is difficult to think of a comparably upmarket option anywhere that offers such an easy introduction to the forest fauna of East Africa. Sykes and colobus monkeys are abundant, and the forest birding is superb, with manically braying hornbills and the lustrous Hartlaub's turaco being especially conspicuous. Every so often, the waterbuck and buffalo that maintain a constant presence in the glade scatter to accommodate an elephant herd as it emerges from a forest path. And when darkness descends, invoking a white noise of insect chatter punctuated by the banshee wailing of tree hyraxes, the pool attracts a remarkably diverse traffic, with giant forest hog, bushpig, genet, white-tailed mongoose and black rhino coming past most nights, and leopard or lion pitching up occasionally. Rounding off the forest experience are excellent morning bird walks, led by a competent local guide, and afternoon forest walks, which focus on insects, small animals, and traditional uses of plants. Another plus of this lodge is that it doesn't operate as an annex of another hotel, so you can come and go as you please, making for a less institutionalised experience.

Naro Moru

The starting point of the most popular hiking route on Mount Kenya, this small market town is also a useful base for birdwatchers and other wildlife enthusiasts who want to explore the Afro-montane forests of the western slopes. More overgrown village than town, it is named after the Naro Moru River, a chilly tributary of the Ewaso Nyiro that rises in the glacial peaks of Mount Kenya. The main tourist focus is the Naro Moru River Lodge, which lies in a lovely wooded riverside garden, and has long been a popular hiking base. For forest wildlife, you need to drive about 10km out of town towards the Naro Moru Entrance Gate, past the Mount Kenya Youth Hostel, from where you can walk freely along the road through the extensive forest bordering the national park. Sykes and colobus monkey are common here, as are buffalo and bushbuck, and you may well see trace of elephant activity. The birdlife is tremendous; there's no better place to seek out the likes of green ibis, bar-tailed trogon, white-headed wood-hoopoe, Waller's chestnut-winged starling and various montane forest warblers and robins.

Nyeri

Situated 135km from Nairobi, Nyeri, the energetic administrative capital of Central Province, is the eighth-largest town in Kenya, supporting a population of 100,000. It is an agreeable place, with a compact commercial centre surrounded by leafy suburbs and flourishing Kikuyu smallholdings. It is also the birthplace of several prominent Kenyans, including President Mwai Kibaki, marathon runner Catherine Ndereba and Nobel laureate Professor Wangari Maathai, who established the admirable Green Belt Movement. The town's most celebrated former resident, however, is Lord Robert Baden-Powell, founder of the international Boy Scout movement, who settled in Nyeri in 1939 and died there two years later. Baden-Powell is buried in St Peter's Anglican Cemetery, facing Mount Kenya, alongside his wife Olave, and their joint grave is now a national monument.

Kikuyu man in traditional regalia, Nyeri (AZ)

The main tourist focus in Nyeri, about 1km from the town centre, is the **Outspan Hotel** (for contacts, see page 213), which dates to 1932. Best known as the base hotel for visits to Treetops, the Outspan is an attractive set-up in its own right, set in leafy landscape gardens offering views towards Mount Kenya. Situated in the hotel grounds, Baden-Powell's former cottage Paxtu is now a small museum, and there is an excellent Kikuyu cultural group that puts on daily performances. A footpath leads from the hotel down to the Chania River, whose forested banks are inhabited by Sykes and colobus monkeys, and dozens of highland bird species.

Nyahururu

Situated 60km northwest of Nyeri, Nyahururu is Kenya's highest town, perched at an altitude of 2,360m on the edge of the Laikipia Plateau, a fresh coniferous setting that's difficult to square with a location practically dead on the Equator. The town itself offers nothing to inspire adjectival outpourings, but it does see quite a bit of passing tourist traffic thanks to its pivotal location along the main road between Lake Nakuru National Park and the central highlands. And if you do pass this way, it's emphatically worth stopping at Thomson's Falls, about 2km out of town along the Nyeri road (see page 10). Named after Joseph Thomson, who stopped there in 1883, this pretty waterfall on the Ewaso Nyiro River is the third highest in Kenya, plummeting 75m over a volcanic ledge in a single drop. The forested gorge below the falls, reached by a slippery footpath from the gardens of the colonial-era Thomson's Falls Lodge, holds black and white colobus monkeys and a varied selection of birds. More birds and a few hippo can be seen at a papyrus-fringed pool 2km upstream; the staff at the lodge can direct you.

Mount Kenya Wildlife Conservancy

☎ 062 32406 📠 www.animalorphanagekenya.com
🕐 10.00–17.00

Established in 1964 in the grounds of the prestigious Mount Kenya Safari Club, this orphanage – which welcomes day visitors – lies on the lower slopes of Mount Kenya about 8km from Nanyuki town. It is involved in several important conservation projects, none more exciting than the Bongo Species Survival Plan, which is currently rehabilitating a herd of 20 captive-born mountain bongos for release into the forests of Mount Kenya, where it has not been recorded in the wild since 1994. The mountain bongo is a beautifully marked antelope, bulkier than the more widespread lowland bongo of West Africa. It is now effectively endemic to Kenya, where fewer than 200 individuals roam freely in Aberdare National Park and the Mau Escarpment, so the re-establishment of a wild population

The endangered mountain bongo (AZ)

on Mount Kenya would be welcome indeed. The sanctuary harbours other mammal species associated with Mount Kenya, including colobus monkeys and eland, and it has bred and intends eventually to release a herd of rare 'white zebras' from a pair captured on the mountain in 1971.

Solio Game Ranch

📞 020 240157 ☀ 06.00-18.00

Running eastward from the Nyahururu road about 35km north of Nyeri, this 70km² fenced sanctuary lies on the saddle dividing Mount Kenya from the Aberdares, making it far more accessible to day visitors than similar reserves on the Laikipia Plateau. Part of the Solio Cattle Ranch, the sanctuary was founded in 1970 as a breeding centre for rhinos, and it also protects substantial numbers of plains zebra, buffalo,

Waterbuck (YM & SE/FLPA)

giraffe, eland, Beisa oryx, waterbuck and impala, all of which are likely to be seen whether you self-drive or take a guided tour. Lion, cheetah, leopard and spotted hyena are resident or regular visitors. But Solio's *raison d'être* remains a rhino breeding programme that has met with remarkable success over the past 40 years. Starting with a combined introduced population of 39 rhinos, the ranch now hosts at least 50 black rhino and 85 white rhino, and another 100 individuals have been translocated from here to Lake Nakuru, Tsavo West and Aberdare national parks, along with various other locations in Laikipia.

LOWIS & LEAKEY
Privately guided safaris

Rutundu

📖 www.rutundu.com

These rustic log cabins sleep eight and are located on the slopes of Mount Kenya, at around 10,000ft. You will certainly find diversity of landscape and experience here - this is a magical wonderland of giant lobelias, scenecios and heather bushes that grow 20ft high. Find here a vastly different side of Africa. The cabins overlook Lake Rutundu which is stocked with trout; keen fisherman might take on the hearty hike to Lake Alice for big rainbow trout. No crowds here.

TRIED & TESTED

Laikipia Plateau

One of East Africa's finest and most exclusive wildlife destinations, the Laikipia Plateau is Kenya's second-largest conservancy after Tsavo, comprising a patchwork of several dozen private and community-owned sanctuaries that extend over a total of 9,500km². Ecologically transitional to the central highlands and northern deserts, this medium-altitude plateau extends northward from Mount Kenya and the Aberdares along the eastern Rift Valley escarpment, an area of flat plains, basaltic outcrops and forested slopes incised by the Ewaso Nyiro and Ewaso Narok rivers, both of which flow through spectacular gorges. The area as a whole is overseen by the Laikipia Wildlife Foundation (LWF; see below for details), which was founded in 1992 as a non-profit organisation whose membership includes all private stakeholders in the region, as well as community groups representing tribes as diverse as the Maasai, Kikuyu, Samburu and Pokot.

Although most of the plateau was given over to livestock during the

Practicalities

Private lodges in Laikipia mostly cater to the top end of the safari market, and almost all of them **fly-in visitors** as part of an all-inclusive package that covers transportation, meals, activities and – in some cases – drinks. Coming from Nairobi, the normal procedure would be to catch a scheduled flight from Wilson Airport to Nanyuki Airport, then to pick up a light aircraft charter to your specific lodge. Coming from somewhere closer, it would usually make greater sense to drive to Nanyuki Airport to pick up a charter flight. It is also possible to **drive** all the way through to your lodge, though in most cases that means a long dusty ride on bumpy and poorly signposted roads, the main exceptions being Sweetwaters and Ol Pejeta, only 25km from Nanyuki town along the C76.

Accommodation

For full details of tour-operator recommended accommodation, see page 224. Here follows a few further suggestions from the author.

Exclusive
Kioja Starbeds ᛙ www.loisaba.com
Loisaba Camp ᛙ www.loisaba.com

The Ewaso Nyiro River incises the Laikipia Plateau. (AZ)

colonial era, it still boasts Kenya's highest level of large mammal biodiversity, as a result of its transitional location. Wildlife viewing can be exceptional. An estimated 6,000 elephant roam the plateau and its environs, along with dry-country specials such as reticulated giraffe, greater and lesser kudu, gerenuk and Beisa oryx, and substantial numbers

Nanyuki Airport stands on the west side of the Mount Kenya ring road, halfway between the towns of Naro Moru and Nanyuki, and a short drive from any of the tree hotels of the Aberdares or Meru. There are good facilities in Nanyuki town, including banks, ATMs, internet cafés, lodges and restaurants. The airport has a great little coffee shop and is the site of the LWF headquarters and information centre. Lodges in Laikipia are all very remote, and while some have satellite internet or phone access, it's easiest to plan around being incommunicado for the duration of your stay there. Links to all lodges, camps, campsites and adventure safari operators based on Laikipia can be found on the superb **Laikipia Wildlife Foundation** website (✆ www.laikipia.org).

Mukutan Retreat ✆ www.gallmankenya.com
Ol Pejeta Ranch House ✆ www.serenahotels.com
Serena Sweetwaters Tented Camp ✆ www.serenahotels.com
Tassia ✆ www.tassiasafaris.com
The Sanctuary at Ol Lentille ✆ www.ol-lentille.com

Moderate
Maralal Safari Lodge ✆ www.angelfire.com/jazz/maralal/

of lion, leopard and cheetah. Laikipia is an important stronghold for several rarities. It provides sanctuary to 70% of the global Grevy's zebra population, more than half of the country's black rhinos, and the northern hemisphere's last remaining viable African wild dog population. In addition, Sweetwaters is home to a captive population of the common chimpanzee, the only place where this endangered ape – which doesn't occur naturally in Kenya, but does in neighbouring Uganda and Tanzania – can be seen in the country.

Horseback safaris are a popular feature of several Laikipia lodges. (BL)

Several of Kenya's most exclusive private reserves and lodges lie on the Laikipia Plateau, including Ol Pejeta, Sweetwaters, Lewa (page 226) and Sabuk (page 227). From a tourist perspective, every ranch is effectively managed as an exclusive and self-contained entity, and the experience offered by most is strikingly different from any other Kenyan reserve, but closer to the famous private game reserves bordering South Africa's Kruger Park. Game drives are almost invariably run by the reserve or lodge management using skilled driver-guides with strong local knowledge. Also on offer is a variety of activities that are generally forbidden in official reserves, such as guided walks and horseback excursions, while spotlighted night drives come with an excellent chance of seeing nocturnal creatures such as leopard, genet, aardvark and bushbaby.

Laikipia Plateau highlights

Ol Pejeta and Sweetwaters
☎ 062 32408 ⌨ www.olpejetaconservancy.org ⏰ 06.00–18.00 for day visits

An important not-for-profit wildlife conservancy, the former ranch of Ol Pejeta protects a 365km² area of semi-arid grassland and acacia woodland flanking the upper reaches of the Ewaso Nyiro River. The most accessible of the Laikipia conservancies, situated only 25km from Nanyuki, it is also the only one open to day visitors, though it is more usual to stay over at one of the property's lodges for two to three nights. Ol Pejeta ranks as the largest black rhino sanctuary in East Africa, with more than 80 black and at least ten white rhino on the property. Ol Pejeta also recently welcomed four of the last eight northern white rhinos left in the world, in a last attempt to save the

A resident at Sweetwaters Chimpanzee Sanctuary (AZ)

sub-species from extinction. Other wildlife includes elephant, buffalo, lion, leopard, cheetah, reticulated giraffe, Jackson's hartebeest, Beisa oryx, gerenuk and 500-plus bird species. In addition to guided drives and walks, activities include lion tracking with researchers and visits to various traditional villages. A very popular activity is the boat trip along the Ewaso Nyiro River to Sweetwaters Chimpanzee Sanctuary, established in 1993 to protect orphans formerly housed at the Jane Goodall Institute in Burundi, and now home to more than 40 chimpanzees, split across two communities, which live in the riparian forest running along either side of the river.

Lewa Wildlife Conservancy
☏ 064 31405 🖰 www.lewa.org
A former cattle ranch reconstituted as a non-profit-making wildlife sanctuary in 1983, this is one of the oldest reserves in Laikipia, and the most accessible by car, situated only 7km along a dirt track signposted from the main road between Nanyuki and Isiolo some 4km north of the junction to Meru. Extending over 263km², Lewa is a crucial stronghold for the endangered Grevy's zebra, supporting approximately 350 individuals, the largest single population in the world. It is also home to more than 65 black and more than 45 white rhino, and an easily seen population of the localised sitatunga antelope, which was translocated from Saiwa Swamp in the 1980s. Specialities aside, Lewa offers good general game viewing, with up to 300 elephant regularly present, along with lion, leopard, spotted hyena, cheetah and a partially resident pack of African wild dogs. Within the reserve is an archaeological site where an abundance of 800,000-year-old hand-axes and other tools made from volcanic rocks has been unearthed. Proceeds all go towards wildlife conservation or local community projects.

Northern Laikipia
The remote and pristine northern sector of the Laikipia Plateau supports several community and private conservancies fronting the spectacular Ewaso Nyiro Gorge. The bush here is thicker and scrubbier than in southern Laikipia, and lodges offer more walking safaris than motorised game viewing, making it an ideal bush retreat at the end of a longer safari. All the Big Five are present, so there is a very real possibility of running into buffalo, elephant or lion on foot, but densities are lower than in other reserves and guides tend to focus more on small mammals and the exceptional birdlife. It is probably the most reliable place in Kenya for the majestic greater kudu.

Samburu women in colourful traditional dress (EL)

Maralal

Perched at an altitude of 1,965m on the northern edge of the Laikipia Plateau, Maralal is the informal capital of the Samburu people and a popular springboard for expeditions to the eastern shore of Lake Turkana. A pleasant and interesting town, it bridges two very different worlds, and impressions of it depend greatly on which you are leaving behind. Coming from Nairobi or the central highlands, Maralal comes across as astonishingly traditional, with an overwhelmingly Samburu character. Yet after a few days in the remote wilds of Turkana, this small town feels like a return to civilisation, and you're more likely to be struck by its built-up nature, cosmopolitan mood and good amenities. Maralal Wildlife Sanctuary, 3km out of town, is home to elephant, plains zebra, eland, impala, olive baboon, spotted hyena and leopard, all of which might be seen at the floodlit waterhole overlooked by Maralal Safari Lodge. Jomo Kenyatta House is a tin-roofed bungalow where its namesake, the future president of Kenya, was detained by the colonial authorities in 1961. The Maralal Camel Derby, held annually over the second weekend in August, is popular with both residents and foreign visitors.

TRIED & TESTED

LOWIS & LEAKEY
Privately guided safari

Borana Lodge
www.borana.co.ke

Located on Borana Ranch, the setting is spectacular - the eight luxurious cottages stretch along the curve of a hill overlooking a valley. We love the flexibility - days here are

arranged around what guests wish to do. Itineraries can include everything from game drives (they offer both night and day game drives) to horseback rides (the stables cater to different levels of experience). The walking is fabulous too, and their special relationship with the local community makes any visit extra special.

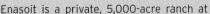

Enasoit Camp
www.enasoit.com

Enasoit is a private, 5,000-acre ranch at
the foot of the Lolldaiga Hills which can be booked on an
exclusive basis. The six rooms have private sitting rooms (with fireplaces)
overlooking the waterhole which is frequented by
myriad animals and birdlife. Quirky and charming,
the greatest appeal here is the wildlife – game
wanders right in front of the tents during the day
and at night there are spotlights overlooking the
saltlick. There is walking, game drives, horseriding,
picnics and a fantastic pool.

Karisia
www.karisia.com

Kerry Glen, James Christian and their team of local guides lead
guests through some of Kenya's most beautiful terrain on superb walking
safaris. Accommodation varies from large walk-in to
light mountain tents depending on the type of trip, and
guests are very comfortably looked after. Camels carry
the equipment but there's always the chance of a ride
for weary legs. The pace is gentle, with safaris
designed to suit different interests – hard to beat for
exploring the Kenyan bush up close.

Kicheche Laikipia Camp
www.kicheche.com

With towering Mount Kenya as a backdrop, this small lodge is
located in a secluded location in the Ol Pejeta Conservancy overlooking a
waterhole. The camp accommodates just 12 guests in
six spacious, L-shaped tents with en-suite facilities
and private verandas. We like that the camp offers
flexible game-viewing excursions including walks and
game drives, and the great hosting by professional
guide Andy Webb and the inimitable Mrs Webb. Arrive
as a guest, leave as a friend.

Laragai House

www.borana.co.ke/laragai-house.html

This private house was built as an escape from the rest of the world. Set on the edge of an escarpment, Laragai enjoys huge vistas. This is

a sumptuous home away from home and an ideal spot to spend time with family and friends in privacy and comfort. There is a private airstrip nearby, helicopter access, tennis court and swimming pool. Built on Borana Ranch you can horseback ride and go on incredible walks and game drives.

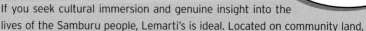

Lemarti's Camp

www.lemartiscamp.com

If you seek cultural immersion and genuine insight into the lives of the Samburu people, Lemarti's is ideal. Located on community land,

this tiny five-tent camp is one of Kenya's most stylish hideaways. Anna Trzebinski and her husband Lemarti Loyapan designed the camp around a cluster of ancient fig trees on the edge of the Ewaso Nyiro River. Days are spent lounging by the river, exploring the area, visiting local Samburu homesteads, and listening to stories from Lemarti and friends.

Lewa Safari Camp

www.lewasafaricamp.com

Set in the Lewa Conservancy, this is one of our regular picks for a great all-round safari experience. 12 comfortable tents, excellent

guiding, spectacular scenery and the chance to see the Big Five – it pretty much ticks all the boxes. Varied activities (including game drives and walks, night drives, horse/camel rides, bush picnics and sundowners) make Lewa ideal even for younger travellers. Relax in the sitting room and eat in a large, thatched dining room or alfresco by the pool.

Lewa Wilderness

🖰 www.lewawilderness.com

Created around one of the original ranch houses owned by the Craig family, Lewa Wilderness usually accommodates 18 guests in five hill rooms (excellent views) and four garden rooms, although two further rooms are available for groups of up to 22. Each spacious room is comfortably furnished and has en-suite facilities. Lewa is a superb conservancy and the great wildlife viewing is enhanced by the range of activities available – walks, camel and horseriding, day and night game drives.

Ol Malo Private House

🖰 www.olmalo.com/ol_house.php

In a private game sanctuary on the Ewaso Nyiro River, Ol Malo is owned and built by the Francombes. It can be booked exclusively with staff, private vehicles and guides all part of the package. Game drives, horse and camel treks and walking are all available. The six rooms are stylishly decorated – the house comfortably sleeps 12. The wildlife is wonderful, and the Francombes' special relationship with the local Samburu community offers an incredible opportunity to observe their colourful culture.

Sabuk Lodge

🖰 www.sabuklodge.com

Sahara meets safari – Sabuk offers a very different Kenya. Magical moments abound – swim the Ewaso Nyiro River or head out on a guided camel safari. Thanks to its setting on private land, Sabuk isn't limited in its range of activities so you're as likely to step out on foot as by vehicle. Perched high above the river, eight guest cottages are individually styled and open fronted, just like sleeping under the stars. Request a night or two fly camping for the ultimate sleep out.

Sirikoi
www.sirikoi.com

Attention to detail and luxurious home comforts are the keynotes here. With free-range chickens and home-grown organic vegetables, Sue and Willie Roberts have created an oasis

of peace overlooking a popular elephant waterhole within the Lewa Conservancy. Accommodation ranges from luxury tented rooms with veranda, living area and elegant bathroom, to an exclusive two-bedroom cottage with its own vehicle. The owners are old safari hands whose experiences ensure many a fascinating story around the campfire. Hosting is top class.

Sosian
www.sosian.com

If anywhere epitomises what's best about a Kenya safari it has to be Sosian with its fantastic hosts, excellent guiding and winning blend of

luxury and traditional safari. Four cottages are set around the beautifully restored African ranch house. Families love the huge selection of activities including horseriding, fishing and archery as well as the pool and tennis court. Honeymooners will be spoilt rotten and the walking safaris are first rate – the best option is the three-night mobile camping affair.

Walking Wild
www.lewawilderness.com

A superb wilderness experience, this traditional walking safari is hosted by one of Lewa Wilderness's premier guides, Lipan Kitonga. Using

simple lightweight tents, these camel-supported trails get you back to nature: choose between shorter three-day safaris (usually spent on Lewa itself), or longer trips (taking in the drier rangelands where meeting local people is as much part of the experience as the wildlife and wilderness). We love the simplicity and the chance to really interact with your surroundings.

Meru National Park

📞 071 3216651 🖰 www.kws.org 🕐 06.00-19.00

This 870km² national park ranked among Kenya's busiest safari destinations in the early 1980s, when its prodigious wildlife and association with the conservationists Joy and George Adamson (see box, page 232) attracted up to 40,000 visitors annually. As with Tsavo, however, Meru was to become a major battleground in the poaching war of the late 1980s, and it practically closed down in 1989 following the fatal shooting of George Adamson outside its borders, and several similar but less publicised incidents. Today, poaching is no longer an issue, wildlife numbers are significantly recovered from their late 1980s nadir, and a few small and exclusive lodges service the park. Nevertheless, Meru has to rank as one of Africa's best-kept wildlife secrets, barely grazing the consciousness of the package safari industry, yet rewarding its few visitors with decent and sometimes exceptional game viewing in a refreshingly untrammelled atmosphere.

Meru highlights

Ecologically transitional to the moist central highlands and arid northern plains, Meru National Park forms the core of a more extensive ecosystem comprising four other national parks and reserves. It receives a relatively high precipitation, since it falls within the eastern rain shadow of Mount Kenya and the Nyambeni Hills, and is also run through by a series of 13 perennial streams that rise in the hills and empty into the muddy Tana River – Kenya's largest waterway – as it runs along the park's southern boundary. Meru consists mainly of open grassland, broken by thick stands of combretum and acacia woodland, but its singular character is perhaps more attributable to the corridors of riparian woodland and tall doum palms that follow its many waterways.

It could be argued that Meru's greatest asset is its uncrowded wilderness atmosphere, which ensures that animal sightings retain an aura of exclusivity rare in more popular reserves. Wildlife, though quite plentiful, is shyer than in busier reserves, and the tall grass and dense thickets aren't especially conducive to spotting game. Nevertheless, the Big Five are all present and correct: large herds of buffalo can be taken for granted, and you'd be unlucky not to come across elephant over the course of an overnight stay, but lion and leopard are less easy to find (as are cheetah and spotted hyena). The endangered black rhino, the park's biggest victim of commercial poaching, had been driven to local extinction by 1990. There's no better measure of the park's recent rehabilitation, however, than that the authorities have seen fit to introduce about 55 individual

Practicalities

Meru is best visited on an organised safari, with **fly-in and drive-in options** both available, though these are best organised through specialist safari companies that run game drives with guides based at one of the park's lodges. It can be visited as a stand-alone destination, or in conjunction with Samburu-Buffalo Springs, Laikipia or one of the 'tree hotels' associated with Mount Kenya or the Aberdares. The park lies about 380km from Nairobi, following the surfaced A2 and B6 via Thika and Embu to the town of Meru, which lies 80km from the main park entrance gate along a partly surfaced road. The drive from Nairobi takes a good half-day and a 4x4 may be required for the park's internal roads, though these are generally well maintained and most junctions are numbered on the ground and on maps, making for easy navigation. There are no shops in the park, so any last-minute shopping should be undertaken in **Meru** town, which boasts an attractive wooded location on the eastern slopes of Mount Kenya and has several banks and ATMs, internet cafés, a few adequate business hotels and a diverting museum.

Accommodation

For full details of tour-operator recommended accommodation, see page 233. Here follows a few further suggestions from the author.

Exclusive
Rhino River Camp ⬧ www.rhinorivercamp.com

Upmarket
Leopard Rock Lodge ⬧ www.leopardmico.com

Budget
Murera Bandas ⬧ www.kws.org

black and white rhinos since 2005. The rhinos are held in a large fenced area that runs south from the main entrance gate past Mururi Swamp, and are quite easily seen from roads through this enclosure.

Meru is a good place to see several large mammals more widely associated with Samburu-Buffalo Springs. The handsome reticulated giraffe is very common, and other dry-country ungulates such as lesser

The strikingly marked reticulated giraffe is one of the more conspicuous residents of Meru National Park. (AZ)

kudu, Grevy's zebra, Beisa oryx and gerenuk occur alongside more widespread species as Burchell's zebra, Coke's hartebeest, waterbuck and bushbuck. Night drives seem to be unusually good for close-up sightings of genet and bushbaby. As for birds, all the traditional safari favourites are abundant – bright blue rollers, bickering starlings, dazzling bee-eaters and the perpetually scurrying yellow-throated spurfowl. It's a good place to see several northern species at the most southerly extent of their range, including Boran cisticola, Somali ostrich and vulturine guineafowl. Hinde's babbler, a very localised endemic, is sometimes noted in thickets along the Murera River.

The largest of the rivers running through the park is the Rojewero, a

Yellow-necked spurfowl frequently call from vantage points at dusk. (AZ)

Joy and George Adamson

Meru's high profile in the 1960s was boosted by its association with Joy and George Adamson, whose pioneering release of captive-raised lions into the wild is recounted in Joy's famous autobiographical book *Born Free* (later made into a film starring Virginia McKenna and Bill Travers). Meru is where Elsa, the leonine subject of *Born Free*, was released by the Adamsons in 1958, it is where she successfully reared three cubs before dying of a tick-borne fever at the age of five, and where her grave stands today (next to the Ura River, south of junction 87).

Although best known for her writing and her work with lions, Joy Adamson was an accomplished artist whose evocative portraits of Kenyan pastoralists are displayed at the Nairobi National Museum. Born Friederike Gessner in Austria-Hungary in 1910, she was sent to Kenya by her Jewish first husband during World War II to escape Nazi persecution. There she met and married her second husband Peter Bally, who gave her the nickname Joy. In the early 1950s she married a third time, to George Adamson, an Indian-born game ranger, four years her senior, then working in northern Kenya.

The Adamsons separated in 1970, but remained strongly intertwined in the public eye for the rest of Joy's life, which ended in tragedy when she was stabbed by a former employee in Shaba National Reserve in 1980. Nine years later, George Adamson, then aged 83, was ambushed and shot dead by Somali poachers whilst driving through a reserve bordering Meru National Park. In addition to the movies *Born Free* and its sequel *Living Free*, the 1999 biopic *Walk with Lions* makes for engaging viewing, largely due to the inspired casting of Richard Harris as George Adamson.

tributary of the Tana. A newly constructed road between junctions 72 and 75 leads past a deep pool in the river where hippos are resident, while a second viewpoint along the same road comprises a wooden boardwalk overlooking a set of rapids – a good site for the endemic golden palm weaver and other riverine species such as African finfoot, Pel's fishing owl and giant kingfisher. The spindly doum palms that stand in stark silhouette against the clear blue sky along this and other rivers often provide refuge to troops of olive baboon and vervet monkey. A more remote goal for a game drive is the forested stretch of the Tana River that runs along the boundary with Mwingi National Reserve – just about the only place where Kenya's largest river is easily accessible, and the site of the rapids known as Adamson's Falls, after George Adamson.

Elsa's Kopje
www.elsaskopje.com

This elegant lodge is named after the orphaned lioness reared by the Adamsons (see box, opposite). Nine stylish open-fronted cottages and one private house have been built into the rocky hillside overlooking the vast plains of the Meru National Park and have some of the finest views in Kenya. Among game highlights here is the opportunity to track some of the rhino protected in Meru's 44km² rhino sanctuary; other activities include day and night drives, bush walks and cultural visits.

Offbeat Meru
www.offbeatsafaris.com

Offbeat is a great-value, seasonal camp set in a picturesque location on the edge of the park within the Bisanadi Reserve. There are six comfortable en-suite living tents, and a pool where you can escape the heat of the day. Game drives take place within the park, whilst nature walks are available from camp. We love the informality, flexible game-viewing activities and traditional bush experience in this seldom-visited, but hugely varied and rewarding area.

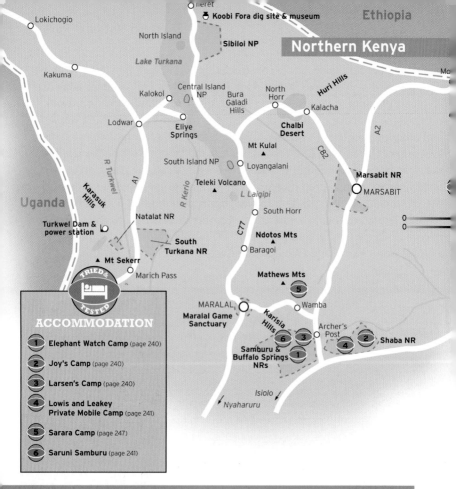

ACCOMMODATION

1 Elephant Watch Camp (page 240)

2 Joy's Camp (page 240)

3 Larsen's Camp (page 240)

4 Lowis and Leakey
Private Mobile Camp (page 241)

5 Sarara Camp (page 247)

6 Saruni Samburu (page 241)

Samburu, Buffalo Springs and Shaba national reserves

Probably the most intriguing of Kenya's protected areas to regular safari-goers, Samburu, Buffalo Springs and Shaba national reserves protect a combined area of 440km² flanking the perennial Ewaso Nyiro River as it flows through the austere badlands north of Mount Kenya. The trio of reserves possesses something of an 'Africa through the looking glass' quality, partly due to the inherent incongruity of seeing this scrubby landscape of rocky plains and bare termite mounds bisected by a lushly forested waterway, but more so because it supports a cast of oddball dry-country variations on familiar safari creatures, most of which are difficult to see elsewhere in their range.

Gazetted as a single entity in 1948 and split in half 15 years later, Samburu and Buffalo Springs respectively lie on the north and south sides of the Ewaso Nyiro, where they are connected by a solitary low bridge. Shaba,

Practicalities

Samburu and Buffalo Springs together form the most important tourist focus in northern Kenya, and they are well developed in terms of lodges and game-viewing roads. Shaba is somewhat less developed, but it feels a lot wilder, the sort of place where you might drive for an hour or two without seeing another sign of human life. This group of reserves is seldom the first choice of first-time safari-goers with limited time, as it doesn't compare to Masai Mara or the other southern reserves for Big Five sightings, but it is included on most longer safaris. It is connected to Nairobi by **regular flights**, but many people visit on a **road safari**, often preceded by a night at one of the tree hotels in the central highlands.

Isiolo, the gateway town to Samburu-Buffalo Springs, lies about 350km from Nairobi via Thika and Nanyuki. Situated at the end of the tarmac, **Isiolo** has a real frontier-town atmosphere, and it could scarcely be more different in character from orderly highland towns such as Nyeri and Nanyuki, with its colourful mix of Somali, Boran, Meru, Samburu and Turkana inhabitants and hot dusty air seemingly infused with the mildly narcotic *miraa* (khat) leaves that are chewed religiously wherever you look. It also has pretty good facilities, including a bank, ATM and several restaurants, but internet access is limited. Note that while the road from Nairobi to Isiolo is surfaced in its entirety, and it can usually be covered in five to six hours, the 40km road from Isiolo to the reserves' entrance gates (and nearby village of Archers Post) is shockingly corrugated and not recommended to anybody with a vulnerable back.

Accommodation

For full details of tour-operator recommended accommodation, see page 240. Here follows a few further suggestions from the author.

Exclusive
Samburu Intrepids ⚲ www.heritage-eastafrica.com

Upmarket
Samburu Game Lodge ⚲ www.wildernesslodges.co.ke
Samburu Serena Safari Lodge ⚲ www.serenahotels.com
Samburu Sopa Lodge ⚲ www.sopalodges.com

Shaba National Reserve protects a habitat of dry acacia-studded plains. (AZ)

which was gazetted in 1974 less than 5km to their east, is neither so well known nor so densely touristed as Samburu-Buffalo Springs. Nevertheless, Shaba has made headlines on several occasions, most notoriously in 1980 when Joy Adamson was murdered at her campsite on its eastern plains. More recently, Shaba served as the setting for the television show *Survivor Africa* and it attracted global attention when a quirky lioness, nicknamed Kamuniak ('Blessed One') by the local Samburu, adopted a succession of half a dozen Beisa oryx calves over a two-year period.

Samburu, Buffalo Springs and Shaba highlights

The three reserves are broadly similar in ecological terms, protecting an area of semi-savanna running either side of the Ewaso Nyiro River. The rocky slopes of Samburu, rising from the north bank of the river, support a cover of shrubby woodland dominated by barbed camelthorns and other acacia species, while the flatter Buffalo Springs and Shaba, running south from the river, are typified by clayey soils and an open cover of lightly wooded grassland. The largest mountain within the reserves' boundaries is the 1,250m Ol Doinyo Koitogorr in Samburu. Several other inselbergs are studded around their immediate vicinity, most notably the 1,624m Shaba Hill outside the southern boundary of Shaba and the 1,880m Ol Doinyo Sabache, on the north bank of the river opposite Shaba, whose basaltic cliffs are the site of a rare Rüppell's vulture breeding colony.

The centrepiece of Samburu-Buffalo Springs is the Ewaso Nyiro River, which might dry up in years of extreme low rainfall, but is essentially perennial, rising from the permanent glaciers atop Mount Kenya whose Samburu name – meaning 'Brown Water' – refers to the rich red-brown top soil it carries down from the Laikipia Plateau. The river flows through the three reserves for a combined total of about 70km, flanked by ribbons of tall riparian forest containing shady *Acacia elatior* trees, buttressed figs, Tana poplars and swaying doum palms. The Ewaso Nyiro is the most important water source for miles around, though there are also a few marshy areas fed by underground water, most notably Buffalo Springs itself, a good place to look for giraffe and various antelope.

Samburu-Buffalo Springs is known for its habituated leopards. (JW/PS)

As for game viewing, Samburu-Buffalo Springs is nothing special when measured in the crudest Big-Five terms. Elephant, buffalo and lion are present but not nearly so common as in the southern reserves, and both species of rhino are absent. The reserves do have a largely justified reputation for good leopard sightings, one that goes back to the outlawed practice of baiting these elusive cats with fresh meat to encourage nocturnal visits to the lodges. Though baiting was discontinued some years back, certain individual leopards resident along the river – presumably the descendants of the ones that used to be baited – remain very habituated to vehicles and people. The best place to look for them is along the network of tracks through the riparian forest in Buffalo Springs, but good sightings are also sometimes to be had in the equivalent habitat in Samburu. The riverine tracks are also the best place to look for elephant, buffalo, hippo, crocodile, waterbuck, bushbuck, olive baboon and vervet monkey.

For many, the biggest attraction of Samburu-Buffalo Springs is its long list of range-restricted and/or endangered dry-country specials. The endangered Grevy's zebra is far bulkier than the familiar common zebra (which also occurs here), and more handsome too, with its dense narrow stripes tapering to a fine circular pattern on the rump. Also common is the reticulated giraffe, distinguished by its neat geometrically marked coat, and now more or less endemic to Kenya as a result of poaching elsewhere in its limited range. Dry-country antelopes includes the regal Beisa oryx, the secretive lesser kudu, Guenther's dik-dik, and local races of Grant's gazelle and impala with unusually long horns. Then there is the bizarre gerenuk, whose distended neck and small head allow it to stretch almost erect on its hind legs to nibble on the leaves that most other browsers can't reach (see page 35). Other dry-country mammals to look out for are the engaging unstriped ground squirrel and the otherwise uncommon striped hyena.

This trio of reserves is the most accessible place to seek out a number of bird species that are almost exclusively associated with northern Kenya

Black-capped social weaver is one of several avian 'specials' associated with Samburu-Buffalo Springs. (AZ)

and bordering parts of Somalia and/or Ethiopia. The literal heavyweights on this list are the Somali ostrich, Abyssinian ground hornbill and spectacular vulturine guineafowl, with its bright cobalt chest (see page 69). Smaller birds include white-headed mousebird, Somali bee-eater, golden pipit, rufous chatterer, bare-eyed thrush, bristle-crowned starling and black-capped social weaver. Samburu-Buffalo Springs is also probably the most reliable site in East Africa for the striking Egyptian vulture. By contrast, the river supports a host of woodland and water-associated species, with African fish eagle and chestnut-bellied kingfisher perching in the trees, yellow-billed stork and African

Yellow-billed storks forage in the shallows of the Ewaso Nyiro River. (GL/FLPA)

spoonbill foraging in the shallows, and flocks of orange-bellied parrot attracting attention with their lively screeching.

Shaba protects a similar range of wildlife to its westerly neighbours, but overall it seems drier and more sparsely vegetated. On the western boundary, a good access point to the river is Sarova Shaba Lodge, whose forested grounds are run through by a sequence of streams and ponds fed by freshwater springs. The main game-viewing loop runs east from here, offering glimpses to the river and passing several hot springs, through a mosaic of lava-strewn plains, grassland, and dry acacia woodland inhabited by Beisa oryx, gerenuk and Grant's gazelle. It's a good place to look for sand-grouse, coursers, bustards and other birds associated with very dry habitats, for instance rosy-patched shrike, golden-breasted starling and the very localised masked lark. More remote still are the starkly scenic eastern plains of Shaba, where all roads gravitate towards Joy's Camp, overlooking a spring-fed waterhole that was once used as a campsite by Joy Adamson and now attracts a steady trickle of elephant, buffalo, lion, reticulated giraffe, Grevy's zebra and antelope. The black lava plains here are home to the ultra-localised Williams lark, while further afield Chanler's Falls lies on the Ewaso Nyiro 32km beyond the reserve's eastern boundary.

Elephant Watch Camp
www.elephantwatchsafaris.com

rainbow tours

Six breezy tents under thatch have gorgeous billowing wall hangings, bright cushions and swathes of colourful fabric. A wealth of birdlife and rare game live in this wild reserve,

but it is the owners' 30-year commitment to understanding the African elephant that infuses and inspires every fibre. The long-standing study programme has helped to promote harmony between the 900-plus elephants and local farmers, and the Samburu staff are devoted to the principles of the camp. The guiding is extraordinary.

Joy's Camp
www.joyscamp.com

LOWIS & LEAKE
Privately guided safar

Built on the site of Joy Adamson's tented home which was also home to Penny the leopard, the heroine of Joy's last book. The camp overlooks

a large natural spring where wildlife endemic to northern Kenya (Grevy's zebra, gerenuk and Somali ostrich) can be seen. The ten Bedouin-style en-suite tents are uniquely decorated with handmade glass and vibrant fabrics from local tribes. Each has its own private deck overlooking the spring. Shaba National Reserve is one of our favourite areas.

Larsen's Camp
www.wildernesslodges.co.ke/larsens_info.html

Africa Sk

Offering the ultimate in safari luxury, this camp is an essential stop on any trip for the more discerning traveller. There are just

20 spacious tents luxuriously decorated in chic safari style, dotted along the banks of the Ewaso Nyiro River in the heart of the Samburu National Park. First-class dining in the beautiful restaurant, lunch along the river and perfect attentive service by the camp's team – all of these things put the cherry on the top of your safari experience.

Lowis and Leakey Private Mobile Camp

www.lowisandleakey.com

A mobile safari is the most authentic African safari experience. The luxury tented camp is built just for you, offering the ultimate in privacy. Areas off the beaten track become accessible, and itineraries can be flexible should weather, game concentrations or other variables change. We also use some of the best small lodges to give maximum breadth to the experience. A typical mobile safari visits a number of different areas showcasing a variety of landscapes, culture and wildlife.

Saruni Samburu

www.sarunisamburu.com

Possibly one of the most romantic places to stay in Kenya – four rooms or 'villas' each with its own private dining and lounge area plus spectacular views over the Kalama Wildlife Conservancy towards Mount Kenya. Linger over meal times - Italian dishes using local produce (excellent coffee guaranteed). A recent addition to the area, Saruni Samburu brings a fresh twist, with professional Samburu guides sharing their local knowledge and heritage. We recommend wallowing in the infinity pool whilst watching the wildlife below.

North of Samburu

The northern half of Kenya is no place for agoraphobics. Arid, sparsely populated and seldom visited by outsiders, it is an uncompromising and time-ravaged land whose expansive horizons and austere volcanic outcrops feel several worlds away from the bustling tourist circuit of the south. Ill-suited to casual exploration, this part of Kenya has much to offer tourists with an adventurous streak or the resources to set up a bespoke safari. Highlights include the remote Mount Marsabit, a forested oasis rising in breezy isolation from the surrounding badlands, and the small village of Kalacha in the heart of the Chalbi Desert. Sibiloi National Park, on the northeast shore of Turkana, is the site of some of the most important hominid fossil finds ever.

The undoubted jewel of the north, however, is Lake Turkana, also known as the Jade Sea, which runs through the Rift Valley floor south of the Ethiopian border for almost 300km to form the eleventh-largest lake in the world, and the only one of comparable size enclosed by a desert. But

Huts built by the nomads living around Lake Turkana reflect their makeshift lifestyle. (NP/C)

Practicalities

There are three possible approaches to exploring northern Kenya. The most comfortable and efficient option is **by air**, using chartered flights to link you to the region's handful of upmarket lodges (one each in Marsabit, Kalacha and Loiyangalani), but this won't come cheaply, and you will miss out on the region's aura of endless space, something that can only really be appreciated at ground level. A second, more adventurous and probably even pricier option is a **bespoke road safari**, which should ideally be undertaken with at least one driver who knows the ground and a support vehicle. A **rougher option** that's well worth considering is an overland truck trip which can be recommended even to those who wouldn't ordinarily join an overland truck as the only affordable way to see this unforgettable part of Kenya. However you travel, tourist facilities are very limited in the region's few towns, and non-existent outside them, so prepare yourself accordingly.

Accommodation

For full details of tour-operator recommended accommodation, see page 247. Here follows a few further suggestions from the author.

Exclusive
Desert Rose Camp ⌐ www.desertrosekenya.com

Upmarket
Kalacha Camp ⌐ www.kalacha.org
Oasis Lodge ⌐ www.oasis-lodge.com
Marsabit Lodge ☎ 069 2102044

while it is the lake that provides the nominal incentive for most trips to this part of Kenya, it is the people of the north that make the most lasting impression – nomadic pastoralists such as the Gabbra, Turkana and Samburu, whose adherence to a strictly traditional lifestyle and dress is practically unique in modern East Africa, creating the impression of travelling not only through space but also through time, to gain a brief glimpse of Africa as it might have been a hundred years ago. That this magnificent wilderness has survived into the modern era is remarkable enough, but that it extends over the better half of one of Africa's most economically developed countries beggars belief.

North Kenya highlights

Mount Marsabit

The largest town in northern Kenya, with a population of 14,000, Marsabit lies about 300km north of Isiolo along the lamentably misnamed Trans-Africa Highway, a back-scrunching series of ruthless corrugations that can take up to six hours to navigate in a sturdy 4x4. The town is perched on the forested slopes of the 1,700m Mount Marsabit, an isolated and long-dormant shield volcano which as its name – literally 'Cold Place' – suggests, is embalmed with cool moist highland air that provides welcome relief coming from the hot low-lying plains below. As towns go, Marsabit is rather humdrum, supporting a mix of Burji, Somali, Rendille, Samburu, Turkana, Borena, Gabbra and Ethiopian migrants, but the lower slopes of the mountain and surrounding plains are protected in the 1,555km² Marsabit National Reserve, and a landscape of extinct volcanic craters (known locally as *gofs*) hosts small populations of reticulated giraffe, Grevy's zebra, gerenuk, lion and cheetah. Culturally, the area is notable for its deep 'singing wells', which are named for the local Borena custom of singing while several dozen people queue up the steep walls to pass along buckets of water.

Enclosed by the eponymous national reserve, the 360km² Marsabit National Park protects the well-watered and lushly forested upper slopes of this isolated massif. In the north of the park, a few kilometres from town, the undersubscribed Marsabit Lodge overlooks an exceptionally beautiful crater lake called Gof Sokorte Dika, which is encircled by forests and cliffs, visited daily by elephants, and supports a varied selection of waterbirds. Higher up the slopes is Lake Paradise, nestled within Gof Sokorte Guda, while the summit is graced by a steep dry crater called Bongole. Marsabit has long been renowned for its heavily tusked elephants, most famously the giant bull Ahmed, whose earth-scraping 3m-

Lake Paradise on the slopes of Marsabit Mountain (SS)

long tusks – now on display at the Nairobi National Museum – were accorded 24-hour armed protection by presidential decree prior to his death of natural causes in 1974. Other wildlife includes greater kudu, bushbuck, black and white colobus, Sykes monkey, leopard, buffalo and isolated populations of many typical various forest birds.

Camels rather than cattle are the main livestock of the Chalbi Desert. (SS)

Chalbi Desert

Turn left at Marsabit, drive west until there are no trees within sight, and you've reached the Chalbi Desert, a vast godforsaken expanse of flat, cracked earth – occasionally transformed into a shallow seasonal lake – where Somali ostriches run off panicked at the rare approach of a vehicle, and the herds of domestic camel are only slightly more habituated. Set in the heart of this desert, Kalacha is a small Gabbra settlement set around a freshwater spring that has supported human habitation for centuries. The only urban punctuation between Marsabit and eastern Turkana, Kalacha has an unusual brick church decorated in the Ethiopian style, but the rest of the village consists of domed Gabbra reed-and-cloth homesteads that show strong affinities to huts built in parts of the Sahara and Kalahari. Excavations at a cairn outside Kalacha unearthed a number of ancient skeletons averaging around 2m in height, lending support to local oral traditions that the area was once inhabited by an extinct race of giants (accredited, among other things, with excavating the deep singing wells around Marsabit).

Lake Turkana

Deep jade waters hemmed in by an apocalyptic moonscape of extinct volcanoes and naked lava flows, the 6,400km² Lake Turkana is the largest desert lake in the world, and one of Kenya's most talked-about off the beaten track goals. Almost 300km long but nowhere more than 32km

UNESCO World Heritage Site

A trio of remote national parks associated with Turkana collectively form one of Kenya's four UNESCO World Heritage Sites. The largest of these is the 1,570km² Sibiloi National Park, gazetted in 1973 on the eastern lakeshore about 120km north of Loiyangalani. Here, the sedimentary rocks at Koobi Fora yielded more than 10,000 vertebrate fossils, including more than 350 hominid specimens that are pivotal to our current scientific understanding of hominid evolution over the last four million years. Sibiloi also protects a rich desert flora, ranging from the pink-flowered desert rose to sky-scraping euphorbia trees. Wildlife includes cheetah, lion, striped hyena, bat-eared fox, Grevy's zebra, gerenuk, lesser kudu, Beisa oryx, reticulated giraffe, the localised tiang (a northern race of topi) and various dry-country bustards, larks and raptors.

The most accessible of the national parks, situated 15km southwest of Loiyangalani, South Island is the largest of three uninhabited volcanic islands that rear up from the lake floor. Gazetted in 1983, the island consists of 16 volcanic craters aligned on a 12km ridge that rises steeply above the lake's surface, and several ancient lava flows can be seen on its northern shore. It supports large numbers of crocodiles, and is an important breeding and alighting point for resident and migratory birds, with a maximum count of 220,000 individual birds comprising 84 species in 1992. African fish eagle, fox kestrel, goliath heron, saddle-billed stork and African skimmer are resident, to be joined seasonally by pink-backed pelican, greater flamingo, spur-winged plover, Caspian plover and little stint. Closer to the western shore, Central Island National Park also supports large bird and crocodile populations.

wide, this soapy soda lake plunges to a depth of 110m on the Rift Valley floor south of the Ethiopian border, where its main inlet it is the Omo River, but has no known outlet, so that the accumulation of soda has made the green water foul-tasting and soapy to the touch. As first seen from the lofty rim of the Rift Valley escarpment, Turkana seems positively primordial, and as you descend to the lakeshore, the stark vegetation defies belief – even the rare patch of grass turns out to be viciously spiky to the touch – and is rendered Infernoesque by the hot, fierce wind that blows relentlessly from across the water. Aptly, this forbidding lake supports the world's largest concentration of Nile crocodile, estimated at 20,000–25,000 (see page 35).

The only substantial settlement on the eastern shore, and main regional tourist centre, Loiyangalani – or Turkana City, if you're feeling facetious – was founded in the 1960s around a palm-fringed freshwater spring and consists of a short main road lined with a few permanent buildings and a sprawl of a reed huts. Home to a mixed community of Rendille, Samburu and Turkana people, Loiyangalani is dominated by staunchly traditional dress codes, though a degree of intertribal fashion exchange appears to take place. The handsome Turkana women are particularly striking with their impressive attire of beaten hides and beaded jewellery, henna-dyed Mohican dreadlocks, and goatee-like lower lip plug (see page 26). These people are all pastoralists by tradition; oddly, it is only the numerically insignificant El Molo that customarily exploit the lake as a source of protein, though many Turkana and Samburu men have recently started catching and eating fish.

The El Molo people live on one tiny island in Lake Turkana. (EL)

The small island inhabited by the Cushitic speaking El Molo – officially listed as the world's least numerous tribe, with a total population of about 300 – is a popular goal for a short day trip out of Loiyangalani, with crocodiles, hippos and various waterbirds likely to be seen in passage. A more demanding outing is the hike up the 2,293m Mount Kulal, a dormant volcano whose upper slopes offer some stunning views across the lake and form the only known habitat of the endemic Kulal white-eye, a small yellow bird that is easily observed in wooded habitats.

TRIED & TESTED

SAFARI CONSULTANTS

Sarara Camp
www.sararacamp.com

Set against the mountainous backdrop of the remote Mathews, Sarara is one of those places you want to keep secret. Six spacious tents (en-suite loos, detached open-air showers), spacious living areas and a pool overlooking a waterhole – this is an oasis of comfort in a hostile environment. The 'singing wells' and elephant interaction are key attractions, but so are the inspiring views. We love the exclusivity, personal service, relaxed atmosphere and cultural experiences of this camp. The animals are the bonus.

Dawn on the Masai Mara National Reserve (SE/D)

Appendix 1

Language

The *lingua franca* of East Africa, **KiSwahili** is the most widely spoken language in Kenya, and it is far more likely to be understood in rural areas than English, the other official language. Mother tongue of the Swahili people, it is a Bantu language that developed on the East African coast about 1,000 years ago, and it has since adopted many words from Arabic, English and to a lesser extent Portuguese, Indian and German. It spread into the interior along with the 19th-century slave caravans and is now widely understood not only in Tanzania and Kenya, but also in Uganda, Rwanda and parts of Malawi, Burundi, Congo, Zambia and Mozambique.

Educated Kenyans and those who deal regularly with tourists will generally speak good English, but visitors who learn a bit of KiSwahili will win plenty of friends and will find it easier to communicate in certain circumstances. Several dictionaries and phrasebooks are available through the usual online booksellers and locally, and the following brief introduction is intended not as a substitute for these, but to help short-stay visitors find their linguistic feet.

Pronunciation

Vowel sounds are pronounced as follows:

a   like the a in *father*
e   like the e in *wet*
i   like the ee in *free*, but less drawn-out
o   somewhere between the o in *no* and the word *awe*
u   similar to the oo in *food*

The double vowel in words like *choo* or *saa* is pronounced like the single vowel, but drawn out for longer. Consonants are in general pronounced as they are in English, though *l* and *r* are often pronounced interchangeably, as are *b* and *v*. Almost all Bantu languages place a stress on the second-last syllable, and KiSwahili is no exception.

Basic grammar

Most words are built from a root with various prefixes, of which the following are the most common:

Pronouns

ni	me	*wa*	they
u	you	*a*	he or she
tu	us		

Tenses   Tenses (negative)

na	present	*si*	present
ta	future	*sita*	future
li	past	*siku*	past
ku	infinitive	*haku*	negative, infinitive

From a root word such as *taka* (want) you might build the following phrases:

Unataka soda	You want a soda
Tutataka soda	We will want a soda
Alitaka soda	He/she wanted a soda

In practice, *ni* and *tu* are often dropped from simple statements; it would be more normal to say *nataka soda* than *ninataka soda*. Negative tenses often change the last syllable of the root word, so that 'don't want', for instance, is not *sitaka* but *sitaki*. In many situations there is no interrogative mode; the difference between a question and a statement lies in the intonation.

Greetings

It is rude to start talking to someone without using a greeting, of which the most common – at least when dealing with tourists – is *Jambo*, a derivative of the more correct *Hujambo*. Another widely used greeting is *Habari?*, which more or less means 'What news?', and is rarely used in isolation but as part of a phrase such as *Habari ya safari?*, *Habari yako?* or *Habari gani?* (very loosely, 'How is your journey?', 'How are you?' and 'How are things?' respectively). *Nzuri* (meaning 'good') is the polite reply to any such request.

Another word often used in greeting is *Salama*, which means 'peace'. When you enter a shop or hotel reception, you will often be greeted by a friendly *Karibu*, which means 'Welcome'. *Asante sana* ('thank you very much') is an appropriate response.

It is respectful to address an old man as *Mzee*. *Bwana*, which means 'Mister', might be used as a polite form of address to a male who is equal or senior to you in age or rank, but who is not a *Mzee*. Older women can be addressed as *Mama*.

The following phrases will come in handy for small talk:

Where have you just come from?	*(U)natoka wapi?*
I have come from Nairobi	*(Ni)natoka Nairobi*
Where are you going?	*(U)nakwenda wapi?*
We are going to Mombasa	*(Tu)nakwenda Mombasa*
What is your name?	*Jina lako nani?*
My name is Philip	*Jina langu ni Philip*
Do you speak English?	*Unasema KiIngereze?*
I speak a little Swahili	*Ninasema KiSwahili kidigo*
Sleep peacefully	*Lala salama*
Bye for now	*Kwaheri sasa*
Have a safe journey	*Safari njema*
Come again (welcome again)	*Karibu tena*
I don't understand	*Sielewi*
Say that again	*Sema tena*

Numbers

1	*moja*	30	*thelathini*
2	*mbili*	40	*arobaini*
3	*tatu*	50	*hamsini*
4	*nne*	60	*sitini*
5	*tano*	70	*sabini*
6	*sita*	80	*themanini*
7	*saba*	90	*tisini*
8	*nane*	100	*mia (moja)*
9	*tisa*	150	*mia moja na hamsini*
10	*kumi*	155	*mia moja hamsini na tano*
11	*kumi na moja*	200	*mia mbili*
20	*ishirini*	1,000	*elfu (moja)* or *mia kumi*

Swahili time

The Swahili clock starts at the equivalent of 06.00, so that *saa moja asubuhi* (hour one in the morning) is 07.00; *saa mbili jioni* (hour two in the evening) is 20.00, etc. To ask the time in Swahili, say *Saa ngapi?*

Days of the week

Monday	*Jumatatu*	Friday	*Ijumaa*
Tuesday	*Jumanne*	Saturday	*Jumamosi*
Wednesday	*Jumatano*	Sunday	*Jumapili*
Thursday	*Alhamisi*		

Shopping

The normal way of asking for something is *Ipo?* or *Zipo?*, which roughly means 'Is there?', so if you want a cold drink you would ask *Soda baridi zipo?* The response will normally be *Ipo* or *Kuna* ('there is') or *Hamna* or *Hakuna* ('there isn't'). Once you've established the shop has what you want, you might say *Nataka koka mbili* ('I want two Cokes'). To check the price, ask *Shillingi ngape?*

Swahili words for non-traditional objects are often similar to the English. Examples are *resiti* ('receipt'), *gari* ('car'), *polisi* ('police') and *posta* ('post office') – in desperation, it's always worth trying the English word with an *i* suffix.

Foodstuffs

avocado	*parachichi*	fruit(s)	*(ma)tunda*
bananas	*ndizi*	maize porridge	*ugali*
beef	*(Nyama ya) ngombe*	meat	*nyama*
bread (loaf)	*mkate*	milk	*maziwa*
bread (slice)	*tosti*	potatoes	*viazi*
chicken	*kuku*	rice	*wali*
coconuts	*nazi*	salt	*chumvi*
coffee	*kahawa*	sauce	*supu*
egg(s)	*(ma)yai*	sugar	*sukari*
fish	*samaki*	tea	*chai*
food	*chakula*	vegetable	*mboga*
		water	*maji*

Family

brother	*kaka*	granddad	*babu*
child	*mtoto*	grandmother	*bibi*
father	*baba*	mother	*mama*
friend	*rafiki*	sister	*dada*

Other useful words and phrases

afternoon	*alasiri*	only	*tu*
again	*tena*	pay	*kulipa*
and	*na*	person	*mtu (watu)*
big	*kubwa*	(people)	
bus	*basi*	please	*tafadhali*
cold	*baridi*	road/street	*barabara/mtaa*
come here	*njo*	shop	*duka*
European(s)	*mzungu (wazungu)*	sleep	*kulala*
evening	*jioni*	slowly	*polepole*
excuse me	*samahani*	small	*kidogo*
far away	*mbale kubwa*	soon	*bado kidogo*
friend	*rafiki*	sorry	*polepole*
good (very)	*mzuri (sana)*	stop	*simama*
goodbye	*kwaheri*	straight	*moja kwa moja*
here	*hapa*	thank you	*asante* (very much)
hot	*moto*		(*sana*)
later	*bado*	there is	*iko/ipo/kuna*
many	*sana*	there is not	*hamna/hakuna*
me	*mimi*	thief	*mwizi (wawizi)*
money	*pesa/shillingi*	(thieves)	
more	*ingine/tena*	time	*saa*
morning	*asubuhi*	today	*leo*
nearby	*karibu/mbale kidogo*	toilet	*choo*
night	*usiku*	tomorrow	*kesho*
no	*hapana*	want	*taka*
no problem	*hakuna matata* or	where	(*iko*) *wapi*
	hamna shida	yes	*ndiyo*
now	*sasa*	yesterday	*jana*
OK/fine	*sawa*	you	*wewe*

Appendix 2

Selected reading

Wildlife

East African Wildlife by Philip Briggs (Bradt, 2008) is a handy and lavishly illustrated one-stop handbook to the region's mammals, birds and other fauna, aimed specifically at one-off or occasional visitors whose interest in wildlife extends beyond the Big Five but who don't want to carry a library of reference books.

For a coffee-table-style introduction to the region's wildlife, *Mara Serengeti: A Photographer's Paradise* (Fountain, 2000) by Jonathan and Angela Scott, of *Big Cat Diary* fame, is difficult to beat.

Mammals

Several are available. The pick is Jonathan Kingdon's immensely detailed *Field Guide to African Mammals* (Christopher Helm, 2003), while the same author's *Pocket Guide to African Mammals* (Christopher Helm, 2004) is a more compact, inexpensive title suited to less dedicated wildlife enthusiasts. Richard Estes's superb *The Safari Companion* (Green Books UK, Chelsea Green USA, Russell Friedman Books South Africa, 1992) is a well-organised and informative guide to mammalian behaviour, but rather bulky for casual safari-goers.

Birds

For serious birders, *Birds of Kenya and Northern Tanzania* by Dale Zimmerman, Don Turner and David Pearson (Christopher Helm, 1996) is a contender for the best single-volume field guide to any African country. If the original hardback edition is too bulky, get the condensed paperback version (Helm Field Guides, 2005). A better choice should your birding itinerary extend into neighbouring countries (except for the far north of Tanzania) is the *Field Guide to the Birds of East Africa* by Terry Stevenson and John Fanshawe (Christopher Helm, 2002, paperback edition 2004).

Other field guides

More specialised titles include Najma Dharani's *Field Guide to Common Trees and Shrubs of East Africa* (Struik, 2002) and a magnificent *Field Guide to the Reptiles of East Africa* by Stephen Spawls, Kim Howell, Robert Drewes and James Ashe (A & C Black, 2004). Alan Channing and

Kim Howell's *Amphibians of East Africa* (Comstock Books in Herpetology, 2006) is also highly worthwhile. Matt Richmond and Irene Kamau's *East African Marine Ecoregion* (World Wide Fund for Nature USA, 2005) examines the whole of the East African coast.

History and biography

Blixen, Karen *Out of Africa* (Penguin, 1937). Famous autobiographical work offering fascinating insight into the colonial era and mindset.

de Vere Allen, J *Swahili Origins* (James Currey, 1992). Good overview of coastal trade and history.

Elkins, Caroline *Imperial Reckoning: The Untold Story of Britain's Gulag in Kenya* (Henry Holt, 2005). Pulitzer-winning, controversy-stirring and harrowing – Britain's brutal suppression of the Mau-Mau uprising.

Hall, Richard *Empires of the Monsoon: A History of the Indian Ocean and its Invaders* (HarperCollins, 1996). Focused and readable, this places the last 1,000 years of East African history in an international framework.

Kenyatta, Jomo *Facing Mount Kenya* (Vintage, 1962). Fascinating overview of Kikuyu culture by the first president of independent Kenya.

Maathai, Wangari *Unbowed: My Autobiography* (Arrow, 2008). Engaging and affirming life story of the Nobel Peace Prize-winning Kikuyu founder of the Green Belt Movement.

Matthiessen, Peter *The Tree Where Man Was Born* (Penguin, 1972). Ruminative and almost poetic introduction to the prehistory and ecology of Kenya and northern Tanzania.

Ochieng, William *A Modern History of Kenya, 1885–1980* (Evans Brothers, 1990). Out of print but worth tracking down as this is (bizarrely) the only one-volume history of Kenya published in modern times.

Pakenham, Thomas *The Scramble for Africa* (Abacis, 1992). Gripping 600-page tome, aptly described by one reviewer as 'Heart of Darkness with the lights switched on'.

Pavitt, Nigel *Kenya: A Country in the Making 1880–1940* (W W Norton, 2008). Fascinating visual account of the early colonial era, complete with more than 700 period photographs and insightful text.

Reader, John *Africa: A Biography of the Continent* (Penguin, 1997). Perhaps the most readable and accurate attempt yet to capture the sweep of African history for the general reader.

Saitoti, Tepilit Ole and Beckwith, Carol *Maasai* (Harry N Abrams, 1990). Visually sumptuous and written with authority, this pricey book offers a peerless introduction to East Africa's most celebrated pastoralists.

Trzebenski, Errol *The Life and Death of Lord Errol* (Fourth Estate, 2000). Latest and best account of the murder that rocked the Happy Valley scene in 1941 (also the subject of the film *White Mischief*).

Fiction

Recommended titles by Kenyan writers include the following:

Kimani, Peter *Before the Rooster Crows* (East African Educational, 2002)

Mwangi, Meja *Going Down River Road* (Heinemann, 1976)

Ngugi wa Thiong'o *A Grain of Wheat* (1967, Penguin Classics edition, 2002) or *Petals of Blood* (1977, Penguin Classics edition, 2002)

Ogola, Margaret *The River and the Source* (1995, Focus Books edition, 2004)

Wainaina, Binyavanga *Discovering Home* (Jovian Books, 2006)

An exciting recent development in Kenyan writing circles is the establishment of the **Kwani Trust** (ᐰ www.kwani.org) by the emerging writers Binyavanga Wainaina and Muthoni Garland in 2003. It has now published four editions of *Kwani?*, Kenya's first literary journal, and it also maintains an interesting website.

Travel magazines

For readers with a broad interest in Africa, an excellent magazine dedicated to tourism throughout Africa is *Travel Africa* (ᐰ www.travelafricamag.com). Recommended for their broad-ranging editorial content and the coffee-table-book standard of photography and reproduction, the award-winning magazines *Africa Geographic* and *Africa Birds and Birding* can be checked out at the website ᐰ www.africageographic.com.

Health

Self-prescribing has its hazards so if you are going anywhere very remote consider taking a health book. For adults there is *Bugs, Bites & Bowels: The Cadogan Guide to Healthy Travel* by Jane Wilson-Howarth (1999); if travelling with the family look at *Your Child Abroad: A Travel Health Guide* by Dr Jane Wilson-Howarth and Dr Matthew Ellis, published by Bradt Travel Guides in 2005.

Index

Samburu girls (CO)

First published November 2010
Bradt Travel Guides Ltd
23 High Street, Chalfont St Peter, Bucks SL9 9QE, England; www.bradtguides.com
Published in the USA by The Globe Pequot Press Inc,
PO Box 480, Guilford, Connecticut 06437-0480

Text copyright © 2010 Philip Briggs; Maps copyright © 2010 Bradt Travel Guides Ltd
Photographs © 2010 Individual photographers (see below)
Managing Editor: Anna Moores

ISBN: 978 1 84162 267 5

British Library Cataloguing in Publication Data
A catalogue record for this book is available from the British Library

Photographs
Aardvark Safaris Ltd: Victoria Langmead (VL), Charlotte Opperman (CO); Alamy: AfriPics.com (AP/A), Images of Africa Photobank (IP/A), Tina Manley (TM/A), PCL (PCL/A); Amboseli Porini (AP); John Berry/Zambezi Safari and Travel Company (JB); Borana Lodge (BL); Campi ya Kanzi (CK); Corbis: Yann Arthus-Bertrand (YAB/C), Chinch Gryniewicz; ecoscene (CG/C), Nigel Pavitt/JAI (NP/C), Swim Ink 2, LLC (SI/C); Wilmar Dik (WD); Dreamstime.com: Agostino (A/D), Tiziano Casalta (TC/D), Neal Cooper (NC/D), Stefan Ekernas (SK/D); Elephant Watch Camp (EWC); FLPA: Neil Bowman (NB/FLPA), Gerry Ellis/Minden Pictures (GE/FLPA), Suzi Eszterhas/Minden Pictures (SE/FLPA), FLPA (FLPA/FLPA), Gerard Lacz (GL/FLPA), ImageBroker/Imagebroker (IB/FLPA), John Karmali (JK/FLPA), Frans Lanting (FL/FLPA), Yva Momatiuk & John Eastcott/Minden Pictures (YM & JE/FLPA), Elliott Neep (EN/FLPA), Paul Sawer (PS/FLPA), Chris & Tilde Stuart (C&TS/FLPA), Richard du Toit/Minden Pictures (RT/FLPA), Winfried Wisniewski (WW/FLPA), Martin B Withers (MW/FLPA); Kenya Tourist Board/www.magicalkenya.com (KTB); Eric Lafforgue (EL); Lions Bluff Lodge (LBL); Manda Bay (MB); Mara Serian (MS); Mary Evans Picture Library: (MEPL), AGIP/Rue des Archives (A/MEPL); National Museums of Kenya (NMK); Photoshot: Lee Dalton/NHPA (LD/PS), James Warwick/NHPA (JW/PS); Rekero Camp (RC); Saruni Mara Camp (SMC); Satao Camp (SC); SuperStock (SS); Wikimedia Commons (WC); Ariadne Van Zandbergen (AZ)

Front cover (Top, left to right) Balloon ride over the Masai Mara (IB/FLPA); Samburu girl (AZ); Male lion, Masai Mara (WW/FLPA); (bottom) Mother elephant and calf, Masai Mara (SE/FLPA)
Back cover Lilac-breasted roller (NC/D); cheetah (AZ); *Front flap* Maasai warrior (EL)
Title page A member of the Samburu tribe (EL); Watamu Beach (TC/D); Cheetah (SE/D)
Part & chapter openers: Page 1: A lappet-faced vulture scans the Mara Plains from an acacia tree, Masai Mara Reserve (AZ); Page 2: Samburu woman (EL); Page 3: Turkana girls in beaded traditional jewellery (EL); Page 28: (top) Little bee-eater (AZ), (bottom) Red-headed agama lizard (EL); Page 29: Plains zebra, Amboseli National Park (EL); Page 58: (top) Black rhino (AZ), (bottom) Landing strip, Laikipia (JB); Page 59: photographer in Amboseli National Park (JB); Page 80: Signpost in Lake Nakuru National Park (WD); Page 81: Tourist truck crossing the Chalbi Desert (AZ); Page 101: Male lions, Masai Mara (GE/FLPA); Page 102: (top) Man feeding giraffe at the AFEW Giraffe Centre (SS), (bottom) Statue of Kenyatta, central Nairobi (SS); Page 103: Eland in Nairobi National Park (LD/PS); Page 116: Maasai man in traditional attire (EL); Page 117: Cheetah, Masai Mara (GE/FLPA); Page 152: (top) Golden pipit (MW/FLPA), (bottom) Baby elephant following mother, Amboseli National Park (GE/FLPA); Page 153: A herd of plains zebra crosses the Amboseli Plains below Kilimanjaro (EL); Page 176: (top): Crab plover (NB/FLPA), (bottom) Women walking along a beach, south of Mombasa (NP/C); Page 177: Shanzu Beach, north of Mombasa (SS); Page 208: The race of Grant's gazelle in northern Kenya has longer horns than its southern counterpart (AZ); Page 209: Turkana women in a characteristic northern setting of rocky earth and cloudless sky (EL)

Maps Artinfusion
Typeset and designed from the author's disc by Artinfusion
Production managed by Jellyfish Print Solutions; printed in Europe